The Programmer's Apprentice

ACM Press

Editor-in-Chief:

Peter Wegner, *Brown University*

ACM Press books represent a collaboration between the Association for Computing Machinery (ACM) and Addison-Wesley Publishing Company to develop and publish a broad range of new works. These works generally fall into one of four series.

Frontier Series. Books focused on novel and exploratory material at the leading edge of computer science and practice.

Anthology Series. Collected works of general interest to computer professionals and/or society at large.

Tutorial Series. Introductory books to help nonspecialists quickly grasp either the general concepts or the needed details of some specific topic.

History Series. Books documenting past developments in the field and linking them to the present.

In addition, ACM Press books include selected conference and workshop proceedings.

The Programmer's Apprentice

Charles Rich
Richard C. Waters
Massachusetts Institute of Technology

ACM PRESS
New York, New York

Addison-Wesley Publishing Company

Reading, Massachusetts • Menlo Park, California • New York
Don Mills, Ontario • Wokingham, England • Amsterdam • Bonn
Sydney • Singapore • Tokyo • Madrid • San Juan

ACM Press Frontier Series

Many of the designations used by manufacturers and sellers to distinguish their products are claimed as trademarks. Where those designations appear in this book, and Addison-Wesley was aware of a trademark claim, the designations have been printed in initial caps or all caps.

The programs and applications presented in this book have been included for their instructional value. They have been tested with care, but are not guaranteed for any particular purpose. The publisher does not offer any warranties or representations, nor does it accept any liabilities with respect to the programs or applications.

Library of Congress Cataloging-in-Publication Data

Rich, Charles, 1951–
    The Programmer's Apprentice / Charles Rich and Richard C. Waters.
    p.   cm. – (ACM Press frontier series)
    Includes bibliographical references.
    ISBN 0-201-52425-2
    1. Computer software–Development. 2. Computer-aided software
engineering. I. Waters, Richard C. II. Title. III. Series.
    QA76.76.D47R53   1990
    005.1–dc20   89-48057
                                                                      CIP

ABCDEFGHIJ-HA-943210

To Candy and Patricia

Preface

How can the next *order of magnitude* improvement in software productivity be achieved? When we first started thinking about this question as graduate students in the mid-1970s, most of the software community considered our notion of an intelligent assistant for programmers—the Programmer's Apprentice—to be rather farfetched. We are happy to observe that much has changed since that time.

Judging from the number of papers on the topic in recent software engineering and CASE (Computer-Aided Software Engineering) conferences, there is now a great deal of interest in applying artificial intelligence to software. We believe that using knowledge-based techniques to support software-engineering problem solving is crucial to developing software tools that are qualitatively better than today's.

In addition, our research has reached an important stage. We have completed a major system-building effort (the Knowledge-Based Editor in Emacs, or KBEmacs) that demonstrates the feasibility of the Programmer's Apprentice. Also, after many years of writing about various aspects of the Apprentice for various audiences, we feel ready to attempt a comprehensive statement of the principles and techniques that underlie the project.

Our first goal in writing this book is to make the techniques we have demonstrated in the laboratory accessible to those who are currently designing the next generation of software tools. We also seek to inspire and excite the wider community of software users about what is possible in the future.

Our second, but no less important, goal is to demonstrate to the artificial intelligence community that software development is a challenging and productive domain in which to pursue fundamental issues in knowledge representation and problem solving. Our project has been driven from the start by the need to represent human knowledge formally (resulting in the development of the Plan Calculus and the cliché library). More recently, the reasoning needs of the Apprentice in the areas of requirements and design have propelled us into the new terrain of hybrid knowledge representation and reasoning systems.

Stepping back a bit, we also want to observe that, although most of this book focuses on software tools, the basic ideas behind the Programmer's Apprentice are relevant to computer-aided design in general—electrical, mechanical, or any other kind. We hope the Programmer's Apprentice can serve as an example of a general methodology to the builders of all kinds of computer-aided design tools.

The book begins in Chapters 1 and 2 with a discussion of the key philosophical and theoretical ideas of the Programmer's Apprentice: intelligent assistance, inspection methods, and clichés. This is followed in Chapters 3–5 by an in-depth presentation of the Plan Calculus, a formal representation we have developed for knowledge about programs and programming. Chapters 6–9 describe KBEmacs, an operational system that demonstrates the key capabilities of the Apprentice in the implementation part of the software process. Chapters 10 and 11 briefly describe our ongoing research in automating the recognition of clichés in existing programs and in demonstrating the capabilities of the Apprentice in the areas of software requirements and design. Chapter 12 summarizes the book from the perspective of how Programmer's Apprentice technology can contribute to the next generation of CASE.

Our final thought on the occasion of completing this book is that, over the years of working together, we have achieved much more than twice what either of us could have done alone. We are sad to see that close collaboration is so rare in our community. We hope that many more researchers will seek out colleagues and make them partners—and friends—as we have.

Acknowledgments

The Programmer's Apprentice project has been a collaboration involving students, faculty, and staff over many years.

We would like to begin (where the project began) by acknowledging Gerry Sussman, who introduced us to engineering problem solving as a domain for artificial intelligence research and who supervised our doctoral dissertations. Carl Hewitt also made important contributions to the intellectual atmosphere that challenged us to attempt what we did. Also present at the beginning was Howie Shrobe, who helped start the project with his dissertation and later moved on to found a similar project in integrated circuit design.

We have been extremely fortunate over the years to have succeeded in convincing many excellent students to share our vision of the Programmer's Apprentice and to work toward making it a reality. These students include Dan Brotsky, Scott Cyphers, David Chapman, Roger Duffey, Greg

Faust, Bob Hall, Bob Handsaker, Tom Kennedy, Ron Kuper, Paul Lefel-hocz, Michael Monegan, Jonathan Orwant, Howard Reubenstein, Patrick Ritto, Rich Robbins, Dan Shapiro, Peter Sterpe, Yang Meng Tan, Elizabeth Turrisi, Jeremy Wertheimer, and Linda Wills.

Large system-development efforts are not possible without the help of full-time staff members. We would like to thank Kent Pitman and Greg Faust for their contributions to KBEmacs and Yishai Feldman for his contributions to Cake.

Large projects are also not possible without administrative support. We would like to thank Crisse Ciro and Rhonda Byrne for providing that support. We also thank Rhonda Byrne for proofreading this manuscript, and Elliot Chikofsky, David Harris, Elaine Kant, William Robinson, and Dick Wray for their editorial suggestions.

The research described here was conducted at the Artificial Intelligence Laboratory of the Massachusetts Institute of Technology. We don't think it could have taken place anywhere else. The intellectual and moral support of our colleagues and the excellent computing facilities of the laboratory were crucial to making this work possible.

Support for the Programmer's Apprentice project has been provided by the following organizations: the Defense Advanced Research Projects Agency (under Naval Research contracts N00014-75-C-0643, N00014-80-C-0505, N00014-85-K-0124, and N00014-88-K-0487), the National Science Foundation (under grants MCS-7912179, MCS-8117633, and IRI-8616644), and the IBM, NYNEX, Siemens, Sperry, and Microelectronics and Computer Technology corporations. The views and conclusions contained in this book are those of the authors and should not be interpreted as representing the policies, expressed or implied, of these organizations.

C.R. and R.C.W.

Cambridge, Massachusetts

Contents

Chapter 1

The Programmer's Apprentice

In the Programmer's Apprentice project, we study how software engineers analyze, synthesize, modify, specify, verify, and document software systems and how these tasks can be automated. From a software-engineering perspective, we use artificial intelligence techniques to support the software-development process. From an artificial-intelligence perspective, we use software engineering as a domain for investigating fundamental issues in knowledge representation and reasoning.

The project's practical goal is to develop a system called the Programmer's Apprentice. Throughout the software life cycle (i.e., during requirements acquisition, design, implementation, testing, and maintenance), the Apprentice will act as a software engineer's junior partner and critic, taking over simple tasks completely and assisting with more complex tasks.

Constructing the Programmer's Apprentice is a long-term undertaking, which is far from complete. However, significant progress has been made. We have articulated two principles (intelligent assistance and inspection methods) that form the foundation of the Programmer's Apprentice. We have developed a knowledge representation (the Plan Calculus) that greatly facilitates the representation and manipulation of knowledge about software systems and commonly used algorithms. We have completed a demonstration system (the Knowledge-Based Editor in Emacs, or KBEmacs) that, although restricted to the task of program implementation, illustrates most of the key capabilities of the Programmer's Apprentice.

Looking into the future, we are currently constructing two new demonstration systems that will support the tasks of requirements engineering and design. These systems are based on the same principles as KBEmacs but will make use of more advanced knowledge representation and reasoning techniques.

1

1.1   Philosophy

Many researchers are seeking to solve current software problems by eliminating software engineers entirely through *automatic programming*. As typically conceived, this approach calls for end-users to write complete specifications for what they want. A fully automatic system then generates a program satisfying these specifications. Program generators along these lines have been successfully developed for a number of specific narrow applications. However, at least in the near-term, a single totally automatic programming system supporting a wide range of applications is not a realistic goal (see [16]).

Intelligent Assistance

We believe it is more fruitful to provide software engineers with intelligent assistance. A provocative example of this approach was put forward by IBM's Harlan Mills in the early 1970s [85, 134]. He advocated the creation of *chief programmer teams* in which expert software engineers were surrounded by support staffs of human assistants, including junior programmers, testers, documentation writers, and program librarians. Experience has shown that this division of labor can dramatically increase the productivity of expert engineers because it allows them to concentrate their effort on the most difficult parts of a given software task without getting bogged down in the routine details that currently eat up most of their time.

Our goal is to provide *every* software engineer with a support team in the form of an intelligent computer program (the Programmer's Apprentice). To date, we have focused on making expert software engineers superproductive. However, the assistant approach is also applicable to the education and support of less-experienced software engineers. (See [116, 149] for examples of current directions in computer-based software-engineering tutors.)

Other work that tries to assist rather than replace software engineers includes the Knowledge-Based Software Assistant [109], which was inspired in part by the Programmer's Apprentice, the Designer/Verifier's Assistant [138], which emphasizes theorem proving and verification, and Grapple [114], which focuses on managing the temporal sequence of events in the software process.

Interacting with the Programmer's Apprentice

The intended interaction between a software engineer and the Programmer's Apprentice (see Figure 1.1) is modeled after interaction with a human assistant. In particular, rather than being a passive tool, the Apprentice will act as an autonomous *agent* in the software process. The Apprentice

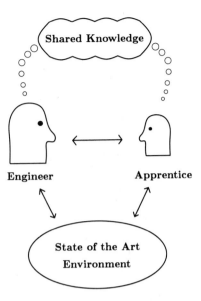

Figure 1.1 Role of the Apprentice.

will assist the engineer by cooperating on or taking over aspects of various software-engineering tasks.

For example, consider the task of program design. The engineer will make the important design decisions and communicate them to the Apprentice. The Apprentice will check for the consistency and reasonableness of these decisions—reporting any problems to the engineer—and make the numerous subsidiary decisions needed to complete the design. Typically, the decisions made by the engineer will be high-level ones, and those made by the Apprentice will be low-level. However, at least when efficiency is important, the engineer will have to make critical low-level decisions as well.

This style of interaction is very different from using a conventional software tool, such as a compiler. When using a compiler, an engineer makes all of the decisions above a certain level of detail without the help of the compiler. The compiler then makes all of the lower-level decisions without any intervention from the engineer.

An aspect of interacting with the Apprentice that we have not concentrated on is the concrete interface between the engineer and the Apprentice. Other than needing to support highly interactive, bidirectional communication, there are few other constraints. One approach, which was taken in KBEmacs, is to leave the interface to the underlying environment undisturbed and support communication with the Apprentice through a separate channel, such as an extra window or command area. Alternatively, the Apprentice might present its own comprehensive interface with a "trap door" to the underlying environment.

Incremental Automation

An easily overlooked, but important, aspect of Figure 1.1 is that the engineer is allowed to use the underlying environment directly. This is notable because many software innovations try to protect engineers from folly by denying them such access. Allowing direct access to the underlying environment has two virtues. First, it means that no old capabilities are lost when new capabilities are added. Second, it provides a clear path for incremental automation.

Initially, the Apprentice will be able to take over only the simplest and most routine parts of the software-engineering process. However, there is no need to wait until the Apprentice can do more because a mechanism is provided for the engineer to do whatever the Apprentice cannot. Therefore, one can immediately obtain a benefit from even a small degree of automation. This is particularly true for large software systems in which there is always plenty of routine work to be done. Subsequently, as technology advances, the proportion of the process handled by the Apprentice can increase.

Shared Knowledge

Between the engineer and the Apprentice, as between two people, the key to effective cooperation is shared knowledge. This knowledge is of two kinds.

First, the software engineer and the Apprentice both must have knowledge about the system being worked on, such as its requirements, its design, its implementation, and the dependencies between them. In order for the Apprentice to share this information, it must be stored on line and in a form that can be reasoned about. This contrasts with current software-engineering environments where, if anything other than code is stored on line at all, it is stored merely as text. As we will see, developing formal representations for software requirements, designs, implementations, and dependencies is a fundamental part of the Programmer's Apprentice project.

Second, the software engineer and the Apprentice must have a large shared vocabulary. It would be impossibly tedious if the Apprentice required engineers to describe everything from first principles. Rather, just as when talking with another person, the engineer using the Apprentice must be able to use common software-engineering terms and concepts. These concepts—what we call *clichés*—range from high-level requirement and design ideas, such as *information system* and *command processor*, to low-level implementation techniques, such as *balanced binary tree* and *linear search*. Identifying and codifying these clichés and the relationships between them is a major activity in the project. A large library of clichés is a central component of the Apprentice.

Maintenance and Evolution

Every aspect of software engineering is colored by the need for continual evolution. Requirements change because the world changes and because it is not possible for requirements analysts or end-users to foresee all of the opportunities for a system's use. Designs change because requirements and technology change. Implementations change because designs change and bugs have to be fixed.

Given the paramount importance of evolution, it is unfortunate that evolution is one of the least well supported aspects of software engineering. In particular, current support for software maintenance is focused almost solely at the level of source code, i.e., implementations. An important goal of work on the Programmer's Apprentice is to actively support the evolution of requirements and designs through the use of formal representations and reasoning.

1.2 Key Capabilities

By way of summary, the following are eight key capabilities of the Programmer's Apprentice:

- *Shared knowledge* — By reference to a library of clichés, the Apprentice will understand commonly used software-engineering terminology. By using these terms, an engineer can work faster and with fewer errors. The engineer and the Apprentice will also share knowledge of the software currently under development.

- *Propagation of decisions* — The Apprentice will automatically make subsidiary decisions that follow from decisions made by the engineer.

- *Error detection* — The Apprentice will check for obvious inconsistencies, both within what an engineer has said and between what the engineer has said and the Apprentice's knowledge of clichés.

- *Support for evolution* — The Apprentice will keep track of dependencies throughout the software-engineering process to help the engineer carry out modifications reliably and assess their potential impact.

- *Explanation* — The Apprentice will be able to explain its decisions and actions so that an engineer can easily override them. Explanations can be interactive or in the form of permanent documentation.

- *Automation of details* — Certain routine aspects of software engineering will be totally automated.

- *Escape to the surrounding environment* — At any time, the engineer will be able to step outside of the Apprentice and use the tools in the surrounding environment.

- *Programming-language independence* — The concepts and the supporting technologies behind the Programmer's Apprentice are predominantly programming-language independent. As a result, the Apprentice will be able to operate in a wide variety of programming languages.

To obtain dramatic improvements in overall software-engineering productivity and reliability, the apprentice must support these capabilities across the full range of software-engineering tasks, from requirements acquisition and analysis to design and implementation.

1.3   Overview of the Project and the Book

As illustrated in Figure 1.2, the Programmer's Apprentice project is pursuing two parallel lines of research: theoretical work leading to the development of supporting technologies (lower arrow) and the construction of demonstration systems (upper arrow). The upward-slanting dashed arrows indicate points at which supporting technology has fed into the construction of demonstration systems.

The first important step in the theoretical line was the development of the notion of clichés. Clichés and their application to problem solving (inspection methods) are discussed in Chapter 2.

Theoretical work continued with the development of a programming-language independent formalism, called the Plan Calculus, for representing the algorithmic structure of software and software clichés. The Plan Calculus is described in Chapters 3–5.

Work on demonstration systems began as soon as the basic outlines of the Plan Calculus were in place. This has culminated in the construction of the Knowledge-Based Editor in Emacs, described in Chapters 6–9. Restricted to the task of program implementation, KBEmacs supports seven of the eight key capabilities of the Programmer's Apprentice. Chapter 7 shows a transcript of KBEmacs being used to implement a Lisp program. Chapter 8 shows the implementation of an Ada program.

KBEmacs supports building a program by combining clichés chosen from a library. Chapter 10 describes a demonstration system that automates the reverse operation—analyzing a program to determine the clichés it is built out of. This kind of design reconstruction has important applications to the maintenance of existing software.

Currently, work in the theory-and-supporting-technology line is concentrating on a hybrid knowledge-representation and reasoning system we

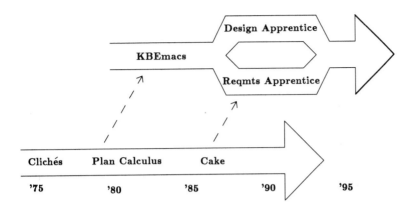

Figure 1.2 Project time line.

call Cake. Cake supports general-purpose logical reasoning, frame-based reasoning, and special-purpose reasoning within the Plan Calculus. The general-purpose capabilities of Cake are motivated by the need to represent and reason about nonalgorithmic aspects of software (e.g., certain aspects of requirements and domain knowledge in general). These capabilities are touched on only briefly in this book both because logic and frames are now standard technology in artificial intelligence and because this book focuses on KBEmacs, which does not make use of these capabilities.

Chapter 11 briefly discusses Cake and reviews work in progress on two new demonstration systems based on Cake. The Design Apprentice will extend KBEmacs into the realm of creating and modifying designs as well as implementations. The Requirements Apprentice will support the creation and evolution of software requirements. Our goal is to eventually merge these systems to achieve a demonstration of the Programmer's Apprentice over the full range of software tasks.

Other work in the Programmer's Apprentice project not covered in this book includes automated techniques for bug localization (see [64]), program translation by abstraction and reimplementation (see [66]), and a new programming-language construct based on loop clichés (see [78]). An annotated bibliography of work in the Programmer's Apprentice project is included at the end of the book.

Finally, Chapter 12 describes how the technology developed in the Programmer's Apprentice project can be applied to overcome the limitations of current CASE technology. The potential benefits are illustrated through a discussion of future tools for systems analysis, program construction, testing, and reengineering.

Chapter 2

Inspection Methods and Clichés

To assist software engineers effectively, one needs a conceptual model of their problem-solving methods. As the basis for this model, we look for analogies with other kinds of engineering activity. In contrast, some researchers (notably Dijkstra; see [94]) look to mathematics. We believe that, while a mathematical viewpoint is appropriate for algorithm discovery (the process of devising a novel algorithm based on a precise specification), it is not appropriate for the construction of large software systems, which typically entails the combination of known algorithms to achieve an only partially explicit specification. (See [119, 125, 146] for examples of current directions in automated assistance for algorithm discovery.)

Within the engineering context, we contrast two very different kinds of problem solving—uniform general methods and inspection methods—and argue that experts mostly use inspection methods. Inspection methods are based on knowledge of commonly used combinations of components, called clichés. These clichés form the bulk of the knowledge shared by expert engineers in any domain.

To deepen the reader's understanding of inspection methods and clichés and to explain the motivation for the Plan Calculus introduced in Chapter 3, this chapter presents informal introspective scenarios of program analysis and synthesis by inspection. The chapter ends with a discussion of issues in the codification and formalization of clichés.

2.1 Engineering Problem Solving

An important property shared by all engineering domains is the existence of standard, well-understood, primitive building blocks. For example, in electrical engineering all circuits are, at the lowest level, built out of resistors, capacitors, inductors, and so on. Similarly, in mechanical engineering, all devices are ultimately based on primitive mechanisms, such as levers, gears, rods, and pulleys. In software engineering, all programs can be constructed out of assignments, conditionals, and recursion. This feature of engineering domains distinguishes them from many other problem-solving domains studied in artificial intelligence (e.g., medical diagnosis) in which there are no well-established primitive levels of description.

A second common property of engineering domains is that the paradigmatic problem to be solved has the following form: Given a vocabulary of primitives and rules for their legitimate combination, devise a composite (usually hierarchical) structure that has some desired behavior. This characterization distinguishes engineering problems from other kinds of problems studied in artificial intelligence (e.g., pattern recognition) in which the relationship between structure and behavior is not the central concern.

In addition to the central synthesis problem described above, engineers must be able to analyze a device (i.e., infer its behavioral properties from its structure) and modify the structure of the device (i.e., debug it) to achieve a desired modification in behavior.

Uniform General Methods

Two different approaches have evolved for solving engineering problems. One approach, *uniform general methods*, takes advantage of the fact that the primitive elements of the domain have well-understood behaviors. For example, in electrical engineering, one way to determine a linear circuit's frequency response is to solve a set of equations derived from the network topology of resistances, capacitances, and inductances in the circuit.

Similarly, in mechanical engineering, one way to analyze the stresses and strains in a mechanical structure is by the *finite element method*. This method comes down to solving (usually by computer) a set of equations derived from viewing the mechanical structure as a grid of primitive geometric elements interacting in simple ways.

Software engineering also has its uniform general methods. For example, in the Floyd-Hoare approach to program verification [103, 113] a theorem is derived from the structure of a program, its desired behavior (specification), and the semantics of the programming-language primitives. The program is verified by proving this theorem (again, usually by computer).

Uniform general methods, such as these examples, have several attractive properties. First, they are based on firm mathematical foundations. As a result, their domain is well defined—you know when they will work and when they will not. Second, the solution process is algorithmic and thus amenable to conventional computerization.

Despite these attractive features, experienced engineers typically use uniform general methods only as a last resort. The reason for this is that these methods typically return only an *answer*. They yield little insight into what the engineer is ultimately concerned with, namely, the detailed relationship between structure and behavior in the device. The engineer needs to understand this relationship in order to modify the structure of the device—for example, to bring its behavior closer to the desired behavior.

Unfortunately, in real engineering applications (including software), a detailed description of how the behavior of a composite device follows from the interaction of the behaviors of its primitive components is extremely complex. In response to this complexity, engineering communities have evolved intermediate vocabularies, giving names to those few out of all possible combinations of primitives that have been useful in practice.

Inspection Methods

Suppose you show an electrical engineer a circuit and ask him to tell you its *gain* (the ratio between the strength of the output signal and the strength of the input signal). The first thing an experienced engineer will do is attempt to *recognize* the form of the circuit. For example, the engineer might identify the circuit as being a two-stage audio amplifier. Given this recognition, answering questions about the circuit's behavior is easy. For instance, given a two-stage audio amplifier, the gain is simply the product of the ratios of pairs of resistors at certain standard points in the circuit.

In electrical engineering, answering questions about a circuit by first recognizing its form is called *analysis by inspection*. Only if you intentionally concoct an obscure circuit can you force an experienced engineer to resort to the general method of translating the circuit into a set of equations.

Similarly in software engineering, suppose you show an experienced software engineer a large data-processing system and inquire as to its maximum running time for given size inputs. Rather than resorting to the first principles of complexity analysis, the experienced engineer will first identify the algorithms being employed and then use their known properties to compute the running time.

There is also *synthesis by inspection*. For example, faced with the task of implementing a common electrical behavior, such as a high-gain, low-impedance amplifier, the hallmark of an experienced electrical engineer is the ability to retrieve from a mental (or actual) "cook book" an appropriate first-cut design, which may subsequently be modified and refined. Similarly, faced with the task of implementing a common software behavior, such as associative retrieval, the hallmark of an experienced software engineer is the ability to call to mind a repertoire of appropriate standard techniques, such as hashing, discrimination nets, and association lists.

We call these engineering problem-solving methods based on the recognition and use of standard forms *inspection methods*; we call the standard forms *clichés*.

Clichés

Examples of clichés in electrical engineering include *two-stage audio amplifier*, *multiplexing*, and *voltage divider*. Examples of clichés in software engineering include *information system*, *associative retrieval*, and *linear search*.

In general, a cliché contains both fixed parts and parts that vary from one occurrence of the cliché to the next. A cliché may also include constraints that restrict the implementation of the parts and/or compute some parts from others.

Clichés form the shared technical vocabulary of a discipline. Although the word cliché has a negative connotation when used in the context of literary criticism, in engineering, the repeated use of the same forms of expression is desirable. Reuse improves productivity in the design process, as well as the ease of comprehension (and thus maintenance) of the resulting devices.

Concepts similar to the idea of clichés appear in software engineering in the work of Arango and Freeman [84] (domain models), Harandi and Young [111] (design templates), and Lavi [122] (generic models); and in artificial intelligence in the work of Minsky [135, 136] (frames, concept germs), Schank and Abelson [145] (scripts), and Chapman [39] (cognitive clichés). Soloway and Ehrlich [148] have conducted a number of empirical studies that support the psychological reality of software clichés.

2.2   Analysis by Inspection

Imagine that you are part of the maintenance team for a large software system. You have been assigned a system-enhancement task that requires a hash table. In the utilities portion of the system sources, you find the code shown in Figure 2.1. (In the interest of brevity, the figure omits definitions for the functions: KEY, which extracts the key field from an entry; HASH, which computes a numerical index from an input key; and MAKE-TABLE, which creates a new empty hash table.) Unfortunately, as you begin to use this hash-table implementation in your application, you realize that the documentation does not answer an important question: How does the implementation handle duplicate keys? More specifically, what will happen if you insert two entries with the same key and then call TABLE-LOOKUP with that key? What will happen if you subsequently call TABLE-DELETE with the same key and then TABLE-LOOKUP? (Perhaps, in the original application, duplicate keys never occurred, so the implementor did not think to document the answers to these questions.)

You might consider solving this analysis problem by formulating it as a set of theorems—something along the lines of proving that for any table t

```
(DEFUN TABLE-LOOKUP (TABLE INPUT)
  (LET ((BUCKET (AREF TABLE (HASH INPUT TABLE))))
    (LOOP
      (IF (NULL BUCKET) (RETURN NIL))
      (LET ((ENTRY (CAR BUCKET)))
        (IF (EQUAL (KEY ENTRY) INPUT) (RETURN ENTRY)))
      (SETQ BUCKET (CDR BUCKET)))))

(DEFUN TABLE-INSERT (TABLE ENTRY)
  (PUSH ENTRY
        (AREF TABLE (HASH (KEY ENTRY) TABLE)))
  TABLE)

(DEFUN TABLE-DELETE (TABLE INPUT)
  (LET* ((INDEX (HASH INPUT TABLE))
         (BUCKET (AREF TABLE INDEX)))
    (IF (EQUAL (KEY (CAR BUCKET)) INPUT)
        (SETF (AREF TABLE INDEX) (CDR BUCKET))
        (BUCKET-DELETE BUCKET INPUT)))
  TABLE)

(DEFUN BUCKET-DELETE (BUCKET INPUT)
  (LET ((PREVIOUS BUCKET))
    (LOOP
      (SETQ BUCKET (CDR PREVIOUS))
      (IF (NULL BUCKET) (RETURN NIL))
      (WHEN (EQUAL (KEY (CAR BUCKET)) INPUT)
        (RPLACD PREVIOUS (CDDR PREVIOUS))
        (RETURN NIL))
      (SETQ PREVIOUS BUCKET))))
```

Figure 2.1 Part of a Common Lisp implementation of a hash table.

and entries e_1 and e_2 with key k:

$$lookup\,(insert\,(insert\,(t, e_2), e_1), k) = e_2$$
$$lookup\,(delete\,(insert\,(insert\,(t, e_1), e_2), k), k) = nil$$

If theorems like these are true, you can feel free to insert and delete entries without worrying about duplicates. However, if they are not true, you need to understand how the proofs fail so that you know which behaviors of TABLE-INSERT and TABLE-DELETE you can rely on.

If you are an experienced programmer, you are more likely to take the approach of first studying the code to discover which clichés were used— sometimes called *reverse engineering*—and then answering the questions based on your understanding of the design. In this example, you know from experience that there are basically two ways to handle duplicate entries: Either check for duplicates at insertion time or search for duplicates at deletion time. The questions then boil down to recognizing which, if either, of these two decisions was made in the code. In addition, by understanding the code completely first, you are in a good position to modify the program to fit your current application.

Let us now proceed step by step through an introspective account of recognizing the clichés in the code in Figure 2.1. As well as introducing further examples of software clichés, this scenario illustrates some important structural aspects of clichés that must be addressed in their formal representation. (Note that Chapter 10 describes a prototype system that automatically performs cliché recognition similar to the recognition illustrated in the scenario below.)

Table Lookup

We begin with the first function in Figure 2.1, TABLE-LOOKUP. This function is essentially a loop. A key feature of a loop is the number and form of its exit conditions. The loop in TABLE-LOOKUP has two exits as indicated in Figure 2.2. More specifically, it is an instance of the cliché *linear search*:

> A *linear search* is a loop in which a given predicate is applied to a succession of values (in this case, the values of the variable ENTRY) until either a value is found that satisfies the predicate, in which case the loop is terminated and the value satisfying the predicate is made available outside the loop (in this case via (RETURN ENTRY)) or the loop is terminated because the search has failed (in this case, because we have reached the end of the list BUCKET).

Figure 2.3 indicates that TABLE-LOOKUP also contains an occurrence of one of the most familiar Lisp clichés, namely, the CAR, CDR, NULL pattern of *cdr enumeration*. Note that *pattern* in this context does not mean a particular configuration of the program string or parse tree, but rather a particular set of operations connected by the appropriate data and control flow. In the case of cdr enumeration, for example, data must flow from the

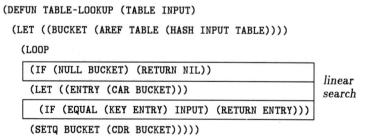

Figure 2.2 Recognition of the cliché linear search.

```
(DEFUN TABLE-LOOKUP (TABLE INPUT)
  (LET ((BUCKET (AREF TABLE (HASH INPUT TABLE))))
    (LOOP
      (IF (NULL BUCKET) (RETURN NIL))
      (LET ((ENTRY (CAR BUCKET)))
        (IF (EQUAL (KEY ENTRY) INPUT) (RETURN ENTRY)))
      (SETQ BUCKET (CDR BUCKET)))))
```

cdr enumeration *linear search*

Figure 2.3 Recognition of the cliché cdr enumeration.

output of CDR to the input of CDR on the next iteration, and control must exit from the iteration when the NULL test succeeds.

An important aspect of clichés illustrated in Figure 2.3 is that occurrences of clichés can overlap. In particular, the NULL exit test is part of two different clichés: It is the failure exit of the linear search and also the empty test of the cdr enumeration. This way of decomposing programs violates the strictly hierarchical approach of most current programming methodologies. However, we will see several examples in which overlapping decomposition is necessary in order to recognize all the clichés in a program.

Table Insert

The code for TABLE-INSERT is a single expression. The only cliché used has already migrated into the programming language: The PUSH macro in Lisp captures the clichéd use of CONS to add an element onto the front of a Lisp list, as in

```
(SETQ L (CONS ... L)).
```

Table Delete

Moving on to TABLE-DELETE (Figure 2.4), we see that the body of this function is a conditional that checks for a common special-case that comes up in the implementation of destructive deletion operations, namely, deleting the element at the head of the data structure. This cliché, called *special-case head deletion*, can be described in English as follows:

> If the head of a data structure (in this case, the car of the list BUCKET) satisfies the criterion for destructive deletion (in this case, its KEY is equal to the input key), then update all pointers to the head of the structure to point instead to the tail of the structure (in this case the cdr of the list); otherwise, use a destructive deletion operation that works for *internal* (nonhead) elements.

```
(DEFUN TABLE-DELETE (TABLE INPUT)
 (LET* ((INDEX (HASH KEY TABLE))
        (BUCKET (AREF TABLE INDEX)))
```

```
  (IF (EQUAL (KEY (CAR BUCKET)) INPUT)
      (SETF (AREF TABLE INDEX) (CDR BUCKET))
      (BUCKET-DELETE BUCKET INPUT)))
```
*special-case
head deletion*

```
 TABLE)
```

Figure 2.4 Recognition of the cliché special-case head deletion.

This example illustrates that abstract data structures need to be part of the formalization of software clichés, since in the definition of this cliché we want to refer abstractly to the *head* and *tail* of a structure, as distinct from any particular implementation, such as the car and cdr of a Lisp list.

Bucket Delete

Moving on to BUCKET-DELETE (Figure 2.5), note that like TABLE-LOOKUP, this function contains a linear search. The syntax in this case is different from the syntax in Figure 2.2. However, the data- and control-flow relationships between the two loop exits are the same.

BUCKET-DELETE also has instances of CAR, CDR, and NULL operations with data and control flow between them satisfying the constraints of the cliché cdr enumeration (see Figure 2.6). However, this occurrence of the cliché has an additional bit of structure, called a *trailing pointer*. On each iteration, there is a pointer (in the variable PREVIOUS) to the cell in the list whose cdr is the current cell being enumerated (in the variable BUCKET). This extension of cdr enumeration, called *trailing cdr enumeration*, is commonly used, as is the case here, in connection with destructive deletion operations. This example illustrates that software-engineering knowledge includes not only

```
(DEFUN BUCKET-DELETE (BUCKET INPUT)
 (LET ((PREVIOUS BUCKET))
  (LOOP
   (SETQ BUCKET (CDR PREVIOUS))
```

```
   (IF (NULL BUCKET) (RETURN NIL))
   (WHEN (EQUAL (KEY (CAR BUCKET)) INPUT)
     (RPLACD PREVIOUS (CDDR PREVIOUS))
     (RETURN NIL))
```
*linear
search*

```
   (SETQ PREVIOUS BUCKET))))
```

Figure 2.5 Recognition of the cliché linear search.

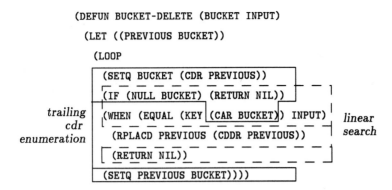

Figure 2.6 Recognition of the cliché trailing cdr enumeration.

clichés, but also relationships between them, such as extension.

The last cliché recognized in BUCKET-DELETE is *splice out* (see Figure 2.7). The use of side effects like RPLACA and RPLACD can lead to extremely hard-to-understand code. However, in this case RPLACD is being used in a very specific context: Its second argument is the current pointer of a cdr enumeration, and its first argument is the corresponding trailing pointer. This use of RPLACD removes the currently enumerated element from the list (as a side effect). It is often the case that recognizing a cliché can bypass reasoning that would otherwise be intractable.

Using the Results of Cliché Recognition

Given the understanding illustrated in Figures 2.2–2.7 of the clichés used in the hash-table functions, it is easy to answer the original question. The implementation does *not* handle duplicate keys, because there is no checking for duplicate keys at insertion time (TABLE-INSERT just does a push) or at deletion time (the linear search cliché used in TABLE-DELETE stops after

```
(DEFUN BUCKET-DELETE (BUCKET INPUT)
  (LET ((PREVIOUS BUCKET))
    (LOOP
      (SETQ BUCKET (CDR PREVIOUS))
      (IF (NULL BUCKET) (RETURN NIL))
      (WHEN (EQUAL (KEY (CAR BUCKET)) INPUT)
        (RPLACD PREVIOUS (CDDR PREVIOUS))      splice
                                               out
        (RETURN NIL))
      (SETQ PREVIOUS BUCKET))))
```

Figure 2.7 Recognition of the cliché splice out.

finding the first value satisfying the predicate). Therefore, to ensure the correct operation of your application, you must call `TABLE-DELETE` before each call to `TABLE-INSERT` in which the entry might have a duplicate key.

Furthermore, with this detailed understanding of the relationship between the structure and behavior of the program, you are also in a good position to modify the program. For example, suppose you decide to handle duplicate keys at deletion time. There are two changes you need to make to the program.

First, you need to replace the cliché linear search used in `BUCKET-DELETE` by a related cliché, *exhaustive linear search*, which does not stop after finding the first value satisfying the predicate, but rather searches for *all* values satisfying the predicate. The splice-out action is then applied to each entry found by the search.

Second, because there could be several duplicate keys at the head of a bucket, the cliché special-case head deletion in `TABLE-DELETE` needs to be replaced by an exhaustive linear search in which the head-deletion action (the `SETF`) is applied to each case found. (As an optimization to save code, this loop could be combined with the loop in `BUCKET-DELETE`.)

When the hash-table functions are viewed as the composition of clichés such as linear search, splice out, and so on, these algorithmic changes are modular—a matter of adding or replacing a small number of conceptual parts—even though this may result in many scattered changes at the code level.

2.3   Synthesis by Inspection

The notion of recognizing familiar forms applies not only to analysis, but also to the synthesis of programs. For example, consider synthesizing a program to satisfy the following specification: Given a set b and a key k, return a value e, such that

$$(e \in b \ \wedge \ key(e) = k) \ \vee \ (e = nil \ \wedge \ \forall x \in b \ key(x) \neq k).$$

A well-known uniform general method for program synthesis is to treat such a specification as a theorem (literally, $\forall bk \exists e \ \dots$). If this theorem can be proved using constructive proof techniques, a program satisfying the specification can be extracted from the proof.

However, if you are an experienced programmer, you will recognize that this specification is not some arbitrary formula in first-order logic, but rather an instance of a common specification cliché called *find if present*: Given an aggregate data structure (such as a set), find an element satisfying some criterion; or if there is none, return a distinguished value. From experience, this specification suggests the combination of a linear search with an enumeration.

The *enumeration* cliché, illustrated by the following code fragment, is a generalization of cdr enumeration. Enumeration is applicable to any data structure that supports the operations of selecting the current element (*current*), computing an aggregate with all but the current element (*rest*), and testing for empty (*empty*).

```
(LET ((X ...))
  (LOOP
    (IF (empty X) (RETURN NIL))
    ... (current X) ...
    (SETQ X (rest X))))
```

Combining linear search with enumeration and choosing variable names based on the specification yields:

```
(LET ((B ...))
  (LOOP
    (IF (empty B) (RETURN NIL))
    (LET ((E (current B)))
      (IF (found E) (RETURN E)))
    (SETQ B (rest B))))
```

The next step in the synthesis is implementing the *found* test of the linear search as $key(e) = k$ (the test in the specification).

```
(LET ((B ...))
  (LOOP
    (IF (empty B) (RETURN NIL))
    (LET ((E (current B)))
      (IF (EQUAL (KEY E) K) (RETURN E)))
    (SETQ B (rest B))))
```

Finally, if the set *b* is implemented as a Lisp list, then *current*, *rest*, and *empty* are filled in with CAR, CDR, and NULL, respectively. This results in the algorithm below, used in the loop body of TABLE-LOOKUP (see Figure 2.1).

```
(LET ((B ...))
  (LOOP
    (IF (NULL B) (RETURN NIL))
    (LET ((E (CAR B)))
      (IF (EQUAL (KEY E) K) (RETURN E)))
    (SETQ B (CDR B))))
```

This example of synthesis by inspection illustrates two kinds of relationships between clichés: implementation of one cliché by another (enumeration and linear search can be used to implement the find-if-present cliché) and specialization (cdr enumerations are a subset of enumerations).

2.4 Codifying Clichés

Figure 2.8 illustrates some of the structure of the space of software clichés by showing the relationship between the clichés used in three areas: statistical programming, graphics programming, and systems programming.

The shaded intersection of the three areas represents basic software-engineering techniques, including common data structures (e.g., arrays,

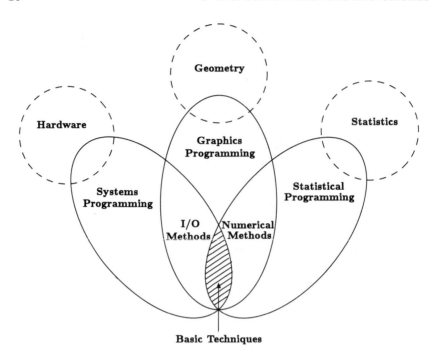

Figure 2.8 A Venn diagram suggesting the structure of software and application domain knowledge.

lists, and sets) and common algorithms (e.g., counting, searching, and sorting). This is the knowledge you find in basic texts, such as [83] or [120]. These clichés are predominantly algorithmic in nature and oriented toward the specification and implementation end of the software process. All the clichés in this chapter fall into this category.

The overlap between each pair of elliptical areas in Figure 2.8 represents clichés of intermediate generality. For example, numerical methods are used in both statistical programming and graphics programming; input/output methods are used in both graphics programming and systems programming.

The remaining part of each area in Figure 2.8 represents the most specialized clichés. Note that as software knowledge becomes more specialized, it begins to overlap with domain knowledge (the dashed circles). For example, in the case of statistical programming, one has to eventually understand the science of statistics; in the case of graphics programming, one eventually gets involved in geometry; in the case of systems programming, one needs to eventually deal with the physical properties of hardware devices, such as printers and disk drives. (See [88] for further discussion of the role of domain knowledge in automatic programming.)

Also, as one moves away from basic techniques toward more specialized areas, the proportion of requirements and specification clichés tends to increase. Certainly, specialized programming areas have specialized algorithmic knowledge, but specialized areas also tend to have more nonalgorithmic, domain-specific clichés.

In the Programmer's Apprentice project, we have begun our codification effort in the central shaded area of Figure 2.8. We have compiled an initial library (see [32]) of several hundred basic clichés including the ones below. (Barstow and Green [87, 108] have codified a similar body of clichés in this same general area using a transformational formalism.)

- Abstract data structures, such as set, graph, mapping, list, sequence, and tree.

- Operations, such as inverting a mapping, modifying arcs in a graph, and addition, deletion, and associative retrieval in a set.

- Data structure implementations, such as indexed sequence and hash table.

- Algorithm fragments, such as searching, enumerating, and accumulating.

Many of these clichés are discussed in this chapter and in the example KBEmacs sessions in Chapters 7 and 8. (The List of Clichés on page 231 lists all the clichés appearing in this book.) We estimate that perhaps a thousand clichés are required to reach a reasonable degree of completeness in basic techniques. Several thousand more clichés in specific areas would be required for a full-scale cliché library.

We are continuing the codification effort in two directions. First, we are expanding the library of basic techniques. This effort is being driven in part by work on program optimization [61]. Second, we are exploring a few application areas. An important focus of this work is on nonalgorithmic clichés such as *information system*. The parts of this cliché include an *information schema*; a set of *transactions* that can create, modify, or delete the data; a set of *reports* that display parts of the data; *integrity constraints* on the data; a *staff* that manages the information system; and *users* who utilize the information system. (Further examples of design and requirements clichés are presented in Chapter 11.)

The next three chapters describe a formalism, called the Plan Calculus, that we have developed to represent algorithmic clichés. Nonalgorithmic clichés are represented in the Programmer's Apprentice using standard frame-based knowledge-representation techniques (see Chapter 11).

Chapter 3

The Plan Calculus

The Plan Calculus is a formal representation for programs and algorithmic clichés. This chapter introduces the basic features of the Plan Calculus and relates the Plan Calculus to alternate formalisms. Chapters 4 and 5 describe the syntax and semantics of the Plan Calculus in greater detail.

3.1 Key Properties

The scenarios in Chapter 2 may create the impression that an algorithmic cliché can be represented most directly as a program template, i.e., a program text fragment with holes to be filled in. Although this is an effective expository technique, program templates lack four key properties essential to a knowledge representation for algorithmic clichés: canonical form, language independence, convenience of manipulation, and expressiveness.

Canonical Form

Consider the cliché linear search from Section 2.2:

> A *linear search* is a loop in which a given predicate is applied to a succession of values until either a value is found that satisfies the predicate, in which case the loop is terminated and the value satisfying the predicate is made available outside the loop or the loop is terminated because the search has failed.

In a library of clichés, one wants a unique representation for this cliché. Unfortunately, in Lisp and other programming languages, the cliché can be

23

written in many ways. It can be written using the `LOOP` macro:

```
(LOOP
  (IF failed (RETURN))
  ...
  (IF (found X) (RETURN X))
  ...)
```

It can be written using `PROG` with only one `RETURN`, instead of two:

```
(PROG ()
  LP (UNLESS failed
      ...
      (IF (found X) (RETURN X))
      ...
      (GO LP)))
```

It can be written tail recursively:

```
(DEFUN SEARCH ()
  (UNLESS failed
     ...
    (COND ((found X) X)
          (T ... (SEARCH)))))
```

As abstract syntax trees, the three templates above have very different structures. Yet, from the point of view of their semantics, all three templates specify the same algorithm, i.e., the same set of computations with the same data and control relationships between them. (Some readers may feel that the tail-recursive version is fundamentally different. However, recent implementations of Lisp treat loops and tail recursion as alternate stylistic expressions of iteration, i.e., the tail recursion is executed without accumulating stack depth.)

The Plan Calculus represents clichés in a more canonical way than program templates because it represents data and control flow explicitly. For example, all three of the templates shown above (and many other textual variants) correspond to the *plan* shown in Figure 3.1.

The notation used in drawing plan diagrams is described in detail in the next chapter. For now, notice that the formalism is inspired by the diagrams programmers scrawl on blackboards and the backs of envelopes. A plan is essentially a hierarchical directed graph. Solid boxes denote operations and tests. Simple arcs between boxes denote data flow. Arcs with double crosshatch marks denote control flow. Dashed boxes denote subplans (in the case of Figure 3.1, a recursive instance of the plan as a whole).

Language Independence

An obvious defect of program templates is their language dependence. Since the compilation of cliché libraries is likely to be expensive, this cost must be

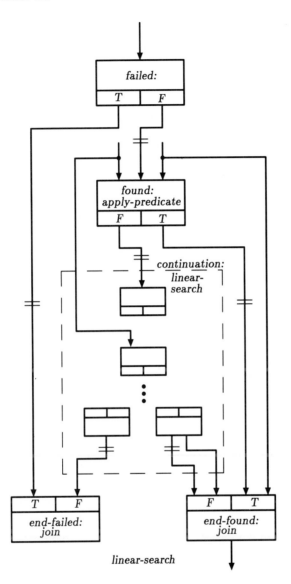

Figure 3.1 Plan for the cliché linear search.

amortized over the broadest possible user community. A separate library for each programming language makes this amortization more difficult.

Beyond this, common experience tells us that if a programmer knows how to use a cliché (such as hash table, linear search, or bubble sort) in one language, he also knows how to use it in other similar languages. From a theoretical point of view, we want the Programmer's Apprentice to have the same capability.

As shown in Figure 3.1, the Plan Calculus abstracts away from the details of algorithms that depend only on how they are expressed in particular programming languages, by omitting these details and representing the algorithms directly in terms of data flow and control flow. A program (or program template) in a conventional programming language is translated into the Plan Calculus as follows. First, the programming-language primitives are divided into two categories:

- *Connective tissue* primitives that are concerned solely with achieving data and control flow (e.g., PROG, COND, SETQ, GO, and RETURN in Lisp).

- *Computational* primitives that operate on the data types of the language (e.g., CAR, CDR, PLUS, NULL, and MINUSP in Lisp) and holes in a program template (e.g., *failed* in the template for linear search).

Each primitive operation, test, or hole is translated into a corresponding box. The connective tissue primitives are then translated into an appropriate pattern of arcs between the boxes. Loops are represented using recursive subplans. To date, we have implemented modules that translate from subsets of Fortran [71], Cobol [67], Lisp (see Chapter 7), and Ada (see Chapter 8) to the Plan Calculus.

Convenient Manipulation

As anyone who has written a complicated macro package can attest, the automated manipulation of program text can be quite tricky. Typical problems include unintended interactions due to accidental duplication of identifiers and awkward constructions due to mismatches of syntactic form. Moreover, manipulations that are simple from an algorithmic point of view are often awkward at the program text level.

For example, consider combining a cliché of the form

```
(A (B ...) (C ...) ...)
```

with another cliché of the form

```
(F (G ...) (H ...))
```

such that the output of G is used as the third input to A.

Using program templates, this combination requires a complicated sequence of rearrangements resulting in code such as the following:

```
(LET ((X (G ...)))
  (A (B ...) (C ...) X)
  (F X (H ...)))
```

In contrast, if these two clichés are represented as plans, they can be combined simply by adding the bold data-flow arc shown in Figure 3.2. The Plan Calculus is easier to manipulate than program text because the

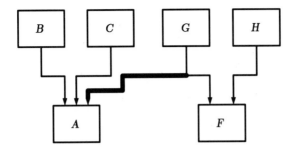

Figure 3.2 Combining two plans by adding a data-flow arc.

kinds of changes one typically wants to apply to an algorithm correspond
to changes that can be easily applied to a graph (i.e., addition and deletion
of arcs and nodes).

The use of data flow in the Plan Calculus also reduces the complexity
of manipulating and reasoning about programs by eliminating many apparent side effects. In the semantics of a conventional programming language,
every assignment statement is a side effect. However, most assignment
statements are merely part of a pattern of assignments and variable references that implement the movement of data from where it is produced to
where it is used. The Plan Calculus models this movement using data-flow
arcs instead.

For example, from a programming-language point of view, the following
code involves a side effect (to the variable X):

```
(SETQ X (P ...))
...
(Q X)
```

The corresponding plan, however, has no side effects in it. The use of
the variable X merely corresponds to a data-flow arc from operation P to
operation Q.

Expressiveness

Consider the template below for the enumeration cliché used in Section 2.3:

```
(LET ((X ...))
  (LOOP
    (IF (empty X) (RETURN))
    ... (current X) ...
    (SETQ X (rest X))))
```

This template captures the data- and control-flow structure of the enumeration cliché, albeit in a language-dependent, noncanonical, and hard-
to-manipulate way. However, the template leaves out an important part
of the content of the cliché, i.e., the constraints on how the three holes
(empty, current, and rest) can be filled in. The plan for the enumeration

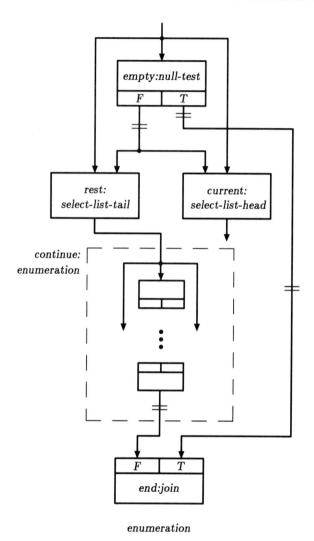

enumeration

Figure 3.3 Plan for the enumeration cliché.

cliché (see Figure 3.3) captures these constraints by restricting the types of the corresponding boxes. Each box is required to be the appropriate operation on a data abstraction called a *list*. A list is recursively defined as having two parts: the head (which has no type constraint) and the tail (which is either a list or the special type *null*, indicating the end of a list). The operations select-list-head and select-list-tail return the head and tail of a list, respectively. Null-test tests whether its input is of type null.

It is important to note that we are using the term *list* here in a very abstract sense. The enumeration plan can be used with any data structure that can be *viewed* as having a head and a tail. For example, a sequence can also be viewed as a list in which the head is the first term of the sequence and the tail is the subsequence starting at the second term. Similarly, *Lisp lists* are an implementation of lists in which the head is the car and tail is the cdr of a given cons cell. The facility in the Plan Calculus for constructing views is called *overlays* and is described in Chapter 5.

3.2 Plans

The choice of the term *plan* for the knowledge representation used in the Programmer's Apprentice is motivated from two directions. The primary meaning of the term comes from an analogy between software engineering and other kinds of engineering. In addition, there are important connections with planning in artificial intelligence.

Engineering Plans

Every engineering discipline has its own specialized schematic languages for representing the structure and behavior of devices and partial designs. For example, an electrical engineer uses circuit diagrams and block diagrams at various levels of abstraction; a structural engineer uses large-scale and detailed blueprints, which show both the architectural framework of a building and also various subsystems such as heating, wiring, and plumbing; and a mechanical engineer uses overlapping hierarchical descriptions of the interconnections between mechanical parts and assemblies. By analogy, software plans are hierarchical descriptions of computations. The Plan Calculus is intended to be a blueprint language for software.

A fundamental characteristic shared by all types of engineering plans is that each level of plan is defined by a set of parts, connections, and constraints. The *parts* of a plan may be specific physical components, such as transistors in a circuit diagram. More often, however, the decomposition is in terms of behavior. For example, a simple amplifier in an electrical block diagram is a box with input and output signals. As far as this level of plan is concerned, the amplification may be implemented in any number of ways. A primitive physical component may be used or another plan may be provided that decomposes the amplifier further. In the Plan Calculus, a part is typically an operation, a test, or a datum.

The *connections* of a plan may also be more or less abstract. In some electrical plans, parts are connected by physical wires. However, in an abstract electrical plan, the connection between parts is signal flow, which may have a more indirect physical realization, such as sharing a multiplexed channel with other signal flows. Connections in the Plan Calculus are expressed by data flow and control flow, which can also be viewed as an abstraction of many alternative realizations. Parts and connections together form the *structural description* of a plan.

The *constraints* of a plan restrict the implementation of the parts. The constraints on an amplifier part of an electrical plan might be $V_2 = kV_1$, where V_1 and V_2 are the input and output signals and k is the amplification factor. The language used in a plan's constraints plan depends on the domain. In electrical engineering, constraints typically involve relationships between continuous functions. Constraints in the Plan Calculus include the preconditions and postconditions of operations and tests, and the invariants of data representations. These constraints are expressed in the Programmer's Apprentice using a standard logical language (see Section 11.1).

Planning in Artificial Intelligence

The second sense of the term *plan* is taken from the planning subfield of artificial intelligence. The goal of a planning algorithm is to find a sequence of actions that transforms a given initial state into a desired final state. This problem is analogous to the synthesis of straight-line programs.

In early planning work (e.g., [102]), a plan was represented simply as a sequence of actions. Sacerdoti [144], however, showed that it was more efficient to use a partially ordered set of actions as the basic representation. In this representation, the planning algorithm needs to consider only those ordering constraints required by the current set of actions, rather than forcing an arbitrary total ordering. Similar benefits are obtained in the Plan Calculus by allowing the partial ordering of operations by data flow and control flow, rather than forcing the total ordering required by conventional programming languages.

The Plan Calculus shares a number of other features with plans used in planning research as well. For instance, the Plan Calculus can be used to represent programs and clichés at various levels of abstraction (as in [143]). In addition, the symbolic evaluation of plans in the Plan Calculus [46] is very similar to symbolic evaluation techniques used in planning in artificial intelligence.

3.3   Relation to Programming Languages

A frequent question is, isn't the Plan Calculus just another very high-level programming language? As with many such questions, the heart of the answer lies in defining the terms. In this case, it depends on exactly what is meant by the term *programming language*. Modern programming languages have two essential goals:

- To describe computations precisely enough to be executed by a machine.

- To serve as a communication medium between program writers and human readers.

In contrast, the two essential goals of the Plan Calculus are:

- To describe algorithmic clichés in a canonical, easy-to-combine, and language-independent form.

- To serve as a medium for the automated manipulation of programs.

The goals of the Plan Calculus are in some ways compatible with and in other ways in conflict with the goals of programming languages. As a result, the answer to the question above is not a simple yes or no.

Conventional programming languages force the programmer to provide enough detail so that a simple local interpreter (e.g., hardware, perhaps with an intermediate compilation step) can execute the code. Unfortunately, much of this detail, such as the choice of special forms used for binding variables, looping, conditional branching, etc., is often irrelevant to the algorithmic content of the code. As discussed earlier in this chapter, this aspect of conventional programming languages conflicts with the Plan Calculus's goal of canonical form.

The goals of human readability and service as a medium for automated manipulation can also conflict. For human reading, a critical restriction is that information must ultimately be laid out on a two-dimensional surface (the retina). In contrast, automated program manipulation systems impose no such intrinsic restriction. In automated systems, it is possible (and often desirable) to have very highly interconnected and tangled information structures, in which many kinds of information are locally available at each point.

Thus, the graphical nature of the Plan Calculus is motivated by a desire for ease of manipulation by an automated tool. As plan diagrams grow in size, however, they very quickly become hard for humans to understand visually. While it may turn out that the Plan Calculus is a good starting point for a graphically oriented human communication environment, this is not a goal of the Plan Calculus. How best to use graphics in software engineering is still an open research question.

Wide-Spectrum Languages

Recently, the notion of programming language has been extended to include so-called very high-level languages (VHLLs). Some of these VHLLs are executable, although not by a simple local interpreter and not very efficiently. Others are really specification languages, in the sense that the compiler is making significant implementation decisions, such as the choice of data structures and algorithms. Furthermore, most VHLLs are also *wide spectrum*, i.e., they include a conventional high-level language as a sublanguage.

The Plan Calculus is also a wide-spectrum language. The input/output and test boxes used in a plan may correspond to operations available in a conventional programming language, or they may be more abstract.

In summary, the answer to the question of whether the Plan Calculus is a programming language is *yes*, the Plan Calculus is a language with the expressive power of a wide-spectrum, very high-level programming language; but *no*, we do not expect programmers to use it directly.

Evolution of Languages

The evolution of programming languages is driven by at least two major forces. One is the desire to move an entire class of decision making from the programmer to the compiler. For example, advancing from machine language to high-level languages moved the task of register allocation to the compiler. Advancing from high-level to very high-level languages involves, among other things, making efficient data structure selection the responsibility of the compiler.

Language evolution is also driven by the recognition of common patterns of usage (clichés) in the current language, which are then incorporated into the syntax of the next language. For example, common patterns of jumps and tests in machine language became the structured control constructs of high-level languages. From this point of view, clichés can be viewed as recommendations for language design. (See [78] for an example of language design based on iteration clichés.) Moreover, this evolutionary process never stops—new clichés always arise at the next higher level.

3.4   Limitations of the Plan Calculus

This section outlines a number of known limitations of the Plan Calculus and suggests some directions for their remedy.

Canonical Form

A desired property of the Plan Calculus is that there be a unique representation for each cliché. Since being a cliché is essentially an empirical, pretheoretic notion, this property is not formally definable. There is, however, a closely related formal property of the Plan Calculus that is also desired (and unfortunately, does not hold in certain cases): Syntactically distinct plans should also be semantically distinct. The reason for desiring this property is illustrated in Figure 3.4.

The two plans on the left of Figure 3.4 have the same meaning, due to the transitivity of control flow. This is more than just a problem of redundancy. The same syntactic manipulation applied to each plan can result in two new plans with *different* meanings. Deleting the control-flow arc between B and C in the top plan results in a plan in which C is unordered with respect to A and B. Deleting the same arc in the bottom plan results in a plan in which C must still follow A. A similar problem arises with control-flow arcs that are redundant with data-flow arcs.

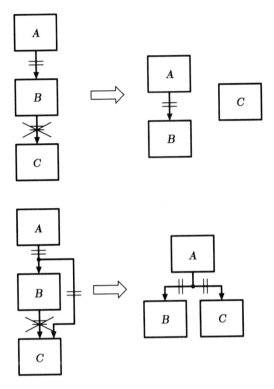

Figure 3.4 Although the two plans on the left have the same meaning and are modified in the same way, the resulting plans have different meanings.

One solution to this problem is to make plan diagrams canonical with respect to the transitive closure of the control flow. Under this solution, the top plan on the left of Figure 3.4 would be syntactically illegal. This restriction would also make it illegal to add a control-flow arc between B and C in the plan at the top-right of Figure 3.4 without adding an arc from A to C as well. The restriction could be conveniently enforced by automatically updating the transitive closure whenever a new control-flow arc is added.

An alternative approach to solving this problem is to move control flow out of the connections of a plan and into the constraints. This is being explored in the most recent implementation of the Plan Calculus (see Section 11.1).

Nonlocal Flow

Consider a program in which data flow is achieved by one module updating a global database and another module querying it. If the Plan Calculus is used straightforwardly, the entire database has to be an input and out-

put to every module that updates it, and an input to every module that
queries it. This representation does not capture the fact that certain modules may produce and consume only certain kinds of data in the global
data base. The intended data-flow graph may therefore be significantly
simpler than the straightforward data-flow graph. One approach to solving
this problem is to view a mutable object (such as a database) as conceptually partitioned into several separate objects, each with a separate data
flow.

A similar problem arises with the use of control-flow arcs to model
exception-handling facilities, such as CATCH and THROW in Lisp. The straightforward use of control-flow arcs requires a multiplicity of special control-flow
exits. For each possible exception, there must be an extra control-flow exit
from each module (and from each of its callers) in which the exception may
occur. Technically, the introduction of an extra control-flow exit makes a
module into a test specification (i.e., either the exception happens or it does
not). Conceptually, however, this seems wrong. What is needed is some
way of viewing the usual control flow separate from the exceptional control flow. Harel's statecharts [112] provide a nice solution to this problem
within a graphical formalism.

The problems described above may be summarized by observing that
the Plan Calculus is oriented toward representing the *local* flow of data and
control, while the examples above are a kind of nonlocal flow.

Other Kinds of Knowledge

There are at least two important kinds of knowledge used in the software
process that the Plan Calculus currently does not express.

The first kind of knowledge concerns the performance properties of algorithms. Performance knowledge is used, for example, to choose between
alternative implementations of an abstract data structure or input/output
specification. The most straightforward idea for adding this kind of information to the Plan Calculus would be to annotate plans with explicit
performance statements, such as "this is a quadratic algorithm," and so on.
However, this approach only scratches the surface of the issue. To make
effective engineering trade-offs, a formal language is also needed for char-
acterizing the distribution of input data to a program. Going even deeper,
a representational framework is needed within which programs can be analyzed to identify bottlenecks and within which potential optimizations can
be evaluated and compared. Recent work in this area by Kant [118] starts
with a program representation similar to the Plan Calculus.

A second important kind of knowledge not represented by the Plan Calculus concerns the structures and constraints of the application domain. For
example, Barstow [88, 89] has studied the role of mathematical models of
physical processes in the synthesis of oil-well-log interpretation software.
Since software can be written in any domain, the problem of represent-

ing domain knowledge in software is in principle equivalent to the general problem of knowledge representation in artificial intelligence. A particular challenge in the case of software, however, is understanding how domain knowledge interacts with computer science knowledge (algorithms, data structures, performance properties, and so on). Neighbors [140] has developed a transformation-based architecture in which domain descriptions can be formalized and combined with software implementation knowledge.

3.5   Other Approaches

Figure 3.5 traces the inheritance of ideas among the major approaches that have been used to represent algorithmic clichés and highlights the place of the Plan Calculus in this genealogy.

The two oldest approaches are subroutines and the encoding of clichés in procedures that generate "the right code" from some convenient input description. Subroutines are easy to combine (by writing programs that call them) but have limited expressive power. For example, it is impossible in many languages to write a subroutine that expresses the matrix multiplication algorithm without committing to a representation for the matrices (e.g., sparse versus dense) and the type of the elements (e.g., real versus complex). In contrast, program generators have essentially unlimited expressive power but are hard to combine. In addition, program generators suffer from the fact that they become increasingly difficult to modify as the number of clichés they encompass grows.

Macros are essentially a restricted and more tractable form of program generator, giving up some expressive power to improve combinability. Macro calls appear similar to subroutine calls, which makes them syntactically convenient to combine. However, the semantics of their combination is not as simple. For example, since a macro can perform arbitrary computation on its calling form to generate the resulting program text, nested macro calls can often have surprising results.

Program schemas (program templates with constraints on the holes) extend the expressive power of subroutines by allowing parameterization of any syntactic subunit of a program. Program schemas have been used by Wirth [157] to catalog programs based on recurrence relations, by Basu and Misra [90] to represent standard loops for which the loop invariant is known, and by Gerhart [105] and Misra [137] to represent and prove the properties of various other algorithmic clichés.

Unfortunately, as illustrated by the linear search example at the beginning of this chapter, the syntaxes of conventional programming languages (and therefore schemas based on them) do not provide a canonical form for clichés. In addition, when two program schemas are used in the same program, there may be unintended interactions between the text that fills the holes—for example, due to the use of the same variables.

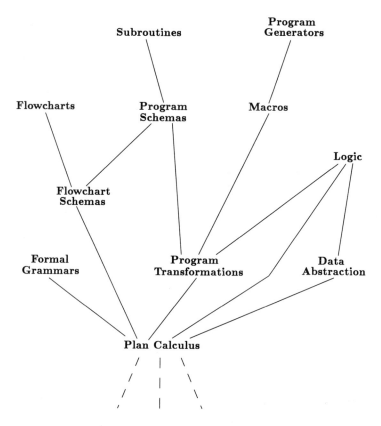

Figure 3.5 Genealogy of representations for algorithmic clichés.

Subroutines, macros, and program schemas all share the undesirable property of being programming-language dependent. One way to alleviate this problem is to use flowcharts. In the simplest version of this idea, there is a node for each program statement (including assignments) and arcs that represent the flow of control in a language-independent fashion. Adding data-flow arcs [95] in place of assignment statements further increases the language independence. Flowchart schemas [115, 129] stand in the same relationship to flowcharts as program schemas stand to subroutines.

Formal logic is another approach to representing clichés, which, like program generators, has unlimited expressive power in principle. Logical formalisms are also inherently programming-language independent. In logic, clichés are represented as sets of logical formulas, which are used as lemmas in the construction of programs. Program synthesis using formal logic has been demonstrated on small examples [130]. However, this approach is severely hampered by the apparent intractability of automatic theorem proving.

A quite successful approach that can be viewed as a restricted use of formal logic is data abstraction [106, 110, 124]. Languages, such as Alphard[158], CLU[123], and Ada[155], have been developed that explicitly support data abstraction. In these languages, one can express algorithmic clichés, such as matrix multiplication, as subroutines without mixing in decisions about data representation.

Program transformations [141], in particular knowledge-based transformations (also called refinement rules [87]), are currently the most commonly used approach for representing and using algorithmic clichés. (Some of the work on program transformations, such as the work on folding and unfolding [91], is aimed at improving the efficiency of programs by applying a fixed set of very general rules, rather than explicitly encoding knowledge of algorithmic clichés.)

A program transformation has three parts: a pattern (which is essentially a program schema), a set of logical applicability conditions, and an action (which is essentially a macro). A number of experimental systems have been developed that demonstrate the synthesis of programs using knowledge-based transformations [86, 92, 147].

A major deficiency of program transformations, in addition to language dependence, is their asymmetry—transformations used to support synthesis by inspection cannot be run in reverse to support analysis by inspection. Using the same clichés for analysis and synthesis is both theoretically desirable and practically important because analysis and synthesis steps are often intermingled in software development. Although it may be necessary for efficiency reasons to use different concrete representations of clichés for different purposes, these should be computed automatically from a single representation in the cliché library.

In contrast to transformations, encoding programming knowledge in a formal grammar is primarily motivated by analysis concerns. For example, Ruth [142] constructed a formal grammar representing the correct answers to an exercise in an introductory PL/1 programming class. Through a combination of top-down, bottom-up, and heuristic parsing techniques, the grammar was used to recognize correct and near-correct programs. Miller and Goldstein [133] also used a grammar formalism (implemented as an augmented transition network) to represent classes of programs in the domain of graphical programming. The major shortcoming of these grammars is that they are string-based and therefore too close to the programming language.

The Plan Calculus combines ideas from most of the representations discussed above. It achieves programming-language independence through the data and control-flow notions of flowchart schemas. It uses aspects of logic and data abstraction to represent data invariants and other constraints. Overlays (see Chapter 5) can be thought of as language-independent, bidirectional program transformations. For the purpose of program analysis, a library of plans can be treated as a formal graph grammar (see Chapter 10).

The Plan Calculus is one of the foundations of work on the Programmer's Apprentice. In addition, representations adopting some or all of the basic ideas of the Plan Calculus are being used by a number of other researchers to support work on program recognition [101, 128], tutoring [96, 121], algorithm design [117, 118], debugging [127], and maintenance [131].

This success notwithstanding, there is still significant work to be done in representing algorithmic clichés. Beyond fixing the specific limitations of the Plan Calculus described in Section 3.4, there are many unanswered general questions regarding the kinds of knowledge used by software engineers and how to represent that knowledge formally.

Chapter 4

Plan Diagrams

A plan diagram is a convenient graphical depiction of the structure (parts and connections) of a plan. This chapter defines the syntax of plan diagrams in detail and gives an informal description of their semantics via an interpreter.

4.1 Atomic Parts

Plans have three kinds of atomic parts: input/output specifications, test specifications, and join specifications (see Figure 4.1).

Input/Output Specifications

The box labeled *set-add* in Figure 4.1 is an example of an *input/output specification*. An input/output specification is drawn as a rectangular box with arcs entering at the top (denoting inputs) and leaving from the bottom (denoting outputs). Each input or output is labeled with a name followed by a colon and (optionally) a type constraint. Set-add has two inputs: *old* (a set) and *input* (no type constraint). The single output of set-add is called *new* (a set). The names of inputs and outputs within an input/output specification must be unique. However, the same names may be reused in other specifications.

The constraints associated with an input/output box typically specify preconditions and postconditions. For example, the postconditions of set-add state that the new set includes the input object, all the elements of the old set, and no others.

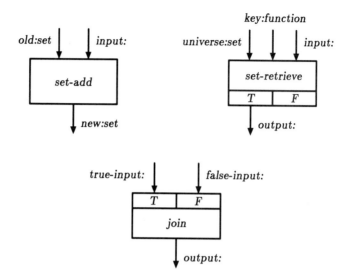

Figure 4.1 Examples of atomic plan diagram parts: an input/output specification (set-add), a test specification (set-retrieve), and a join specification (join).

Test Specifications

The box labeled *set-retrieve* in Figure 4.1 is an example of a *test specification*. A test specification is drawn as a rectangular box, with the bottom part divided into two sides labeled T and F. The inputs to a test specification are just like the inputs to an input/output specification. The outputs of a test specification are divided into two groups. The outputs produced when the test succeeds leave from the side labeled T. The outputs produced when the test fails leave from the side labeled F. Set-retrieve has three inputs: the *universe* (a set), the *key* (a function), and the *input*. The output of the set-retrieve box is called *output* and is defined only when the test succeeds.

As with input/output specifications, the constraints associated with a test specification typically include preconditions and postconditions. The preconditions of set-retrieve specify that the universe is a subset of the domain of the key function and that the input is a member of the range of the key function. The postconditions of set-retrieve specify that the output (when it is produced) is a member of the universe and that applying the key function to the output yields the input.

Test specifications also include a *test condition*, which is true if and only if the test succeeds. The test condition of set-retrieve specifies that there exists an element of the universe with the input key. (The generalization of test specifications to n mutually exclusive conditions is straightforward.)

Join Specifications

The box labeled *join* in Figure 4.1 is an example of a *join specification*. A join specification is drawn as a rectangular box with the top part divided into two sides labeled T and F. Join specifications are used to end conditional blocks. The inputs to a join specification are grouped similarly to the outputs of a test specification. The inputs on either the T or the F side are consumed only when the corresponding branch of the conditional block is executed. The constraints associated with the join box state that the output is equal to the true-input when the T case holds, or the false-input when the F case holds.

The join specification in Figure 4.1 has one input on each side and one output. There can be more inputs and outputs, but there must be the same number on each side and at the bottom. (Join specifications can be generalized to n mutually exclusive cases in a way analogous to test specifications.)

Unlike input/output and test specifications, join specifications do not correspond to any real computation. Rather, they specify how the data available for further computation depends on the prior flow of control.

4.2   Connections

Input/output specifications, test specifications, and join specifications are combined to form plan diagrams using two kinds of connections.

Data Flow

The first kind of connection is *data flow*. In plan diagrams, data flow is depicted using arcs connecting outputs to inputs. Data-flow arcs may fan out (i.e., there may be several arcs originating at a given output) but may not fan in (i.e., there may be only one arc terminating at a given input). Directed cycles are not allowed. (Loops are represented using tail recursion, as described in Section 4.6.)

The right side of Figure 4.2 shows a simple plan diagram constructed using data flow. This plan, equality-within-epsilon, checks whether two quantities are equal within some tolerance. Each box in a plan has a unique name, so that multiple instances of boxes with the same type can be referred to unambiguously. These names identify the *parts* of the plan. The parts of the plan equality-within-epsilon are *subtract*, *normalize*, and *compare*. These parts are constrained to have the types difference, absolute-value, and less-than, respectively. To reduce clutter in plan diagrams, the names and type constraints on the inputs and outputs of the boxes are usually omitted. This information can be determined by looking at the definition of the box type. (See the left side of Figure 4.2.)

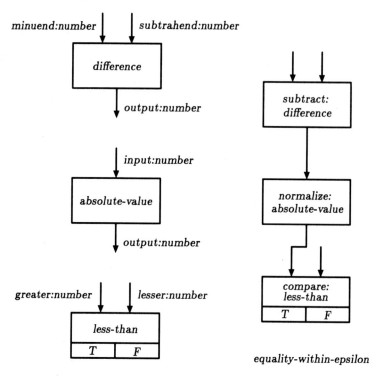

Figure 4.2 The box types on the left are used to construct the plan on the right.

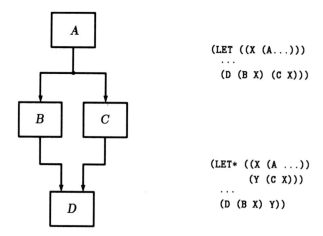

Figure 4.3 A partially ordered plan and two possible code realizations.

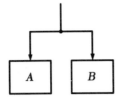

Figure 4.4 A plan in which two inputs are "wired together."

Data-flow arcs in plan diagrams are an abstraction of various data-flow mechanisms in programming languages, such as nesting of expressions, intermediate variables, and special forms. For example, in the following Lisp realization of equality-within-epsilon, all the data flow is achieved by nesting:

```
(< (ABS (- ... ...)) ...)
```

The same data flow could be coded using an intermediate variable,

```
(LET ((X (- ... ...)))
  (< (ABS X) ...)))
```

or a combination of nesting, an intermediate variable, and a special form:

```
(LET ((Y (PROG ...
              (RETURN (ABS (- ... ...)))))))
  (< Y ...))
```

Data-flow connections provide a second kind of abstraction of program text as well. Any order of steps is allowed in a program using the cliché, as long as the order is compatible with (i.e., a completion of) the partial order specified by the data flow. The left side of Figure 4.3 shows a plan diagram in which the data flow only partially constrains the order of steps in the computation. Both of the code realizations at the right of the figure are allowed by this plan.

A different kind of structural feature involving data flow is illustrated in Figure 4.4. In this plan, the inputs to A and B are "wired together." This means that when this plan is combined with other plans, the data flow to A and B must come from the same place.

Control Flow

The second kind of structural connection in plans is *control flow*. In plan diagrams, control flow is depicted using arcs with double crosshatch marks between *exit points* and *entry points*. Input/output specifications have a single entry point (at the top of the box) and a single exit point (at the bottom of the box). Test specifications have a single entry point (at the top of the box) and an exit point for each case (along the bottom of the

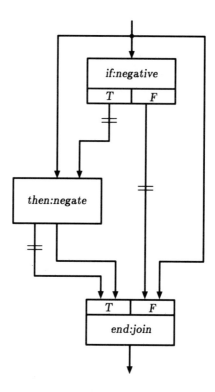

negate-if-negative

Figure 4.5 A plan diagram illustrating control flow and data flow.

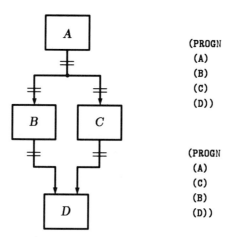

```
(PROGN
 (A)
 (B)
 (C)
 (D))


(PROGN
 (A)
 (C)
 (B)
 (D))
```

Figure 4.6 A plan partially ordered by control flow and two code realizations.

box). Join specifications have an entry point for each case (along the top of the box) and a single exit point (at the bottom of the box). Control-flow arcs may both fan in and fan out. Directed cycles are not allowed.

Figure 4.5 shows a simple plan diagram, negate-if-negative, constructed using control flow and data flow. This plan computes the absolute value of a number by negating it if it is negative.

Note that absolute-value is an input/output specification (used, for example, in the plan equality-within-epsilon in Figure 4.2), which has the postcondition that the output is the absolute value of the input. In contrast, negate-if-negative is a plan (combination of steps) that implements absolute-value. In general, several different plans may implement a given specification. (The notion of a plan implementing a specification is captured in overlays; see Chapter 5.)

Control-flow arcs in plan diagrams are an abstraction of various control-flow mechanisms in programming languages, such as nesting of expressions, sequencing primitives, and special forms. For example, in the following Lisp realization of negate-if-negative, the necessary control flow is achieved using the special form IF:

```
(IF (MINUSP X) (SETQ X (- X)))
```

The same control flow is achieved in a more complicated way in the following code through the interaction of the special forms COND, PROG, and RETURN:

```
(PROG ...
   (COND ((MINUSP X) ...)
         (T (RETURN)))
   (SETQ X (- X)))
```

Control flow in plan diagrams has a different meaning than control flow in typical flowchart languages. In the semantics of the Plan Calculus, a control-flow connection is a restriction on possible execution orders, whereas in flowcharts, control flow is an abstract "go to" instruction. A control-flow arc between box A and box B in a plan diagram means that B *eventually* follows A, not that B immediately follows A. Control flow, unlike data flow, is therefore transitive. (See next section for another way of understanding the meaning of control-flow arcs.)

Like data flow, control flow provides a partial-order abstraction of program text. Conventional programming languages do not distinguish between the necessary orderings of program steps and those that are chosen arbitrarily. Using the Plan Calculus, however, any order of steps is allowed in the final program, as long as it is compatible with (i.e., a completion of) the partial order specified by the data and control flow. The left side of Figure 4.6 shows a plan diagram in which control flow only partially constrains the order of steps in the computation. Both of the code realizations at the right of the figure are allowed by this plan.

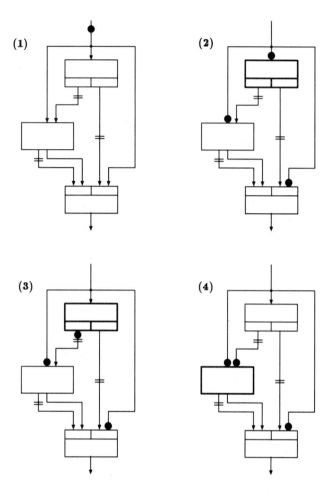

Figure 4.7 An example (continued in Figure 4.8) of executing the plan diagram for negate-if-negative (see Figure 4.5) according to the parallel execution model.

4.3   A Parallel Execution Model for Plan Diagrams

The meaning of a plan diagram is defined formally as the set of computation sequences the plan allows (see [32, 34]). However, a useful intuitive model for plan diagrams is to imagine their direct execution as parallel data-flow programs. This section describes a set of rules for executing plan diagrams. Figures 4.7 and 4.8 show an example execution of the negate-if-negative plan. The large solid circles represent data and control tokens flowing along arcs. Activated boxes are indicated in bold. A symbolic interpreter for plan diagrams along these lines was implemented by Shrobe [46].

Basically, plan diagrams are executed by having *tokens* flow between boxes along the data- and control-flow arcs in a plan. Boxes consume tokens at the top and produce tokens at the bottom. The tokens that flow

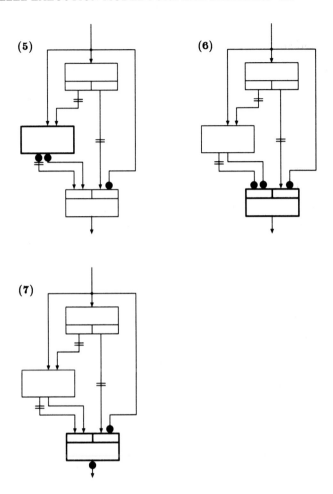

Figure 4.8 Continuation of Figure 4.7, showing an example of executing the plan diagram for negate-if-negative according to the parallel execution model.

along data-flow arcs are data objects with the appropriate properties. The tokens that flow along control-flow arcs control conditional execution; they have no other properties.

Execution is initiated by supplying tokens representing the starting data. These tokens come from outside of the diagram and are provided at each input that does not have a data-flow arc terminating on it. Execution then proceeds in parallel according to the rules below.

An input/output specification is activated as soon as a token has arrived over each of its incoming arcs. If there is fan-in of control flow, a token must arrive on *each* control-flow arc. (Since there are no directed cycles, it is not possible for two tokens to be transmitted over the same arc.)

When activation occurs, the input data is checked to see whether the preconditions are satisfied. If they are not satisfied, execution terminates abnormally; otherwise, output data satisfying the postconditions is produced at each output and a control token is produced at the exit point.

When tokens are produced at an output or exit point, they are propagated along the data-flow and control-flow arcs to the inputs and entry points at the destinations of the arcs. Where there is fan-out of data-flow arcs, multiple pointers to the same data are created, as opposed to multiple copies. (This allows the modeling of side effects. See Section 4.5.) Where there is fan-out of control-flow arcs, it does not matter whether you copy or create pointers, since control tokens have no distinct properties.

Test specifications are activated in the same way as input/output specifications. When activation occurs, the input data is checked to see whether the preconditions are satisfied. If they are not satisfied, execution terminates abnormally; otherwise, the test condition is checked. If the test condition is true, output data and a control token are produced on the T side; otherwise, output data and a control token are produced on the F side.

A join specification is activated when tokens are present on all the incoming arcs for one of the input sides. When this occurs, a control token is produced at the exit point, and the appropriate data tokens are passed through to the corresponding outputs.

A few points are worth noting about the parallel execution model described above. First, the purpose of the model is to provide intuition into the meaning of the diagrams, not to provide a formal foundation. Formally proving properties of plans (such as whether a given plan terminates normally for all possible inputs) requires manipulating the logical statement of the constraints (e.g., preconditions, postconditions, and test conditions), which is outside of the parallel execution model.

Second, the simplicity of the parallel execution model depends critically on the absence of cycles in the data and control flow. (Loops are modeled using recursively defined plans, as described in Section 4.6.)

Finally, note that the Plan Calculus is a wide-spectrum language. Depending on how specific the input data is and whether the steps of the plan are totally ordered, executing a plan can be like executing a conventional program or symbolically evaluating a specification.

4.4 Hierarchical Plans

Plans may contain other plans as parts. This makes it possible to reuse already defined clichés to build larger clichés in a hierarchical fashion. Figure 4.9 shows a plan, approx-and-retry-sqrt, that has the plan equality-within-epsilon (Figure 4.2) as a subplan. Approx-and-retry-sqrt is a somewhat contrived plan that computes the square root of a number using an approximation operation and retries the approximation with greater precision if necessary.

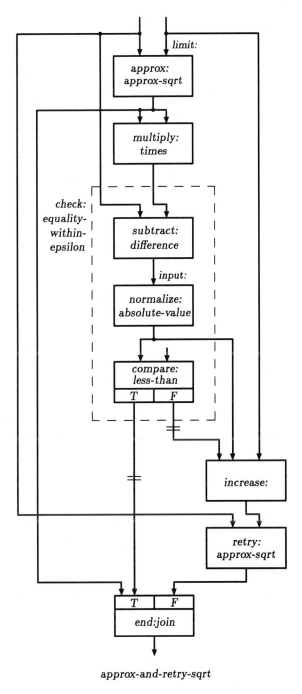

approx-and-retry-sqrt

Figure 4.9 An example of a hierarchical plan.

The square-root approximation operation (approx-sqrt) in Figure 4.9 has an input (limit) specifying the maximum number of steps to be used in the approximation. If the result of the operation is not within tolerance (check), the iteration limit is increased (increase), and the approximation is tried again (retry). The check part is itself a plan (equality-within-epsilon) with parts: subtract, normalize, and compare. In the interest of brevity, the formula for computing the new, increased limit (from the old limit and the absolute value of the error) is not specified in Figure 4.9.

Within hierarchical plans, it is convenient to refer to parts at different levels in the structure by combining part names into *paths*. The path

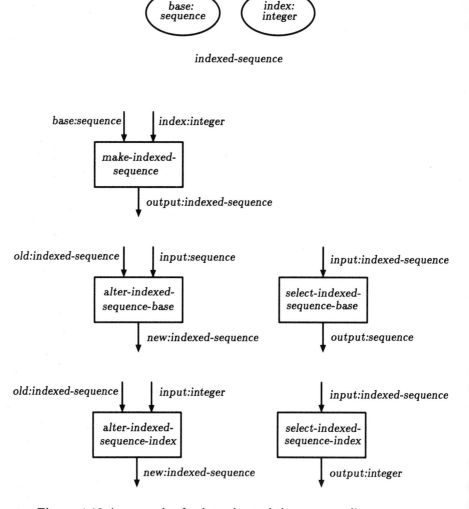

Figure 4.10 An example of a data plan and the corresponding accessors.

approx.limit in Figure 4.9 refers to the *limit* input of the *approx* part. Similarly, *check.normalize.input* refers to the *input* input of the *normalize* part of the *check* part.

In plan diagrams, dashed boxes are used to delimit subplans. This boundary is not, however, a barrier to establishing connections between the parts of the subplan and the surrounding plan. Inputs to intermediate steps of a subplan can come from the surrounding plan and intermediate results in the subplan can be used by the surrounding plan. For example, note the data-flow connection between the output of *check.normalize* and the first input of increase in Figure 4.9.

Data Plans

Parts of a plan may also be constrained to be data, such as integers, sequences, or sets. If all of the parts of a plan are data (or, hierarchically, data plans), then the plan is a *data plan*. Data plans are used to represent clichéd aggregations of data. For example, Figure 4.10 shows the data plan indexed-sequence, which represents the cliché of a sequence (base) with an associated index pointer (index). (The sequence is typically implemented concretely as an array.) This data plan is part of many implementations of buffers, queues, and stacks.

The constraint associated with a data plan is the *invariant* of the data structure. For example, the invariant of indexed-sequence states that the index must be between zero and the length of the base.

A data plan automatically defines a corresponding collection of input/output specifications for standard data structure accessors:

- A *constructor*, which takes an instance of the appropriate type for each part and produces a new instance of the aggregate. The operation requires that the inputs satisfy the invariant of the data plan.

- A *selector* for each part, which takes an instance of the aggregate and returns the corresponding part.

- An *alterant* for each part, which takes an instance of the aggregate and an instance of the appropriate type for the part and destructively modifies the data aggregate by replacing the part with the new item. A precondition of this operation is that the new item together with the other old parts satisfy the invariant of the data plan.

The naming conventions for these accessors, their inputs, and their outputs, are illustrated in Figure 4.10.

Implicit Accessors

In general, a hierarchical plan may have a mixture of data and computational parts. Figure 4.11 shows the hierarchical plan bump-and-update,

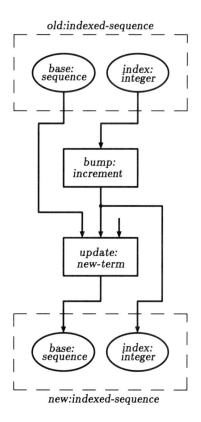

bump-and-update

Figure 4.11 A hierarchical plan with data and computation parts.

which has the data plan indexed-sequence as a subplan (twice). This plan expresses the clichéd pattern of operations on an indexed sequence in which the index is incremented (bump) and a new term is stored at the new location (update), as in the following code:

```
(DEFSTRUCT INDEXED-SEQUENCE BASE INDEX)

(DEFUN NEW-TERM (SEQUENCE INDEX TERM)
  (SETQ SEQUENCE (COPY-SEQ SEQUENCE))
  (SETF (ELT SEQUENCE INDEX) TERM)
  SEQUENCE)

(LET ((I (1+ (INDEXED-SEQUENCE-INDEX Q))))
  (MAKE-INDEXED-SEQUENCE
    :BASE (NEW-TERM (INDEXED-SEQUENCE-BASE Q) I X)
    :INDEX I))
```

New-term (the type of the update step) is a predefined input/output specification associated with the primitive data type sequence. It returns

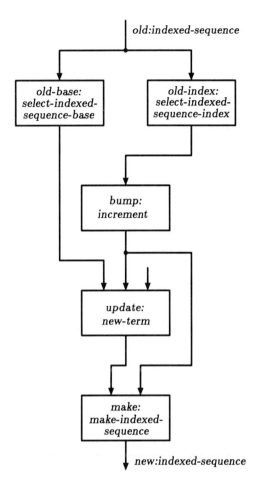

old:indexed-sequence

| old-base: select-indexed-sequence-base | old-index: select-indexed-sequence-index |

bump: increment

update: new-term

make: make-indexed-sequence

new:indexed-sequence

bump-and-update

Figure 4.12 A depiction of bump-and-update (see Figure 4.11) that uses explicit accessors instead of data plans.

a *copy* of the input sequence, with one term changed. Due to the use of new-term, the bump-and-update plan is purely functional, i.e., there are no side effects. (A related plan that uses side effects is discussed in the next section.)

Notice that the selector and constructor operations in the code above do not appear explicitly as boxes in the plan diagram. It is a convenient feature of plan diagrams that these accessors are implicit in the way data flow is connected to the parts of a data plan. The depiction of bump-and-update in Figure 4.11 can be taken as an abbreviation for Figure 4.12, in which the accessors are explicit.

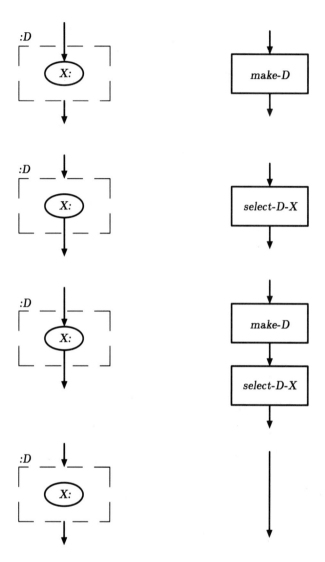

Figure 4.13 Four examples of translation between data flow connected to a one-part data plan and explicit use of accessors.

The general rules for interpreting data flow involving data plans are illustrated in Figures 4.13 and 4.14. Figure 4.13 shows how each of the four possible ways of connecting data flow to a data plan D with a single part X (on the left side of the figure) can be translated into explicit accessors (on the right). Figure 4.14 shows how various combinations of data flow to a data plan with two parts can be translated into explicit accessors. The last combination on the left in Figure 4.14 is illegal.

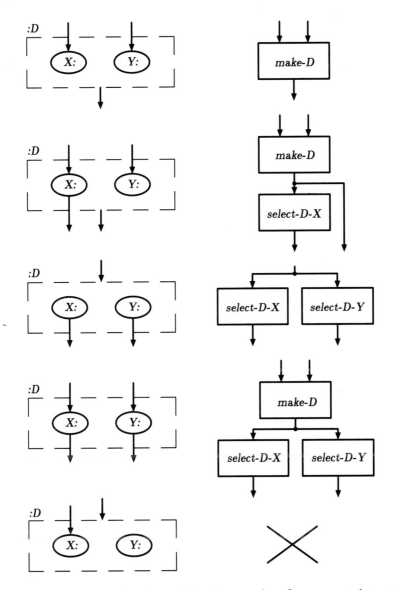

Figure 4.14 Five examples of translation between data flow connected to a two-part data plan and explicit use of accessors.

4.5   Side Effects

Side effects are modeled in the Plan Calculus by introducing input/output specifications that destructively modify their inputs. For example, the destructive variant of new-term, called alter-term, has the same inputs and outputs, but specifies that the old sequence is destructively modified to

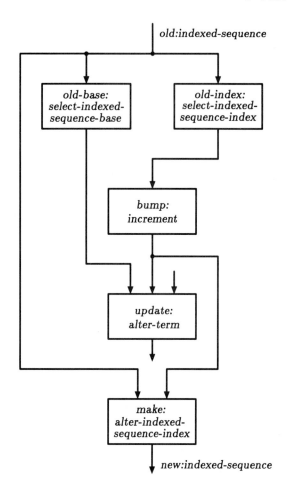

destructive-bump-and-update

Figure 4.15 The destructive version of bump-and-update.

obtain the new sequence. (The formal statement of this condition involves use of a situational calculus for modeling mutable objects; see [32, 34].)

Figure 4.15 shows an example of a plan involving side effects, called destructive-bump-and-update. This plan is the destructive counterpart of bump-and-update, corresponding to the following code:

```
(LET ((I (1+ (INDEXED-SEQUENCE-INDEX Q))))
  (SETF (ELT (INDEXED-SEQUENCE-BASE Q) I) ITEM)
  (SETF (INDEXED-SEQUENCE-INDEX Q) I))
```

(Cross-references between the destructive and nondestructive versions of plans are part of the taxonomic structure of the cliché library.)

The plan diagram for destructive-bump-and-update has explicit accessors, such as alter-indexed-sequence-index, for the parts of the indexed sequence. The abbreviated data-flow notation for data plans described above cannot be used in plans with side effects because the correct expansion of the abbreviations in the presence of side effects requires nonlocal reasoning. For example, in destructive-bump-and-update, there is no alterant for the base of the indexed sequence because the destructive modification of the sequence in the update step (alter-term) also achieves the destructive modification of the indexed sequence containing it.

In the Plan Calculus, side effects arise only in connection with the destructive modification of arrays, records, and other mutable data structures. Most assignment statements that would appear in the corresponding program text are replaced by the use of data flow. (An exception is the use of global variables, whose current value is best thought of as part of the state of the system. These are modeled using the primitive mutable data plan, *cell*, which has a single part called *contents*.) This is advantageous because reasoning about side effects is complex, especially if mutable objects can overlap (see [46, 47]).

4.6 Recursively Defined Plans

Hierarchical plans can be recursively defined, i.e., the type of a subplan can be the same as the type of the plan. Figure 4.16 shows recursive data plans defining the list and binary-tree abstractions. (Note the use of disjunctive types.) Figure 4.17 shows a recursively defined computational

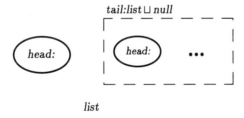

list

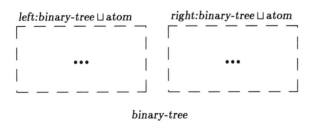

binary-tree

Figure 4.16 Two examples of recursively defined data plans.

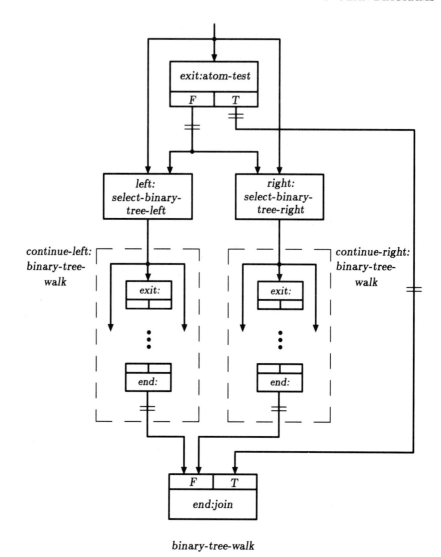

binary-tree-walk

Figure 4.17 The recursive definition of the plan for walking a binary-tree.

plan, called binary-tree-walk, that visits every node of a binary-tree. In the usual Lisp implementation, in which a binary-tree is made up of cons cells, the following code is an implementation of this plan:

```
(DEFUN WALK (TREE)
  ...
  (UNLESS (ATOM TREE)
    (WALK (CAR TREE))
    (WALK (CDR TREE))))
```

Notice, however, that WALK makes an ordering commitment that is not required by the binary-tree-walk plan. In WALK, the nodes of the tree are walked in left-to-right order (assuming car corresponds to left and cdr to right). The binary-tree-walk plan is more general—it does not force the traversal to occur in any particular order. An advantage of the Plan Calculus over conventional program text is that it allows the expression of more general clichés, such as this. Furthermore, to constrain the binary-tree-walk plan to the traversal order used in WALK, you need only add a control-flow arc from *continue-left.end* to *continue-right.exit.*

Iterative Computations

Because iteration is equivalent to tail recursion, recursively defined plans can be used to represent iterative computations. (See [82], pp. 32-33, for a complete discussion of the relationship between iteration, tail recursion, and looping constructs.) For example, consider the following iterative program for computing factorial and the corresponding plan in Figure 4.18:

```
(DEFUN LOOP-FACTORIAL (N)
  (LET ((F 1))
    (LOOP
      (IF (= N 1) (RETURN F))
      (SETQ N (1- N))
      (SETQ F (* N F)))))
```

The loop in the body of this program can be coded alternatively in the following tail-recursive form, which mirrors more closely the structure of the plan in Figure 4.18:

```
(DEFUN ITERATIVE-FACTORIAL (N)
  (ITERATIVE-FACTORIAL-BODY N 1))

(DEFUN ITERATIVE-FACTORIAL-BODY (N F)
  (IF (= N 1)
      F
      (ITERATIVE-FACTORIAL-BODY (1- N) (* N F))))
```

The two versions of factorial above encode the same algorithm, i.e., the same set of computations performed in the same order. (It is a defect of some Lisp compilers and interpreters that these two versions are not executed in the same way.) This algorithm is iterative because the amount of storage required is independent of the size of the input. A singly recursive program, such as ITERATIVE-FACTORIAL-BODY, that encodes an iterative algorithm is called *tail-recursive*. Although iterative computations are often loosely referred to as *loops*, the essential characteristic of iteration is not the existence of a cycle in control flow, but rather the fixed storage requirements.

A singly recursive plan is tail-recursive when there is no computation to be performed "on the way up," i.e., after the recursive invocation. This point is illustrated by comparing the tail-recursive plan in Figure 4.18 with

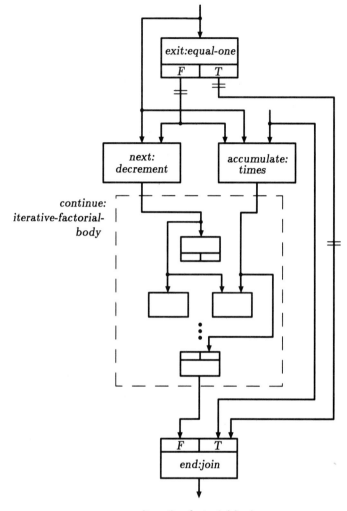

Figure 4.18 Iterative (tail-recursive) plan for the computation of factorial. An auxiliary plan definition (not shown here) is required to specify the initialization of the accumulated product to 1.

the singly recursive, but not tail-recursive, plan in Figure 4.19 corresponding to the following program. The program below encodes a *different* algorithm, which (due to the associativity and commutativity of multiplication) also computes factorial.

```
(DEFUN RECURSIVE-FACTORIAL (N)
   (IF (= N 1)
       1
       (* N (RECURSIVE-FACTORIAL (1- N))))))
```

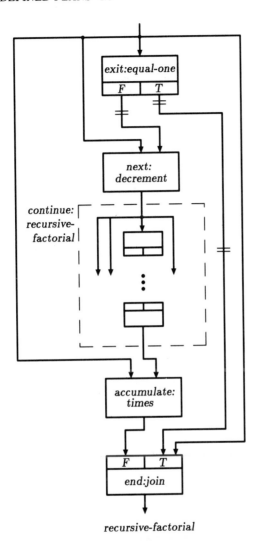

Figure 4.19 Linearly recursive plan for the computation of factorial.

The multiplication (accumulate) step in Figure 4.19 requires input from the end of the recursive invocation and therefore must come *after* the recursion, whereas, in Figure 4.18 there are no computations to be performed after the recursive invocation. (Joins do not count as computations. For this purpose, they are best thought of as part of the data flow.) The computation in Figure 4.19 is not iterative, but linearly recursive—storage grows linearly with the size of the input.

Chapter 5

Overlays

Programming knowledge includes understanding many kinds of relationships between algorithmic clichés, such as how an instance of one cliché can be viewed as an instance of another. Overlays are the general facility in the Plan Calculus for representing such shifts of viewpoint. (The idea of overlays was stimulated in part by Sussman's slices [152], which he used to represent equivalences between electronic circuits.)

An *overlay* is a pair of plans with a set of *correspondences* between their parts. Overlays are depicted, as shown in Figure 5.1, as two plan diagrams side by side with a dashed vertical line separating them; the correspondences are drawn as hooked lines between the corresponding parts of each plan. Basically, an overlay asserts that an instance of a plan on the left, viewed through the correspondences, satisfies the constraints of the plan on the right.

Overlays are used to represent knowledge about implementing specifications, implementing data abstractions, and optimization. Overlays are also used to represent *temporal abstraction* (see Section 5.5), in which an iterative program is viewed as a composition of operations on sequences.

5.1 Implementing a Specification

Figure 5.1 is an example of a simple overlay representing implementation knowledge. The right side of the diagram is the input/output specification absolute-value. The left side of the diagram is the plan negate-if-negative, which tests whether a number is negative and if so negates it. This overlay represents the knowledge that negate-if-negative is a correct implementation of the absolute-value specification. Implementation overlays always have an atomic plan (i.e., an input/output or test specification) as their right side.

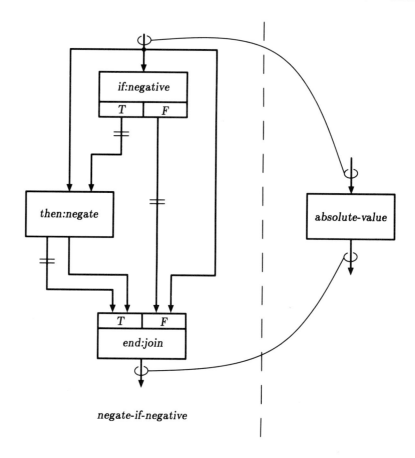

Figure 5.1 Overlay for implementing absolute value by testing and negating.

The correspondences in Figure 5.1 identify the input of absolute-value with the input of the test in the implementation plan, and the output of absolute-value with the output of the join in the implementation plan. An unlabeled correspondence, such as in this figure, indicates identity. A correspondence labeled with a function name (see Section 5.3) indicates that the part on the right side is equal to the result of applying the named function to the corresponding part on the left side.

Note the distinction being made here between the specification for absolute value and methods of computing absolute value. Although negate-if-negative is the most obvious method of implementing absolute-value, there are other methods—for example, squaring the number and then taking the square root. Each implemention method is represented by a separate overlay that has the absolute-value specification as its right side.

Correctness Conditions

Formally, an overlay defines a mapping between the set of instances of the left side plan (the domain) to the set of instances of the right side plan (the range). For an overlay to be correct, the mapping must be *single-valued*, *total*, and *onto*. Automated verification of these conditions for overlays in the cliché library is the focus of ongoing research. (See Section 11.1 for a description of the automated reasoning system being used.)

The single-valued condition (every domain element maps to at most one range element) guarantees that the implementation process loses no information, i.e., for a given overlay, the specification can always be recovered from the implementation. However, the mapping may be many-to-one, in which case the implementation is not uniquely determined by the specification.

The total condition (the mapping is defined for every domain element) guarantees that each implementation instance corresponds to some specification instance. This property is important for using overlays in analysis (see next section).

Finally, the onto condition (each range element is the image of some domain element) guarantees that all instances of the specification are implemented.

5.2   Using Overlays in Analysis and Synthesis

The knowledge encoded in an overlay can be used in both the analysis and synthesis of programs. In analysis by inspection, the left side of an overlay is matched against the plan representation of the program under analysis. (For example, the left side of the overlay at the top of Figure 5.2 matches the bold part of the plan at the lower left of the figure.) When a match is found, the matching section can be replaced by the right side of the overlay (as indicated at the bottom right of Figure 5.2). The correspondences provide the information needed to connect the right side of the overlay with the appropriate parts of the surrounding plan.

The repeated application of this recognition process can be thought of as parsing, where each overlay defines a grammar rule. (The sides are reversed: The right side of the overlay corresponds to a nonterminal; and the left side of the overlay corresponds to the expansion of the nonterminal.) The grammar will typically be ambiguous (allow multiple parses) because there may be several overlays with the same left side and also because there may be many ways of matching a left side against a plan. Chapter 10 describes a system that performs this kind of parsing automatically.

In synthesis by inspection, the right side of an overlay is matched against a plan representing the current synthesis state. (For example, the right side of the overlay at the top of Figure 5.2 matches the bold part of the plan at the lower right of Figure 5.2.) The section of the plan matching the

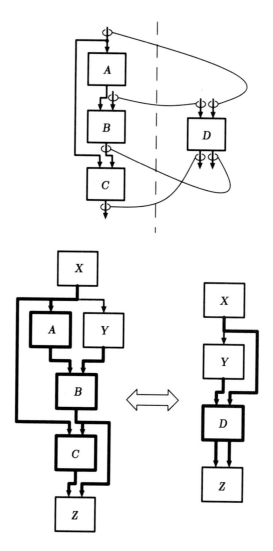

Figure 5.2 Overlays can be used for both analysis and synthesis.

overlay's right side is then replaced by the overlay's left side (as indicated at the bottom left of the figure). Again the correspondences are used to get the right connections. In the grammar metaphor, synthesis by inspection corresponds to using the grammar to generate sentences. Synthesis by inspection under user guidance is supported by KBEmacs.

In the matching and replacement process, parts of the matching section of a plan may need to be copied. An operation must be copied if it has an output p such that (1) there is data flow from p that goes outside the matched area and (2) p does not correspond to an output on the other

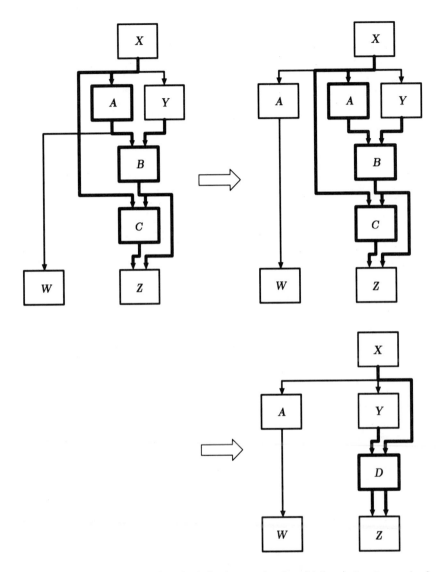

Figure 5.3 An example of analysis by inspection in which copying is required.

side of the overlay. When this situation occurs, the operation must be copied and the offending data flow moved to the copy before replacement can occur. For example, the left side of the overlay in Figure 5.2 matches against the plan at the top left of Figure 5.3, as indicated in bold. However, box *A* must be copied (as shown at the top right of Figure 5.3) before the matched section of the plan can be replaced by the right side of the overlay (as shown at the bottom right).

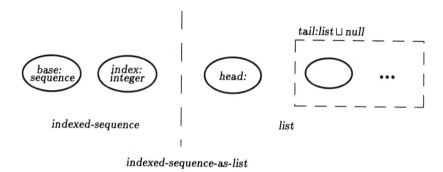

Figure 5.4 An example of implementation knowledge involving data structures.

5.3   Implementing an Abstract Data Structure

Implementations of abstract data structures are represented in the Plan Calculus by overlays between data plans. The data plan on the overlay's left side is the concrete (or implementation, or representation) data structure; the data plan on the overlay's right side is the abstract data structure. Using different data overlays, a given abstract data structure can be implemented differently in different contexts. This is awkward in some programming languages.

As with overlays in general, a data overlay must be a single-valued, total, and onto mapping from instances of the concrete data structure to instances of the abstract data structure. In the data abstraction literature (e.g., [123]), this mapping is typically called the *abstraction function*. Only the domain and range of a data overlay can be indicated in plan diagrams. A logical language is required to define the abstraction function.

Figure 5.4 shows the data overlay, indexed-sequence-as-list, which represents one method of implementing a list using an indexed sequence. The abstraction function of this overlay is defined as follows: The head of the list corresponds to the term of the base sequence indexed by the index i. The tail of the list is recursively defined as the list implemented by the indexed sequence with the same base and index $i - 1$. An empty list (null) is implemented by an indexed sequence with index zero.

As shown in Figure 5.5, data overlays are often used to label correspondences in the definition of other overlays. The overlay bump-and-update-as-push represents an implementation of the push operation, in which the list is implemented as an indexed sequence. (The postconditions of push specify that the head of the new list is equal to the input and that the tail of the new list is equal to the old list.) In the overlay, the old and new indexed sequences of the implementation plan (bump-and-update; see Figure 4.11) correspond to the old and new lists of the push operation, respectively. These correspondences are labeled with the data overlay indexed-sequence-as-list (see Figure 5.4). This means that the old indexed sequence

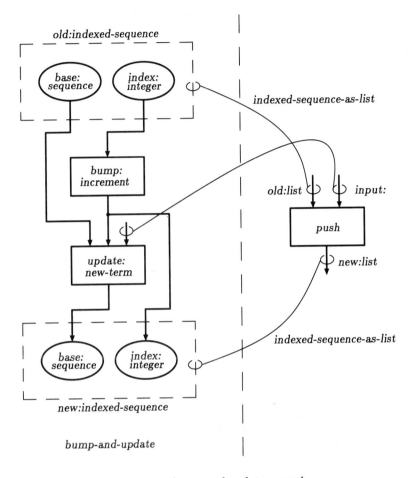

old:indexed-sequence

indexed-sequence-as-list

bump-and-update

bump-and-update-as-push

Figure 5.5 An overlay in which correspondences are labeled with data overlays.

of bump-and-update *viewed as a list* corresponds to the old input of push and similarly for the new indexed sequence and the new output of push.

Recall that the plan diagram shown for bump-and-update is actually an abbreviation for the diagram with explicit accessors shown in Figure 4.12. With explicit accessors on the left side of the overlay, the correspondence involving the old indexed sequence would connect to the input of the selectors at the top of the plan; the correspondence involving the new indexed sequence would connect to the output of the constructor at the bottom.

Finally, note that the overlay bump-and-update-as-push represents the simplest version of this implementation. Both the list and the sequence involved are unbounded (so there is no overflow case) and there are no side effects (new-term copies its input). The cliché library also contains

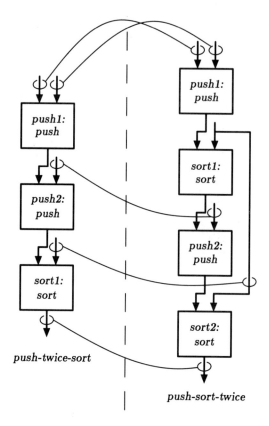

push-twice-sort

push-sort-twice

push-sort-optimization

Figure 5.6 An example of an overlay encoding optimization knowledge.

overlays showing how to implement push when the list is bounded and when a destructive operation is desired.

5.4 Optimization

The most general form of an overlay has a nonatomic plan diagram on each side. Such overlays are most often used to capture optimization knowledge. The overlay in Figure 5.6 involves the optimization of a certain pattern of operations on a list. The overlay's right side is a plan in which an object is pushed onto a list, the list is sorted, another object is pushed onto the sorted list, and then the list is sorted again. This pattern of operations can be optimized as shown by the plan on the overlay's left side, in which one of the sorting operations is eliminated. One can think of this overlay as embodying a lemma in the theory of lists and sorting.

One would not expect a programmer to write code matching the right side of this overlay. However, patterns requiring optimization can easily arise in automated synthesis, when higher level operations are expanded into implementations. For example, a reasonable implementation for the operation of adding an object to a sorted list is to push the object onto the list and then resort the list. Two such operations on the same sorted list would give rise to the pattern on the right side of Figure 5.6.

Using an overlay such as Figure 5.6 in the synthesis direction, i.e., matching the right side and replacing it by the left side, amounts to applying an optimization. Using such an overlay in the analysis direction, i.e., matching the left side and replacing it by the right side, amounts to "undoing" an optimization. It is often necessary to undo optimizations to facilitate further recognition.

In the grammar metaphor, an overlay with nonatomic plans on both sides corresponds to a context-sensitive grammar rule. Undoing optimizations as part of recognition is therefore an inherently expensive process.

5.5   Temporal Abstraction

Temporal abstraction is a technique for viewing clichéd fragments of iterative computation as operations on a sequences of values. This makes it possible to reason about most iterative programs just as simply as programs without iteration (see [46, 78]). The use of overlays for temporal abstraction is illustrated below in conjunction with the following (somewhat contrived) example program, which computes the product of the prime numbers between 1 and n:

```
(DEFUN PRIME-PRODUCT (N)
  (LET ((P 1))
    (LOOP
      (IF (ZEROP N) (RETURN P))
      (IF (PRIMEP N) (SETQ P (* N P)))
      (SETQ N (1- N))))))
```

An empirical study [71] has shown that iterative programs, such as PRIME-PRODUCT, can almost always be decomposed into a small set of basic iteration clichés, including generation, filtering, accumulation, and termination. Before discussing temporal abstraction in more detail, it is useful to take a look at these iteration clichés.

Iteration Clichés

The *generation* cliché illustrated by the following code template is represented formally by the plan diagram on the left of Figure 5.7. (Note that we first look just at the plans on the left sides of Figures 5.7–5.10; later, we discuss the complete overlays.) On each iteration, a function *next* is applied to the result of the previous application. (Apply-function applies its first in-

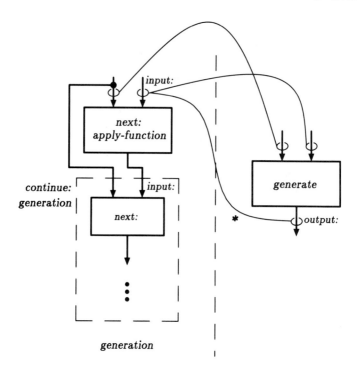

Figure 5.7 Overlay viewing the generation cliché as a generate operation.

put, a function, to its second input.) Generation appears in PRIME-PRODUCT with the Lisp decrementing function (1-) filled in for *next*. This instance of generation is called *counting-down*. If *next* is CDR, we have *cdr-generation*, the familiar pattern of "cdr-ing down a list."

```
(LOOP
  ...
  (SETQ X (next X))
  ...)
```

The *filtering* cliché illustrated by the following code template is represented formally by the plan diagram on the left of Figure 5.8. On each iteration, a test *if* is applied to some value. (Apply-predicate applies its first input, a predicate, to its second input.) If the test succeeds, an operation *then* is applied to the value. Filtering appears in PRIME-PRODUCT with the Lisp function PRIMEP (a user-defined function that tests whether a number is prime) filled in for *if* and an operation involving multiplication filled in for *then*.

```
(LOOP
  ...
  (IF (if Y)
      (then ... Y ...))
  ...)
```

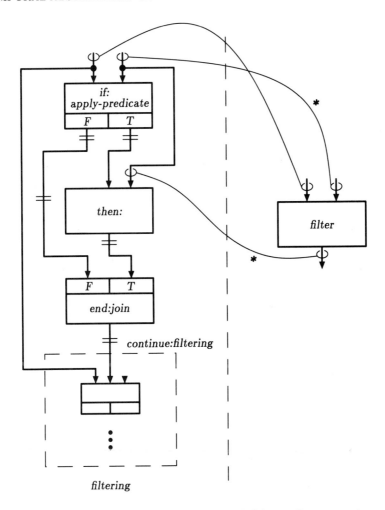

Figure 5.8 Overlay viewing the filtering cliché as a filter operation.

The *accumulation* cliché illustrated by the following code template is represented formally by the plan diagram on the left of Figure 5.9. On each iteration, a function *next* of two arguments is applied to the result of the previous application and a new value. When the iteration terminates, the result of the last application of *next* is returned. Accumulation appears in PRIME-PRODUCT with multiplication filled in for *next*, computing a product. If + is filled in for *next*, a sum is computed.

```
(LOOP
   ...
   (IF ... (RETURN Z))
   ...
   (SETQ Z (next ... Z))
   ...)
```

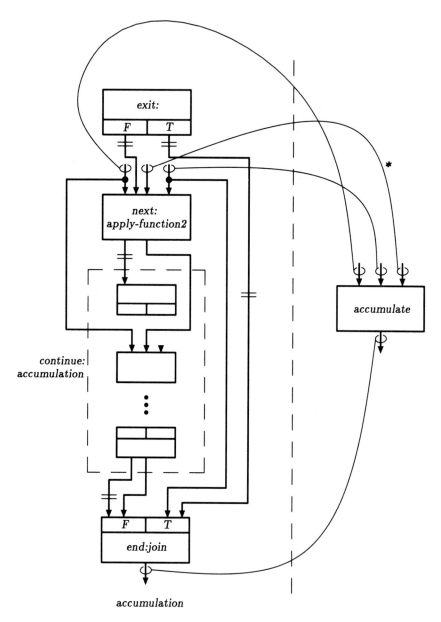

Figure 5.9 Overlay viewing the accumulation cliché as an accumulate operation.

The *termination* cliché illustrated by the following code template is represented formally by the plan diagram on the left of Figure 5.10. On each iteration, a test *exit* is applied to a value. When the test succeeds, the iteration is terminated; otherwise, the value is used by some other computation *step*. The placement of the test guarantees that *step* sees only

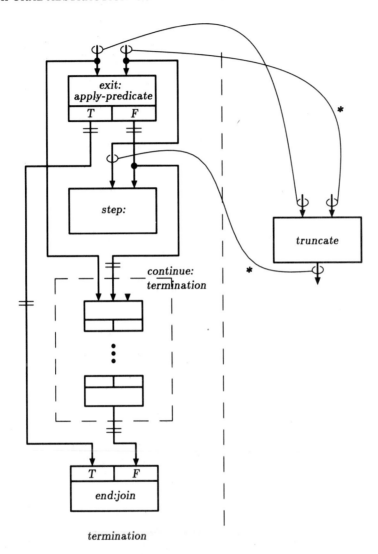

Figure 5.10 Overlay viewing the termination cliché as a truncate operation.

values up to, but not including, the first value for which the test succeeds. Termination is often used to stop generation when some particular value is reached. In PRIME-PRODUCT, termination appears with the Lisp function ZEROP filled in for *exit*.

```
(LOOP
  ...
  (IF (exit W) (RETURN ...))
  ...
  (step ... W ...)
  ...)
```

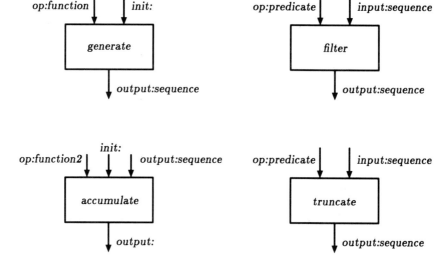

Figure 5.11 Some sequence input/output specifications that are used in temporal abstraction.

Sequence Operations

A key aspect of the iteration clichés just discussed is that they can be viewed as operating on sequences of values spread out through time—one value is processed on each iteration. In particular, the generation, filtering, accumulation, and termination clichés are closely related to the following four sequence operations (see Figure 5.11):

- *Generate* – given a function (*op*) and an initial value (*init*), generate produces the sequence [*init, op(init), op(op(init)), ...*].

- *Filter* – the output sequence consists of the terms of the input sequence that satisfy the given predicate, in the order they appear in the input sequence (including duplicates).

- *Accumulate* – the output is the result of *reducing* (in the sense of APL) the input sequence using the given binary function (*op*) and initial value (*init*). For example, if the input sequence is [a b c], the output is *op(c, op(b, op(a, init)))*.

- *Truncate* – the output sequence is the longest initial subsequence of the input sequence that does not include a term satisfying the given predicate.

Temporal Overlays

Temporal overlays formalize the temporal abstraction of iteration clichés as sequence operations. As an example, consider the overlay in Figure 5.7 on page 72, which shows the temporal abstraction of the generation cliché as a generate operation. Two of the correspondences in the overlay are the usual (unlabeled) identity correspondences: The function applied at each step of the generation corresponds to the function input of the generate box; the input to the function application on the first iteration of the generation corresponds to the initial value of generate.

The third correspondence in Figure 5.7, labeled with an asterisk, is what we call a *temporal correspondence*. A temporal correspondence links a data part in an iterative plan on the left side of an overlay with a part of type sequence on the right side. The first term of this *temporal sequence* is equal to the indicated part of the iterative plan; the second term is equal to the same part of the recursively defined subplan; and so on recursively. (For a discussion of generalizing temporal abstraction to arbitrary recursive plans, see [32, 70].)

In Figure 5.7, the input to the function application in the generation plan is abstracted as the temporal sequence output of the generate operation. The elements of this sequence are [*next.input, continue.next.input, continue.continue.next.input, ...*].

A *temporal overlay* is an overlay that includes at least one temporal correspondence. As shown in Figures 5.7–5.10, there is a temporal overlay in the cliché library for each of the four iteration clichés discussed above.

The benefit of temporal overlays is that they make it possible to view a program composed of iteration clichés as a composition of sequence functions, which is much easier to understand and reason about. To illustrate, Figure 5.12 shows how the four temporal overlays in Figures 5.7–5.10 can be used to view PRIME-PRODUCT as a composition of sequence operations. The left side of the figure is the plan for PRIME-PRODUCT. The right side of the figure is the corresponding plan in terms of sequence operations. The temporal correspondences are indicated with asterisks.

Because plans like the one on the right of Figure 5.12 are much easier to manipulate than the one on the left, temporal overlays play an important role in the Programmer's Apprentice. In particular, KBEmacs automatically applies temporal abstraction to all iterative programs.

A programming-language extension (see [78]) based on temporal abstraction has also been developed, which allows programmers to work directly at the level of sequence operations, without incurring any additional cost in efficiency. When using this extension, expressions equivalent to the composition of sequence operations on the right side of Figure 5.12 are automatically compiled into iterative programs equivalent to the plan on the left.

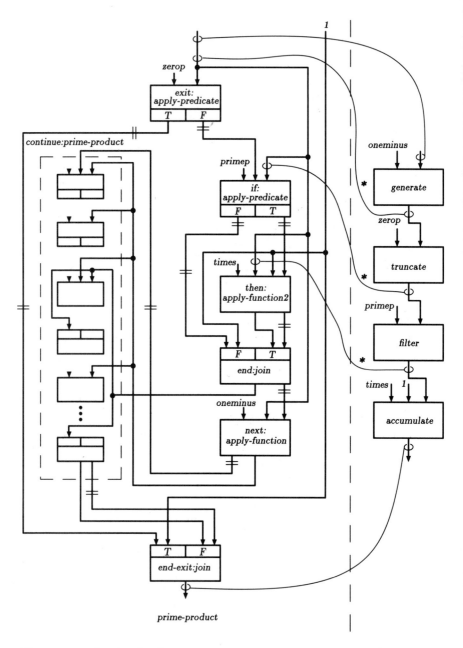

Figure 5.12 Overlay for the temporal abstraction of PRIME-PRODUCT (page 71) as a composition of operations on sequences.

Chapter 6

KBEmacs:
An Implementation Apprentice

KBEmacs demonstrates seven of the eight key capabilities of the Programmer's Apprentice (see Section 1.2) in the context of program implementation. In particular, KBEmacs can be used to implement a program rapidly and reliably by combining clichés. In Figure 6.1, three simple commands (referring to the clichés linear-search and cdr-enumeration) suffice to implement the TABLE-LOOKUP program discussed in Section 2.2.

The principal benefit of KBEmacs is illustrated by the ratio between the size of the program produced and the size of the commands used to produce it. This ratio is seldom less than 2 to 1 and, as shown by the implementation of the 57-line Ada program UNIT_REPAIR_REPORT using 6 commands in Chapter 8, can reach 10 to 1 when constructing large programs. This size reduction is important because programmers seem to produce a more or

```
Define a program TABLE-LOOKUP with parameters TABLE and INPUT.
Insert a linear-search of a cdr-enumeration of
  (AREF TABLE (HASH INPUT TABLE)).
Fill the predicate with (EQUAL (KEY ELEMENT) INPUT).

                        ⇓
(DEFUN TABLE-LOOKUP (TABLE INPUT)
  (LET ((LIST (AREF TABLE (HASH INPUT TABLE))))
    (LOOP
      (IF (NULL LIST) (RETURN NIL))
      (LET ((ELEMENT (CAR LIST)))
        (IF (EQUAL (KEY ELEMENT) INPUT) (RETURN ELEMENT)))
      (SETQ LIST (CDR LIST)))))
```

Figure 6.1 The KBEmacs commands at the top produce the program shown.

less constant number of lines of code per day independent of the language being used. As a result, reductions in size should translate directly into reductions in implementation time.

A second benefit of KBEmacs is that it enhances the reliability of the programs produced. Since a cliché is used many times, it is economically feasible to lavish time on it to ensure that it is general-purpose and bug-free. This reliability is inherited by the programs that use the cliché.

Using ordinary implementation methods, programmers make two kinds of errors: They choose incorrect algorithms and they fail to correctly render algorithms as program code. A third benefit of KBEmacs is that it eliminates algorithm rendering errors by automatically writing the code for the algorithms selected by the programmer.

6.1 Approach

KBEmacs is implemented as an extension to an existing state-of-the-art program editor. A good way to compare KBEmacs with other program editors (and other programming tools in general) is to consider the level at which programs are manipulated (see Figure 6.2).

The simplest program editors are ordinary text editors used to edit programs. These editors know nothing about programming or programming languages. The operations they support are therefore limited to operations on strings, such as inserting, deleting, and locating characters.

Syntax editors incorporate knowledge about the syntax of programming languages (see, for example, [97, 132, 150, 154]). This allows them to support operations based on the parse tree of a program, such as insertion, deletion, and editing-cursor motion, based on the syntactic structure of the program. An important benefit of syntax editors is that they can ensure that the program being edited is always syntactically correct.

KBEmacs incorporates knowledge about the semantics of algorithms and programming languages. In addition to syntax editing and textual editing, KBEmacs supports operations based on algorithmic structure, such as instantiating algorithms and modifying their parts. These operations are

Tool	Level of Manipulation
⋮	⋮
Design Apprentice	Design Decisions
KBEmacs	Algorithmic Structure
Syntax Editor	Parse Trees
Text Editor	Character Strings

Figure 6.2 Levels of manipulation supported by programming tools.

supported through the use of the Plan Calculus and a library of algorithmic clichés. Using constraints, KBEmacs can ensure certain aspects of the semantic correctness of the program being edited.

The Design Apprentice (see Section 11.2) will go a step further by incorporating knowledge of the trade-offs underlying the decisions required when designing a program. This will allow the programmer to converse with the system in terms of design decisions rather than specific algorithms.

Levels of manipulation even higher than those shown in Figure 6.2 are possible, e.g., dealing directly with the requirements that underlie design decisions. Reaching these higher levels is a long-term goal of the Programmer's Apprentice project.

Architecture

Figure 6.3 shows the architecture of KBEmacs. Two representations are maintained for the program being manipulated: program text (displayed to the programmer) and a plan (used to support KBEmacs's internal operation). At any moment, the programmer can modify either the text or the plan. If the text is modified, the *analyzer* is used to create a new plan. If the plan is modified, the *coder* is used to create new program text.

The program text can be modified using a standard program editor. Since KBEmacs is implemented on the Symbolics Lisp Machine [153], Symbolics's standard Emacs-style [150] editor is used. This editor supports both text- and syntax-based program editing.

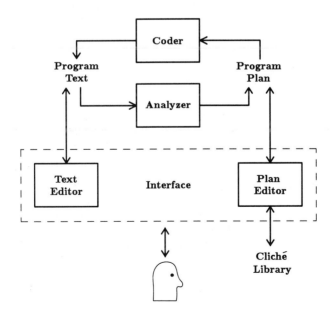

Figure 6.3 Architecture of KBEmacs.

The Plan can be modified using *knowledge-based* commands supported by the *plan editor*. These commands rely on two kinds of knowledge. First, the commands can refer to clichés in the *cliché library*. Second, the plan editor itself contains a significant amount of procedurally embedded knowledge about manipulating and combining clichés.

While plans are crucial to the internal operation of KBEmacs, program text is used as the primary user interface. This allows a programmer to interact with KBEmacs using a familiar programming language and without studying the Plan Calculus. Further, since KBEmacs produces ordinary source code, standard programming tools (e.g., the compiler) can be used without any kind of special interface.

KBEmacs's interface unifies text-, syntax-, and knowledge-based editing so that they are all conveniently accessed through the standard Emacs-style editor. The knowledge-based commands are supported as a pseudo-English extension of the standard editor's command set. The results of knowledge-based commands are visible to the programmer as alterations in the program text in the editor buffer. The effect is as if a human assistant were modifying the text under the programmer's direction. The programmer can fall back on direct text- and syntax-based editing at any time.

Representation Shift

One of the most powerful problem-solving strategies in artificial intelligence is *representation shift*—shifting from a representation in which a problem is easy to state but hard to solve to a less obvious representation in which the problem is easy to solve. Much of the power of KBEmacs is due to the representation shift from program text (or parse trees) to the Plan Calculus. Additional power is derived from the further representation shift (within the Plan Calculus) of temporal abstraction.

As discussed at length in Chapter 3, using the Plan Calculus as a representation has many advantages. It allows a wide variety of clichés to be represented in a canonical, language-independent way. Further, program modifications are much easier to perform on plans than on program text or parse trees.

6.2   Capabilities

The capabilities of KBEmacs are illustrated in detail in the next two chapters. However, before proceeding, it is useful to summarize and evaluate what KBEmacs can do from the perspective of the key capabilities of the Apprentice presented in Section 1.2. Restricted to the domain of program implementation, KBEmacs goes a long way toward demonstrating the potential of these capabilities and the feasibility of supporting them.

Shared knowledge. Programmers can use standard programming terminology because these terms are defined in KBEmacs's cliché library. This allows efficient and accurate communication between the programmer and KBEmacs. Programmers can extend KBEmacs into new programming domains and tailor the system to their particular programming styles by entering new clichés into the library.

Propagation of decisions. Using simple constraints, KBEmacs automatically determines some of the consequences of the programmer's design decisions. This reduces the number of decisions that have to be made explicitly by the programmer.

Support for evolution. KBEmacs keeps track of the clichés used to construct a program and supports commands that can modify the program in terms of these clichés. Programmers can edit at the level of the algorithm underlying a program, rather than merely at the level of programming-language syntax. In addition, simple algorithmic changes can often be stated as simple knowledge-based commands even when the changes require widespread textual alterations in the program.

Explanation. Based on its knowledge of the clichés used to construct a program, KBEmacs can create a comment describing the program's algorithmic structure. It can also highlight the location of clichés and their parts in a program.

Automation of details. When using KBEmacs, the programmer must make the key decisions about which clichés to use. However, KBEmacs handles the details of ensuring that the clichés are combined correctly. This is true during both program implementation and modification. KBEmacs takes care of several other kinds of details as well. For example, when working with Ada programs, KBEmacs automatically generates most of the variable declarations.

Escape to the surrounding environment. KBEmacs provides a new set of facilities without blocking the use of preexisting facilities. At any moment, the programmer can use any of the standard Symbolics Lisp Machine programming tools. In particular, text- and syntax-based editing can be freely intermixed with knowledge-based editing.

Programming-language independence. Because KBEmacs is based on the Plan Calculus, its internal operation is substantially programming-language independent. In particular, the same set of commands can be used to operate on both Lisp programs and Ada programs. However, while KBEmacs can be used in one language as well as in any other, KBEmacs by itself cannot translate programs between programming languages. Translation is beyond the capabilities of KBEmacs because clichés in different programming languages can differ semantically as well as syntactically (see Section 8.1). Therefore translation is not merely a question of recoding a plan in a different language; the source language clichés must be changed to appropriate target language clichés. Methods for doing this conversion based on a library of clichés represented using the Plan Calculus are discussed in [66].

6.3 Limitations

One key capability of the Apprentice—*error detection*—is absent from the discussion in the preceding section. The lack of error detection is a symptom of the central weakness of KBEmacs—it has no general-purpose reasoning facilities. This and other limitations are discussed below. As the successor to KBEmacs, a primary goal of the Design Apprentice (see Section 11.2) is removing these limitations.

No general-purpose reasoning. All of KBEmacs's reasoning is achieved via special-purpose procedures. This approach made it possible to construct KBEmacs without waiting for an appropriate general-purpose reasoning system. However, it significantly limits the capabilities of KBEmacs.

Because it has no general-purpose reasoning component, KBEmacs has no general way to evaluate the reasonableness of a programmer's commands. Except in a few specialized situations, KBEmacs merely does whatever the programmer says, whether or not it is reasonable.

KBEmacs implements Plan Calculus constraints as procedures, rather than using a general-purpose logical language. Each constraint procedure operates directly on the internal plan representation and is responsible for propagating the effects of the constraint. In principle, this allows arbitrarily complex constraints to be supported. However, in practice, it significantly limits the constraints that can be used because the requisite constraint procedures are not easy to write.

By incorporating a general-purpose reasoning system (Cake), the Design Apprentice will surmount these problems. In particular, the Design Apprentice will support several kinds of error detection and the propagation of design decisions via logical constraints.

Limited cliché library. KBEmacs's cliché library is limited in two respects. First, KBEmacs does not support taxonomic relationships between clichés such as specialization and extension. As a result, an important source of information relevant to the propagation of design decisions is missing. In addition, programmers must refer to low-level clichés explicitly by name.

The Design Apprentice will have a taxonomically organized library. Programmers will be able to phrase their commands in terms of a small number of high-level clichés. The Design Apprentice will determine which of the various low-level clichés are appropriate in a given situation.

The second limitation of KBEmacs's current cliché library is that it contains only a few dozen clichés. These are sufficient to support the demonstrations in the following chapters. However, for KBEmacs to be useful in a wide range of situations, the library will have to contain hundreds, if not thousands, of clichés. There is no fundamental reason why the appropriate clichés could not be entered into the system; however, this will require a significant amount of effort.

Incomplete analysis. Although the analyzer module is capable of making a new plan whenever the text representation of a program is modified, this plan does not, in general, include a complete analysis of the changed program in terms of clichés. This means that after the program text has been modified, KBEmacs's ability to explain the program and modify the program using knowledge-based commands is subsequently reduced. (Other knowledge-based editing operations, such as adding new clichés and filling previously unfilled roles, remain fully effective.) This limitation of KBEmacs could be removed by incorporating the kind of analysis module discussed in Chapter 10.

Needs reimplementation. Even with the limitations above, KBEmacs would be a useful programming tool, if it were not for the fact that the whole system must be reimplemented. As demonstrated by the transcripts in the next two chapters, KBEmacs is a real running system that can operate on programs of moderate size and complexity. Unfortunately, the current implementation of KBEmacs has two problems that preclude its use as anything other than a demonstration. First, KBEmacs is too slow. Knowledge-based commands can take several minutes to execute. For KBEmacs to be convenient to use, this time must be reduced to a matter of seconds. Second, KBEmacs has evolved over a number of years in a very untidy fashion and is full of bugs.

An experimental reimplementation of the plan editor (see Section 9.7) has shown that both of these problems can be fixed by rewriting the modules in the system. However, since KBEmacs consists of some forty thousand lines of Lisp code, this will not be a trivial task.

Chapter 7

Implementing a Lisp Program

The first section of this chapter shows how Lisp clichés are defined in KBEmacs. The second section then presents a transcript showing the construction of a report program through the top-down combination of clichés. The third section shows the use of KBEmacs to construct a numerical program through the bottom-up combination of clichés. The final section shows KBEmacs assisting in program modification and documentation.

7.1 Lisp Clichés

The plans in the cliché library embody most of KBEmacs's knowledge of programming. A basic assumption underlying KBEmacs is that the knowledge of these clichés is shared between man and machine—i.e., that the programmer is aware of at least the basic features of the various clichés. Thus, it is important for the reader to gain an understanding of some of these clichés before looking at the transcript shown in Screens 7.1–7.19.

A Simple Cliché

Figure 7.1 shows an example of defining the plan for a Lisp cliché in KBEmacs. The first argument of the macro DEFINE-PLAN is the name of the cliché. The second argument is a list of declarations giving information about the cliché. The remainder of the form is a body specifying the computation corresponding to the cliché. The macro creates a plan for the cliché by analyzing the body. In addition, the macro creates an input/output specification summarizing the inputs and outputs of the cliché, and an overlay between the plan and the specification.

A typical cliché contains some parts that remain fixed from one use to the next and other parts that are implemented differently on different oc-

```
(DEFINE-PLAN SQUARING
   (PRIMARY-ROLES (NUMBER)
   DESCRIBED-ROLES (NUMBER)
   COMMENT "computes the square of {the number}")
  (EXPT {the input number} 2))
```

Figure 7.1 A cliché for squaring a number.

casions. In KBEmacs, the variable parts are called *roles*. Since KBEmacs's interface is oriented around the metaphor of textual templates, the act of implementing a role is called *filling* it. In KBEmacs, the term *role* is also used to refer to the input and output ports of a cliché's input/output specification. This is done both to highlight their importance when combining clichés and to give them short names for easy reference.

In the body of a DEFINE-PLAN, roles are defined by the form {...}. This *role annotation* acts as a placeholder showing where the role fits into the computation. The phrase inside the braces names the role. Lowercase is used when printing this phrase to differentiate it from the surrounding code. (As discussed below, role annotation is used in other contexts to refer to roles rather than define them.)

Annotation of the form {the input ...} is used to define input roles. In addition, any free variables that are referenced in the body of a DEFINE-PLAN automatically become input roles that have the same names as the variables. In Figure 7.1, the only input role is the number to be squared.

Annotation of the form {the output ...} is used to define output roles. In addition, the return value of a cliché (i.e., the result of the last form in the body of a DEFINE-PLAN) and any free variables that are modified by the body automatically become output roles. (The words input and output are not required when referring to an input or output role as opposed to defining it.)

When communicating with KBEmacs, indefinite noun phrases such as "a squaring of X" are used to create instances of a cliché. These phrases give the name of the cliché and may indicate values that fill some of its roles. The PRIMARY-ROLES declaration in a DEFINE-PLAN specifies which roles can be filled this way and in what order. (KBEmacs's command language is described in detail in Section 9.5.)

The COMMENT declaration in a DEFINE-PLAN is used to generate brief descriptions of cliché instances. Within the comment string, role annotation is used to refer to roles. When a description is generated, each instance of {...} is replaced by a description of the filler of the indicated role. For example, the phrase "computes the square of X" would be used to briefly describe the cliché instance created by the phrase "a squaring of X".

The DESCRIBED-ROLES declaration in a DEFINE-PLAN is used to generate longer descriptions of instances of a cliché. It specifies which roles should be described in detail when constructing a comment (see Section 7.4).

```
(DEFINE-PLAN CDR-ENUMERATION
    (PRIMARY-ROLES (LIST)
     DESCRIBED-ROLES (LIST)
     COMMENT "enumerates the elements of {the list}")
   (LET* ((LIST {the input list}))
     (LOOP
       (IF ({NULL, the empty} LIST) (RETURN))
       {({CAR, the current} LIST), the output element}
       (SETQ LIST ({CDR, the rest} LIST)))))
```

Figure 7.2 A cliché for enumerating a Lisp list.

The Cdr-Enumeration Cliché

Figure 7.2 shows how the plan for the cdr-enumeration cliché is defined. Like all enumeration clichés, cdr-enumeration has an input role, three operation roles, and a temporal-sequence output role.

The definition of the operation roles in Figure 7.2 utilizes role annotation of the form {*filler*, `the` ... }. This indicates both the name of the role and the computation that fills the role. The *empty* role (filled with `NULL`) tests whether or not the list has run out. The *current* role (filled with `CAR`) accesses the individual elements of the list. The *rest* role (filled with `CDR`) steps from one list element to the next.

The Simple-Report Cliché

The central cliché used in the transcript below is simple-report, which captures the high-level structure of a simple reporting program (see Figure 7.3). This cliché has seven roles. The *file-name* is the name of the file that will contain the report being produced. The *title* is printed on a title page and, along with the page number, at the top of each succeeding page of the report. The *enumerator* enumerates the elements of some aggregate data structure. The *print-item* prints information about each enumerated element. The *line-limit* is used to determine when a page break should be inserted in the report. The *column-headings* are printed at the top of each page of the report to explain the output of the print-item. The *summary* prints some summary information at the end of the report.

Much of the computation in simple-report is there to keep track of the page number and the line number and to determine when page breaks should occur. (Unlike some other languages, Common Lisp does not provide automatic support for these operations.) Under the assumption that only 66 lines (numbered 0–65) can be printed on a page, the line number (`LINE`) is initially set to 66 to force a page break after the title page is printed. Whenever the line number is greater than the line-limit, the page number is incremented by one, a new page is started with the appropriate page headings, and the line number is reinitialized.

```
(DEFINE-PLAN SIMPLE-REPORT
   (PRIMARY-ROLES (ENUMERATOR PRINT-ITEM SUMMARY)
   DESCRIBED-ROLES (FILE-NAME TITLE ENUMERATOR
                        COLUMN-HEADINGS PRINT-ITEM SUMMARY)
   COMMENT "prints a report of {the input data of the enumerator}"
   CONSTRAINTS
     ((DEFAULT {the file-name} "report.txt")
      (DERIVED {the line-limit}
               (- 65
                  (SIZE-IN-LINES {the print-item})
                  (SIZE-IN-LINES {the summary}))))))
   (WITH-OPEN-FILE (REPORT {the file-name} :DIRECTION :OUTPUT)
     (LET* ((DATE (TIME:PRINT-CURRENT-TIME NIL))
            (LINE 66)
            (PAGE 0)
            (TITLE {the title})
            (DATA {the input data of the enumerator}))
       (FORMAT REPORT "~5%~60:@<~A~>~2%~60:@<~A~>~%" TITLE DATE)
       (LOOP
         (IF ({the empty of the enumerator} DATA) (RETURN))
         (WHEN (> LINE {the line-limit})
           (SETQ PAGE (+ PAGE 1))
           (FORMAT REPORT "~|~%Page:~3D~44:@<~A~>~17A~2%"
                     PAGE TITLE DATE)
           (SETQ LINE 3)
           ({the column-headings} {REPORT, modified}
                                  {LINE, modified}))
         ({the print-item} {REPORT, modified}
                           {LINE, modified}
                           ({the current of the enumerator} DATA))
         (SETQ DATA ({the rest of the enumerator} DATA)))
       ({the summary} {REPORT, modified}))))
```

Figure 7.3 A cliché for printing a simple report.

Simple-report makes use of several additional forms of role annotation. When used in the form of a function call (e.g., ({the operation} DATA)), role annotation specifies the arguments that are expected to be used by the computation filling the role. For instance ({the operation} DATA) indicates that the function filling the operation role should use as an input the value of the variable DATA.

Annotation of the form {variable, modified} indicates that the enclosing function call modifies variable—i.e., assigns a new value to it or has a side effect on the object that is its value. For example, the print-item, column-headings, and summary all modify the report file by sending output to it. In addition, the column-headings and the print-item are both expected to update the line number. This information is used by KBEmacs as part of the basis for its understanding of the data flow in the program.

The enumerator is a *compound* role that has the five subroles (empty, current, and rest along with an input role and an output role) typical of all enumerations. This is indicated in Figure 7.3 using annotation of the form {the *subrole* of the *compound-role*}. The subroles can be filled individually, or they can be filled simultaneously using an enumeration cliché (such as cdr-enumeration).

The CONSTRAINTS declaration in a DEFINE-PLAN defines a set of constraint procedures. When the plan is used during the construction of a program, these procedures are used to monitor the evolving program and, when necessary, modify the contents of roles to ensure that the constraints are satisfied.

Constraint procedures are defined using a combination of ordinary Lisp code and {...} annotation referring to roles. In Figure 7.3, the DEFAULT constraint specifies that "report.txt" should be used as the name of the file containing the report, unless the programmer specifies something else.

The DERIVED constraint specifies that the line-limit should be computed from the print-item and the summary. The function SIZE-IN-LINES analyzes the code filling a role and determines the maximum number of lines it can print. (A number of functions are provided by KBEmacs specifically for use in constraints.)

The expression in the DERIVED constraint guarantees that, whenever the line number is less than or equal to the line-limit, there will be room for both the print-item and the summary to be printed on the current page. This ensures that neither the print-item nor the summary will ever be broken over a page boundary and that the summary will never appear on a page by itself.

Because the line-limit role is derived by a constraint, the programmer never has to fill it explicitly. Furthermore, the role is automatically updated if the column-headings, print-item, or summary are changed. This increases the productivity of the programmer and the reliability of the program produced.

A final aspect of simple-report is that, while it is primarily written using Common Lisp [151], it makes use of a function that is defined only in Symbolics Lisp. The expression (TIME:PRINT-CURRENT-TIME NIL) returns a string of the form "mm/dd/yy hh:mm:ss" specifying both the current date and time.

Suites of Clichés

Clichés are not designed in isolation; rather they are typically conceived of in tightly knit groups, or *suites*, that are intended to be used together. One example of this is the way the cdr-enumeration cliché and the enumerator role of the simple-report cliché are designed to fit together. Another example can be seen in the cliché print-out (see Figure 7.4).

The print-out cliché prints an item using the standard Common Lisp function FORMAT. The cliché has three roles: the input *item* to be printed; the *format-string*, which specifies how to print the item; and the *size-in-lines*, which specifies how many output lines are used by the format-string.

```
(DEFINE-PLAN PRINT-OUT
    (PRIMARY-ROLES (FORMAT-STRING ITEM)
    DESCRIBED-ROLES (FORMAT-STRING ITEM)
    COMMENT "prints {the item}"
    CONSTRAINTS
      ((DEFAULT {the format-string} "~%~A")
       (DERIVED {the size-in-lines}
                (SIZE-IN-LINES {the format-string})))))
    (FORMAT REPORT {the format-string} {the input item})
    (SETQ LINE (+ LINE {the size-in-lines})))
```

Figure 7.4 A cliché for printing an item.

The role size-in-lines is automatically derived from the format-string by a constraint. An essential property of print-out is that it has free variable inputs and outputs that match variables used in the simple-report cliché. In addition, print-out increments the line number in the way expected by simple-report. The interaction of these two clichés is illustrated in the next section.

7.2 Top-Down Implementation

This section begins the presentation of a transcript illustrating the use of KBEmacs. In the first part of the transcript, the programmer constructs a program REPORT-TIMINGS, which prints a report. Given a list of timings (e.g., from an experiment), the program prints the timings followed by their mean and standard deviation. To implement this program, the programmer proceeds in a top-down fashion—first specifying the top-level cliché to use, then filling its roles (sometimes using other clichés), and so on. (Bottom-up program construction is illustrated in the next section.)

Directions for a Human Assistant

Suppose that an expert programmer were asked to write the program REPORT-TIMINGS and decided to delegate the task to an inexperienced assistant. To tell the assistant what to do, the expert might give directions like the ones in Figure 7.5.

These directions assume a significant amount of shared knowledge between the expert and the assistant. In particular, they assume that the assistant understands the term *simple report*. Presumably, this includes understanding how to print a title page, how to print headings at the top of the subsequent pages of the report, and how to determine when page breaks should be introduced. This knowledge is captured in KBEmacs via the cliché simple-report. By using clichés like simple-report, a programmer can tell KBEmacs how to produce the program REPORT-TIMINGS by giving directions at a level of detail similar to those in Figure 7.5.

Define a simple report program REPORT-TIMINGS with one parameter, a list of timings. Print the title "Report of Reaction
Timings (in msec.)". Print each timing and a summary showing the mean and deviation of the timings. Do not print column
headings.

Figure 7.5 Directions for a human assistant.

Layout of the Screen Images

The transcript in this chapter is a sequence of nineteen screen images taken
from a Symbolics Lisp Machine. Most of these screens show the Emacs-
style editor in which KBEmacs is embedded. Each editor screen has three
parts (see Screen 7.1). The first few lines show the commands typed by
the programmer since the previous screen (if any). Underlining is used to
indicate output typed by the system (e.g., in response to commands) as
opposed to what the programmer types.

The main body of each editor screen has a box drawn around it and
shows the state of the editor buffer after executing the commands. (To
save space, the buffer is abbreviated by omitting excess blank lines at the
bottom.) The position of the editing cursor is indicated by the symbol ▯.
The symbol ⟪ in the left margin is used to indicate lines that have changed
since the previous screen (if any).

The line below the editor buffer box shows the editor mode line, which
is composed of the name of the system (i.e., KBEmacs), the editing mode
(e.g., (LISP) or (TEXT)), and the name of the file being edited.

Integration with Emacs

Before beginning to construct REPORT-TIMINGS, the programmer uses the
standard Emacs command c-X c-F to create a file to contain the program,
as shown in Screen 7.1. The use of this standard Emacs command illustrates

```
c-X c-F Find file <KBE.DEMO>TIMINGS.LISP
(New File)
s-X Define a program REPORT-TIMINGS with a parameter TIMINGS. <end>
```

⟪ | ▯DEFUN REPORT-TIMINGS (TIMINGS))

KBEmacs (LISP) <KBE.DEMO>TIMINGS.LISP

Screen 7.1 Beginning the definition of a program.

the tight integration of KBEmacs with Emacs. KBEmacs adds a variety of new editor commands without interfering with (or rendering obsolete) any of the standard commands.

(In the interest of saving space, the various standard Emacs commands used in the transcript are only briefly described here; see [153] for complete documentation. Command characters of the form c- are typed by holding the keyboard shift key CONTROL. The command c-X c-F reads a file into Emacs, creating it if it does not already exist.)

Beginning the Definition of a Program

To begin the construction of REPORT-TIMINGS, the programmer uses the knowledge-based command Define to specify the name of the program and its parameter (see Screen 7.1). KBEmacs communicates the results of knowledge-based commands to the programmer (and to the rest of the programming environment) by directly modifying the text in the editor buffer. To draw the attention of the programmer to changes, the cursor is moved to the first important change in the buffer (if any). (KBEmacs considers changes to the body of a program more important than changes to variable declarations or initializations.) In Screen 7.1, the empty program definition (DEFUN REPORT-TIMINGS (TIMINGS)) is inserted into the buffer and the cursor is placed before it.

The special commands supported by KBEmacs make use of the keyboard shift key SUPER (indicated here by s-). The command character s-X is used to enter knowledge-based commands. After typing s-X, the programmer can type one or more knowledge-based commands. The end of command entry is signaled by typing the key <end>, which causes the commands to be executed.

As discussed in detail in Section 9.5, knowledge-based commands are specified using a simple pseudo-English command language. Each command is a verb followed by one or more noun phrases. If a word is typed using capital letters (e.g., TIMINGS as opposed to parameter) it is assumed to be a name (e.g., of a program or parameter) or a code fragment. Automatic word completion is supported to facilitate typing of the command language.

Inserting a Cliché into a Program

In Screen 7.2, the programmer uses the Insert command to insert an instance of the simple-report cliché into REPORT-TIMINGS. In general, the Insert command places an instance of a cliché in a program at the position indicated by the editing cursor.

The code produced in Screen 7.2 is the same as the code in the body of the definition of simple-report (see Figure 7.3) except that three roles have been filled via constraints and some of the role annotation has been suppressed. The file-name and line-limit have been filled with their default values. The line-limit has been given the value 63 under the assumption, made by the function SIZE-IN-LINES, that the print-item and summary will each produce only one output line.

Suppressing Annotation

Once a role such as the file-name has been filled, the annotation indicating where it is located is no longer displayed by KBEmacs. For the task of program construction, suppressing this annotation is helpful, because it reduces visual clutter and highlights the roles that still need to be filled. In other situations (e.g., documentation), it might be beneficial for KBEmacs to redisplay this annotation.

Note that while KBEmacs does not display annotation for filled roles, it retains a knowledge of these roles as part of its plan for the program. The plan typically contains a lot of information that is not directly displayed. In particular, the plan contains complete information about the clichés used to construct the program including their roles and constraints. As illustrated later in this chapter, there are a number of ways KBEmacs can use this information to assist the programmer.

With regard to the display of annotation, output roles are treated differently from other roles. In particular, output role annotation is retained to remind the programmer of the name of the role, unless the output is

```
s-X Insert a simple-report. <end>
(DEFUN REPORT-TIMINGS (TIMINGS)
  (WITH-OPEN-FILE (REPORT "report.txt" :DIRECTION :OUTPUT)
    (LET* ((DATE (TIME:PRINT-CURRENT-TIME NIL))
           (LINE 66)
           (PAGE 0)
           (TITLE {the title})
           (DATA {the input data of the enumerator}))
      (FORMAT REPORT "~5%~60:@<~A~>~2%~60:@<~A~>~%" TITLE DATE)
      (LOOP
        (IF ({the empty of the enumerator} DATA) (RETURN))
        (WHEN (> LINE 63)
          (SETQ PAGE (+ PAGE 1))
          (FORMAT REPORT "~|~%Page:~3D~44:@<~A~>~17A~2%"
                  PAGE TITLE DATE)
          (SETQ LINE 3)
          ({the column-headings} {REPORT, modified}
                                 {LINE, modified}))
        ({the print-item} {REPORT, modified}
                          {LINE, modified}
                          ({the current of the enumerator} DATA))
        (SETQ DATA ({the rest of the enumerator} DATA)))
      ({the summary} {REPORT, modified}))))
```

KBEmacs (LISP) <KBE.DEMO>TIMINGS.LISP

Screen 7.2 Inserting a cliché into a program.

assigned to a variable. This guarantees that an easy way to refer to the
output role is always evident to the programmer.

Navigating Between Roles

In keeping with the general Emacs philosophy of providing a wide variety of
convenient one-character commands for moving the editor cursor—e.g., c-N
(move to next line) and c-P (move to previous line)—KBEmacs provides a
number of commands for navigating in a program based on role annotation.
The command s-N moves to the first occurrence of role annotation after the
current cursor position. (In Screen 7.3, the programmer uses the command
s-N to move to the title role. Ordinary Emacs cursor motion commands
could also have been used.) The command s-P moves the editing cursor to
the first occurrence of role annotation prior to the current cursor position.

Direct Editing

To fill the title role, the programmer uses ordinary Emacs commands to
type in the title string. (In the command area of the screen, the phrase
direct editing is used in lieu of an explicit listing of these commands since
only the net effect of the commands is interesting.)

s-N
direct editing

```
(DEFUN REPORT-TIMINGS (TIMINGS)
  (WITH-OPEN-FILE (REPORT "report.txt" :DIRECTION :OUTPUT)
    (LET* ((DATE (TIME:PRINT-CURRENT-TIME NIL))
           (LINE 66)
           (PAGE 0)
           (TITLE "Report of Reaction Timings (in msec.)"▯)
           (DATA {the input data of the enumerator}))
      (FORMAT REPORT "~5%~60:@<~A~>~2%~60:@<~A~>~%" TITLE DATE)
      (LOOP
        (IF ({the empty of the enumerator} DATA) (RETURN))
        (WHEN (> LINE 63)
          (SETQ PAGE (+ PAGE 1))
          (FORMAT REPORT "~|~%Page:~3D~44:@<~A~>~17A~2%"
                          PAGE TITLE DATE)
          (SETQ LINE 3)
          ({the column-headings} {REPORT, modified}
                                 {LINE, modified}))
        ({the print-item} {REPORT, modified}
                          {LINE, modified}
                          ({the current of the enumerator} DATA))
        (SETQ DATA ({the rest of the enumerator} DATA)))
      ({the summary} {REPORT, modified})))))
```

KBEmacs (LISP) <KBE.DEMO>TIMINGS.LISP

Screen 7.3 Direct editing.

The programmer could have used a knowledge-based command to fill the title—i.e., "Fill the title with "Report of ...":" However, using ordinary text editing is simpler. An important goal of KBEmacs is to provide assistance to programmers without preventing them from doing simple things in simple ways. Programmers are encouraged to use ordinary text editing whenever that is the easiest thing to do.

Filling a Role with a Cliché

When a role is to be filled with an instance of a cliché, it becomes profitable to use a knowledge-based command rather than direct editing. In Screen 7.4, the Fill command is used to fill the enumerator with an instance of cdr-enumeration. This causes REPORT-TIMINGS to enumerate (and therefore report on) the list of TIMINGS. Note that the enumerator is a compound role and all its subroles have been simultaneously filled.

The Fill command fills an unfilled role (specified by a definite noun phrase beginning with *the*) by inserting an instance of a cliché (specified by an indefinite noun phrase beginning with *a*). The definite noun phrase is disambiguated with respect to the position of the cursor. The phrase "the enumerator" in the command in Screen 7.4 is interpreted to mean the enumerator in REPORT-TIMINGS because the cursor was positioned in this program when the command was typed (see Screen 7.3). If there were

```
s-X Fill the enumerator with a cdr-enumeration of TIMINGS. <end>
```
```
(DEFUN REPORT-TIMINGS (TIMINGS)
  (WITH-OPEN-FILE (REPORT "report.txt" :DIRECTION :OUTPUT)
    (LET* ((DATE (TIME:PRINT-CURRENT-TIME NIL))
           (LINE 66)
           (LIST TIMINGS)
           (PAGE 0)
           (TITLE "Report of Reaction Timings (in msec.)"))
      (FORMAT REPORT "~5%~60:@<~A~>~2%~60:@<~A~>~%" TITLE DATE)
      (LOOP
        (IF (NULL LIST) (RETURN))
        (WHEN (> LINE 63)
          (SETQ PAGE (+ PAGE 1))
          (FORMAT REPORT "~|~%Page:~3D~44:@<~A~>~17A~2%"
                         PAGE TITLE DATE)
          (SETQ LINE 3)
          ({the column-headings} {REPORT, modified}
                                 {LINE, modified}))
        ({the print-item} {REPORT, modified}
                          {LINE, modified}
                          {(CAR LIST), the output element})
        (SETQ LIST (CDR LIST)))
      ({the summary} {REPORT, modified})))))
```

KBEmacs (LISP) <KBE.DEMO>TIMINGS.LISP

Screen 7.4 Filling a role with a cliché.

more than one enumerator in the program, the programmer would have
had to explicitly state which one was being referred to (see Section 9.5).

A subsidiary, but important, change in Screen 7.4 from Screen 7.3 is
that the variable name DATA has been changed to the more informative name
LIST. The readability of a program depends to a surprising extent on how
the data flow is implemented and, in particular, on what variable names are
used. Therefore KBEmacs works hard to use nesting of expressions where
appropriate and to pick reasonable variable names. In this case, the variable
name LIST is chosen because it is suggested by the code in the definition of
cdr-enumeration.

An additional minor change in the program in Screen 7.4 is that the
order of the bound variables in the LET* has been changed. Within the limits
of data-flow constraints, KBEmacs puts the bound variables in alphabetical
order. The only exception to this is that uninformative variable names,
such as DATA, are put at the end of the list (see Screen 7.3).

Removing a Role

After filling the enumerator, the programmer proceeds to complete the rest
of the program. In Screen 7.5, as no column headings are desired, the
programmer uses the Remove command to get rid of the column-headings
role. In general, clichés (such as simple-report) are defined so that they
include a wide variety of features, on the theory that it is easier for a
programmer to prune things away than to think them up.

```
s-X Remove the column-headings. <end>
```

```
(DEFUN REPORT-TIMINGS (TIMINGS)
  (WITH-OPEN-FILE (REPORT "report.txt" :DIRECTION :OUTPUT)
    (LET* ((DATE (TIME:PRINT-CURRENT-TIME NIL))
           (LINE 66)
           (LIST TIMINGS)
           (PAGE 0)
           (TITLE "Report of Reaction Timings (in msec.)"))
      (FORMAT REPORT "~5%~60:@<~A~>~2%~60:@<~A~>~%" TITLE DATE)
      (LOOP
        (IF (NULL LIST) (RETURN))
        (WHEN (> LINE 63)
          (SETQ PAGE (+ PAGE 1))
          (FORMAT REPORT "~|~%Page:~3D~44:@<~A~>~17A~2%"
                  PAGE TITLE DATE)
          (SETQ LINE 3))
        ({the print-item} {REPORT, modified}
                          {LINE, modified}
                          {(CAR LIST), the output element})
        (SETQ LIST (CDR LIST)))
      ({the summary} {REPORT, modified})))))
```

KBEmacs (LISP) <KBE.DEMO>TIMINGS.LISP

Screen 7.5 Removing a role.

An Abbreviated Command for Filling Roles

In addition to the basic command s-X, KBEmacs supports a number of abbreviated commands that make it easier to type particular knowledge-based commands. Each of the abbreviated commands is the same as s-X, except that a partial (or complete) knowledge-based command is automatically generated by the system.

The command s-F sets up the initial part of a Fill command for the first unfilled role that textually follows the current cursor position. The programmer has to complete the command by indicating what cliché to fill the role with. In Screen 7.6, s-F generates the first half of a Fill command for the print-item role, since this is the first role following the cursor in Screen 7.5.

The programmer fills the print-item with a print-out. The format-string role of print-out is filled with a literal string in the command. (The string used forces a new line, prints five spaces, and then prints an eight-digit decimal number.) The fact that program text can be directly included in a knowledge-based command is convenient in many situations.

Deducing Data-Flow Connections

For KBEmacs, the most difficult part of filling a role with an instance of a cliché is deciding how to connect up the data flow. This is done by comparing the data-flow environment of the unfilled role with the data-flow requirements of the cliché.

s-F Fill the print-item with a print-out of "~&~5T~8D". <end>

```
(DEFUN REPORT-TIMINGS (TIMINGS)
  (WITH-OPEN-FILE (REPORT "report.txt" :DIRECTION :OUTPUT)
    (LET* ((DATE (TIME:PRINT-CURRENT-TIME NIL))
           (LINE 66)
           (LIST TIMINGS)
           (PAGE 0)
           (TITLE "Report of Reaction Timings (in msec.)"))
      (FORMAT REPORT "~5%~60:@<~A~>~2%~60:@<~A~>~%" TITLE DATE)
      (LOOP
        (IF (NULL LIST) (RETURN))
        (WHEN (> LINE 63)
          (SETQ PAGE (+ PAGE 1))
          (FORMAT REPORT "~|~%Page:~3D~44:@<~A~>~17A~2%"
                         PAGE TITLE DATE)
          (SETQ LINE 3))
        (FORMAT REPORT "~&~5T~8D" {(CAR LIST), the output element})
        (SETQ LINE (+ LINE 1))
        (SETQ LIST (CDR LIST)))
      ({the summary} {REPORT, modified})))))
```

KBEmacs (LISP) <KBE.DEMO>TIMINGS.LISP

Screen 7.6 An abbreviated command for filling roles.

The annotation on the print-item role in Screen 7.5 (reproduced at the end of this paragraph) specifies that the role takes as inputs the output file REPORT, the line number variable LINE, and the output element of the enumerator. In addition, it specifies that REPORT and LINE are modified by the print-item and therefore are also outputs of the role.

```
({the print-item} {REPORT, modified}
                  {LINE, modified}
                  {(CAR LIST), the output element})
```

The definition of print-out (Figure 7.4 on page 92) specifies three input roles—item, report, and line—and three output roles—report, line, and the return value. (REPORT and LINE are free variables that are read and written in the body of the definition.)

When the print-item role is filled with an instance of print-out, KBEmacs connects up the data flow as follows: The report and line inputs of print-out are connected to the report and line inputs of the print-item role because the names match. The report and line outputs of print-out are connected to the modified outputs of the print-item role for the same reason. The input item of the print-out is connected to the output element of the enumerator because this element is the only argument of the print-item that has not yet been accounted for. The return value of the print-out is not connected to anything because the return value of the print-item role is not used.

The heuristics illustrated in the previous paragraph work quite well most of the time. However, sometimes the programmer has some other pattern of connection in mind. When this happens, the programmer has to either restate what is wanted using a more detailed knowledge-based command or use textual editing to fix the connections.

Asking What Needs to be Done

KBEmacs keeps track of which roles remain to be filled in. In Screen 7.7, the programmer asks the system to report this information for the program REPORT-TIMINGS. (The abbreviated command s-W.is used to save typing.) KBEmacs reports that the summary role still needs to be filled. In addition to unfilled roles, the system will list any output roles that have not been used for anything.

To fill the summary, the programmer moves the cursor to the position of the summary role and uses ordinary editing commands to type in an expression that prints the mean and deviation of the timings. The code uses a subroutine MEAN-AND-DEVIATION, which returns the mean and deviation of a list of numbers.

Telling KBEmacs that a Program is Finished

In Screen 7.8, the programmer uses the Finish command (triggered by the abbreviated command s-<end>) to signal that the implementation of

REPORT-TIMINGS has been completed. This command first checks that all the roles have been filled and all the output roles have been used for something. (An error message is issued if this is not the case.) Next, the command removes all role annotation (in this case, for the role element), so that the code can be read by the standard Lisp compiler. (The annotation can be reintroduced at a later time if the programmer desires.)

After signaling that the implementation of REPORT-TIMINGS has been finished, the programmer uses the standard Emacs command c-shift-C (compile definition) to compile the program REPORT-TIMINGS. As part of its normal functioning, this command warns the programmer that the function MEAN-AND-DEVIATION has not yet been defined. This is another example of the way KBEmacs takes advantage of the standard programming environment wherever possible.

Analyzing Direct Editing

When direct editing is performed by the programmer, KBEmacs waits until the next knowledge-based command is used before considering the changes made. This is done to avoid analyzing partially edited programs that are in inconsistent states.

```
s-W What needs to be done? <end>
for the function REPORT-TIMINGS
 Fill the summary.
s-N s-N direct editing
```

```
(DEFUN REPORT-TIMINGS (TIMINGS)
  (WITH-OPEN-FILE (REPORT "report.txt" :DIRECTION :OUTPUT)
    (LET* ((DATE (TIME:PRINT-CURRENT-TIME NIL))
           (LINE 66)
           (LIST TIMINGS)
           (PAGE 0)
           (TITLE "Report of Reaction Timings (in msec.)"))
      (FORMAT REPORT "~5%~60:@<~A~>~2%~60:@<~A~>~%" TITLE DATE)
      (LOOP
        (IF (NULL LIST) (RETURN))
        (WHEN (> LINE 63)
          (SETQ PAGE (+ PAGE 1))
          (FORMAT REPORT "~|~%Page:~3D~44:@<~A~>~17A~2%"
                         PAGE TITLE DATE)
          (SETQ LINE 3))
        (FORMAT REPORT "~&~5T~8D" {(CAR LIST), the output element})
        (SETQ LINE (+ LINE 1))
        (SETQ LIST (CDR LIST)))
      (FORMAT REPORT "~2&~{mean:~11,2F    (deviation: ~,2F)~}"
                     (MEAN-AND-DEVIATION TIMINGS))))
```

KBEmacs (LISP) <KBE.DEMO>TIMINGS.LISP

Screen 7.7 Asking what needs to be done.

For instance, KBEmacs takes no notice of the direct editing in Screen 7.7 until the knowledge-based command in Screen 7.8 is typed. When this happens, KBEmacs analyzes the effects of the direct editing before executing the `Finish` command. (Although it did not lead to any changes in the program, analysis also occurred after Screen 7.3.)

Often direct editing can be understood as filling one or more roles because the changes are confined solely to replacing one or more unfilled roles textually. (This is true both here and after Screen 7.3.) When this is the case, the direct editing is processed as if the equivalent `Fill` commands had been used. This guarantees that the plan for the program will be updated correctly. In other situations, more complicated analysis has to be used to update the plan (see Section 9.3).

Checking Constraints

Whenever the plan for a program is modified by a knowledge-based command (or altered due to the analysis following direct editing), KBEmacs checks to see that the constraints on the clichés in the plan are still satisfied. Looking at the plan that results from the analysis of Screen 7.7, KBEmacs notes that the DERIVED constraint on the line-limit role is no longer satis-

```
s-<end> Finish editing the function REPORT-TIMINGS. <end>
c-shift-C Compiling REPORT-TIMINGS
The following functions were referenced but do not seem defined:
  MEAN-AND-DEVIATION referenced by REPORT-TIMINGS
```

```
(DEFUN REPORT-TIMINGS (TIMINGS)
  (WITH-OPEN-FILE (REPORT "report.txt" :DIRECTION :OUTPUT)
    (LET* ((DATE (TIME:PRINT-CURRENT-TIME NIL))
           (LINE 66)
           (LIST TIMINGS)
           (PAGE 0)
           (TITLE "Report of Reaction Timings (in msec.)"))
      (FORMAT REPORT "~5%~60:@<~A~>~2%~60:@<~A~>~%" TITLE DATE)
      (LOOP
        (IF (NULL LIST) (RETURN))
        (WHEN (> LINE 62)
          (SETQ PAGE (+ PAGE 1))
          (FORMAT REPORT "~|~%Page:~3D~44:@<~A~>~17A~2%"
                         PAGE TITLE DATE)
          (SETQ LINE 3))
        (FORMAT REPORT "~&~5T~8D" (CAR LIST))
        (SETQ LINE (+ LINE 1))
        (SETQ LIST (CDR LIST)))
      (FORMAT REPORT "~2&~{mean:~11,2F    (deviation: ~,2F)~}"
              (MEAN-AND-DEVIATION TIMINGS)))))
```

KBEmacs (LISP) <KBE.DEMO>TIMINGS.LISP

Screen 7.8 Analyzing direct editing.

```
Define a program REPORT-TIMINGS with a parameter TIMINGS.
Insert a simple-report.
Fill the title with "Report of Reaction Timings (in msec.)".
Fill the enumerator with a cdr-enumeration of TIMINGS.
Remove the column-headings.
Fill the print-item with a print-out of "~&~5T~8D".
Fill the summary with
  (FORMAT REPORT "~2&~{mean:~11,2F   (deviation: ~,2F)~}"
          (MEAN-AND-DEVIATION TIMINGS)).
```

Figure 7.6 Command summary.

fied. The constraint is violated because the summary requires two output lines rather than one output line as initially assumed by SIZE-IN-LINES in Screen 7.2. (The FORMAT code ~2& causes two blank lines.)

To satisfy the constraint, KBEmacs changes the line-limit from 63 to 62. The line-limit did not change when the programmer filled the print-item because the print-item was filled with a computation that requires one output line.

The automatic updating of the line-limit role is a good example of the way KBEmacs can enhance program reliability. The main leverage KBEmacs applies to the reliability problem is that each cliché in the library is internally consistent. The use of constraints can help maintain this consistency.

It is interesting to note that if KBEmacs did not update the line-limit role, the programmer might not have realized that it needed to be updated. The bug that would result, though minor, would have the pernicious quality of being rather hard to detect during program testing, since the bug manifests itself only when the program attempts to print the summary as the last line of a page.

Evaluation of the Commands Used

The set of knowledge-based commands used to implement the program REPORT-TIMINGS is summarized in Figure 7.6, with direct editing recast as equivalent uses of the Fill command.

It is interesting to compare these commands with the hypothetical set of directions for an inexperienced assistant programmer (Figure 7.5 on page 93). The two sets of directions are quite similar in tone and rely heavily on terms such as *simple report.*

However, the knowledge-based commands are more detailed. For example, when using KBEmacs, the programmer must explicitly refer to cdr-enumeration. In addition, the programmer must specify the exact format strings to use for printing timings and the summary. An important future direction of work on the Programmer's Apprentice is reducing the detail that has to be specified by the programmer.

Define a program MEAN-AND-DEVIATION with one parameter, a list of timings. Return a list of the mean and deviation of the timings. The mean is the sum of the timings divided by the number of timings. The standard deviation is the square root of the difference between the second moment and the square of the mean. The second moment is the sum of the squares of the timings divided by the number of timings.

Figure 7.7 Directions for a human assistant.

7.3   Bottom-Up Implementation

In the next part of the transcript, the programmer implements the function MEAN-AND-DEVIATION, using a rather different style of interaction with KBEmacs. Instead of constructing the program in a top-down fashion starting from a high-level cliché, the programmer builds the program from the bottom up by combining various low-level clichés. This bottom-up approach is appropriate for the function MEAN-AND-DEVIATION because there is no high-level cliché that captures the overall structure of the program.

Consider the kind of directions an expert programmer might give to an assistant regarding MEAN-AND-DEVIATION. The directions shown in Figure 7.7 assume that the assistant understands how to count the number of elements in a list and how to compute a sum. However, they do not assume that the assistant knows the mathematical definitions of the mean and standard deviation.

It would have been equally plausible to assume that the assistant *did* know how to compute the mean and deviation (and that KBEmacs has clichés for computing the mean and deviation). However, the goal of this part of the transcript is to illustrate how low-level clichés can be combined to construct a more complex computation. Thus, the transcript assumes that clichés for computing the mean and deviation are not known.

direct editing

```
《  (DEFUN MEAN-AND-DEVIATION (TIMINGS) [])



```

KBEmacs (LISP) <KBE.DEMO>TIMINGS.LISP

Screen 7.9 Beginning the definition of a program.

```
(DEFINE-PLAN SUM
    (PRIMARY-ROLES (NUMBER)
    DESCRIBED-ROLES (NUMBER)
    COMMENT "accumulates the sum of {the number}")
  (LET* ((SUM {0, the zero}))
    (LOOP
      (SETQ SUM ({+, the accumulator} SUM {the input number})))
    SUM))
```

Figure 7.8 A cliché for computing a sum.

The Sum Cliché

To begin the implementation of the program MEAN-AND-DEVIATION, the programmer simply types a functional header for the program (see Screen 7.9). This is at least as easy as using the Define command.

To compute the mean of the timings, the program MEAN-AND-DEVIATION must first compute their sum. Since this is a stereotyped computation, the programmer asks KBEmacs to insert it into the program (see Screen 7.10). The programmer specifies the appropriate algorithm by combining two clichés: cdr-enumeration and sum.

The plan for the sum cliché (Figure 7.8) specifies how to accumulate the sum of a temporal sequence of numbers. Sum is a member of a general class of clichés called accumulation clichés, all of which have the following roles: An input role (here the *number*) is the temporal sequence of values to be aggregated. The *accumulator* (here +) is a function that adds successive input values into the aggregate. The *zero* (here 0) is the left identity of the accumulator. The final aggregate value becomes the return value output.

Flexible Interaction

The programmer continues the implementation of MEAN-AND-DEVIATION by moving the cursor to the end of the program and starting to type an expression specifying the return value (see Screen 7.11). This value is a

```
s-X Insert a sum of a cdr-enumeration of TIMINGS. <end>
```

```
(DEFUN MEAN-AND-DEVIATION (TIMINGS)
  [LET* ((LIST TIMINGS)
         (SUM 0))
    (LOOP
      (IF (NULL LIST) (RETURN))
      (SETQ SUM (+ SUM {(CAR LIST), the output element}))
      (SETQ LIST (CDR LIST)))
    SUM))
```

```
KBEmacs (LISP) <KBE.DEMO>TIMINGS.LISP
```

Screen 7.10 Inserting a cliché into a program.

list whose first element is the mean (the sum of the timings divided by the number of timings).

Screen 7.11 is frozen at the moment where the programmer needs to enter the computation of the number of timings. In Screen 7.12, this computation is introduced using the `Insert` command and the count cliché.

The use of `Insert` in Screen 7.12 is a good example of the kind of flexible interaction between man and machine that KBEmacs strives for. In the middle of typing an expression, the programmer issues a request to KBEmacs that is easy to conceive and state, but requires a significant number of changes scattered throughout the program—e.g., in addition to adding computation into the main loop, two new variables are created. The programmer can construct a program by combining whole algorithms in the order in which they naturally come to mind.

(Like the sum cliché, the count cliché is an accumulation. The input role is a temporal sequence of values to be counted. The *accumulator* increments a counter by one each time an element of the sequence is encountered. The *zero* initializes the counter to zero.)

Using Common Sense

An interesting aspect of Screen 7.12 is that, while the changes in the program satisfy the programmer's intent, they do not correspond to the most literal interpretation of the knowledge-based command given. In general, the `Insert` command inserts code at the place where the cursor is positioned. Therefore, the most straightforward thing for KBEmacs to have done would have been to create the program in Figure 7.9.

There are situations where inserting a separate loop would be the right thing to do. However, in Figure 7.9 it seems unreasonable. (Among other things, the loop does not terminate.) KBEmacs reasons that since the programmer's command refers to a temporal sequence of values computed in the main program loop ("`the element`"), the count cliché should be inserted in the main loop, with only the final value of the count inserted at the cursor position.

direct editing

```
(DEFUN MEAN-AND-DEVIATION (TIMINGS)
  (LET* ((LIST TIMINGS)
         (SUM 0))
    (LOOP
      (IF (NULL LIST) (RETURN))
      (SETQ SUM (+ SUM {(CAR LIST), the output element}))
      (SETQ LIST (CDR LIST)))
    (LIST (/ SUM ▯))))
```

KBEmacs (LISP) <KBE.DEMO>TIMINGS.LISP

Screen 7.11 Direct editing.

```
(DEFUN MEAN-AND-DEVIATION (TIMINGS)
  (LET* ((COUNT 0)
         (LIST TIMINGS)
         (SUM 0))
    (LOOP
      (IF (NULL LIST) (RETURN))
      (SETQ SUM (+ SUM {(CAR LIST), the output element}))
      (SETQ LIST (CDR LIST)))
    (LIST (/ SUM (PROGN (LOOP (SETQ COUNT (+ COUNT 1)))
                        COUNT)))))
```

Figure 7.9 Naive interpretation of the command in Screen 12.

This is an example of a deep problem—the need for *common sense*—which KBEmacs only solves in a few limited situations. As with any assistant, the programmer wants KBEmacs to exhibit common sense. The system tries to do this by rejecting interpretations of knowledge-based commands that are obviously unreasonable. However, KBEmacs's abilities in this respect are quite limited. What may appear to the programmer as *merely* common sense may in fact require an understanding of programming that is much deeper than that possessed by KBEmacs.

Aesthetic Quality of the Code Produced

As will be discussed in Section 9.4, producing reasonably aesthetic code is the most difficult task KBEmacs has to perform. The code in Screen 7.12 is a good example of what KBEmacs can do. The code is clearly readable, but it has many small problems. For instance, a variable is used to hold the output of the enumerator even though this is not actually necessary. Further, while the variable name used (ELEMENT) is plausible, it is not particularly informative in the context of this program. Finally, as mentioned earlier,

```
s-X Insert a count of the element. <end>
```

```
(DEFUN MEAN-AND-DEVIATION (TIMINGS)
  (LET* ((COUNT 0)
         (ELEMENT)
         (LIST TIMINGS)
         (SUM 0))
    (LOOP
      (IF (NULL LIST) (RETURN))
      (SETQ ELEMENT (CAR LIST))
      (SETQ COUNT (+ COUNT 1))
      (SETQ LIST (CDR LIST))
      (SETQ SUM (+ SUM ELEMENT)))
    (LIST (/ SUM COUNT))))
```

```
KBEmacs (LISP) <KBE.DEMO>TIMINGS.LISP
```

Screen 7.12 Inserting a cliché into a program.

KBEmacs orders the variables bound by the LET* alphabetically rather than by using some criterion based on meaning.

One way to think about the code produced by KBEmacs is to realize that like any programmer, KBEmacs has an identifiable style. If you were using KBEmacs, you would probably prefer to have it produce code in your own style. However, if you ask someone else to write some code for you, it is only reasonable to expect the code to come out largely in their style. Beyond this, the stylistic uniformity introduced by KBEmacs could be quite useful in a project involving many programmers.

By using textual editing, programmers have the option of changing the code produced by KBEmacs to suit their aesthetic desires. For instance, in Screen 7.13, the programmer uses the standard Emacs command m-% (query replace) to rename the variable ELEMENT to TIMING.

Embedded Cliché Instance Phrases

The programmer finishes the program MEAN-AND-DEVIATION by specifying how to compute the deviation. This is done by using standard Emacs commands to edit the program code.

The expression typed by the programmer at the bottom of Screen 7.13 illustrates a different mode of interaction with KBEmacs: Annotation describing a computation in terms of clichés is inserted directly in the program. When the direct editing is later analyzed, KBEmacs replaces the annotation with the appropriate code (see Screen 7.14). This is equivalent to using the Insert command but can be more convenient.

The next to last line of Screen 7.14 contains a cliché instance phrase specifying how to compute a sum of the squares of the individual timings.

```
m-c-H c-U m-% replace some occurrences of: ELEMENT with: TIMING
direct editing
```

```
(DEFUN MEAN-AND-DEVIATION (TIMINGS)
   (LET* ((COUNT 0)
《         (TIMING)
          (LIST TIMINGS)
          (SUM 0))
      (LOOP
        (IF (NULL LIST) (RETURN))
《       (SETQ TIMING (CAR LIST))
        (SETQ COUNT (+ COUNT 1))
        (SETQ LIST (CDR LIST))
《       (SETQ SUM (+ SUM TIMING)))
      (LIST (/ SUM COUNT)
《            (SQRT (- (/ {a sum of a squaring of TIMING} COUNT)
《                     (EXPT {the return-value of the first /} 2)))》))
```

KBEmacs (LISP) <KBE.DEMO>TIMINGS.LISP

Screen 7.13 Embedded cliché instance phrases.

It uses the sum and squaring clichés. The last line specifies how to compute the square of the mean. In addition to referring to the result value of a cliché, one can use the phrase "the return-value of ..." to refer to the output of any function. The phrase "the first /" identifies the function in question as the first (in execution order) division operation.

Replacing Embedded Cliché Instance Phrases with Code

In Screen 7.14, the programmer tells KBEmacs that the program has been completed. The major effect this has is triggering an analysis of the direct editing in Screen 7.13. The results of this analysis lead to three changes in the program.

First, to maintain its stylistic constraints, KBEmacs reorders the bound variables so that they are alphabetical. (They got out of order due to the variable renaming in Screen 7.13.)

Second, the embedded phrase "a sum of a squaring of TIMING" is replaced by ordinary program code. As part of this, a second summation is inserted into the main loop. This summation computes the sum of the squares of the timings. Due to the fact that the variable name SUM is already used in the program, KBEmacs uses the name SUM1 for the accumulation variable of this second summation.

Third, a variable is introduced so that the mean can be used in two places in the computation. The name X is used for this variable because KBEmacs has no basis for determining a better name to use.

In Screen 7.15, the programmer uses textual editing to give better names to the variables SUM1 and X and compiles the program so that it can be tested.

s-<end> Finish editing the function MEAN-AND-DEVIATION. <end>

```
(DEFUN MEAN-AND-DEVIATION (TIMINGS)
  (LET* ((COUNT 0)
         (LIST TIMINGS)
         (SUM 0)
         (SUM1 0)
         (TIMING)
         (X))
    (LOOP
      (IF (NULL LIST) (RETURN))
      (SETQ TIMING (CAR LIST))
      (SETQ SUM1 (+ SUM1 (EXPT TIMING 2)))
      (SETQ COUNT (+ COUNT 1))
      (SETQ LIST (CDR LIST))
      (SETQ SUM (+ SUM TIMING)))
    (SETQ X (/ SUM COUNT))
    (LIST X (SQRT (- (/ SUM1 COUNT) (EXPT X 2))))))
```

KBEmacs (LISP) <KBE.DEMO>TIMINGS.LISP

Screen 7.14 Replacing embedded cliché instances phrases with code.

Testing

In Screen 7.16, the programmer uses the standard Lisp Machine context-switching command `<select>` L to switch to the Lisp execution environment. The programmer then defines a test program TEST-REPORT-TIMINGS and tests the program REPORT-TIMINGS. The program DISPLAY-REPORT displays the report produced. To save space in the figure, groups of blank lines are abbreviated using the form *<n blank lines>*. Page breaks are represented by `<page>`.

Evaluation of the Commands Used

As shown in Figure 7.10, the KBEmacs commands used in this part of the transcript can be nicely summarized by pretending that all of the clichés were inserted using embedded annotation. This annotation has much the same flavor as the hypothetical set of directions for a human assistant (Figure 7.7 on page 104).

(If embedded annotation had actually been used as shown in Figure 7.10, it would have resulted in a correctly running program. However, the program would have been quite inefficient because there would have been four separate cdr-enumerations and two separate counts. KBEmacs is not capable of automatically determining that these computations should be shared. Achieving this sharing is an important reason why the transcript in Screens 7.9–7.15 took the form it did.)

```
m-c-H c-U m-% replace some occurrences of: SUM1 with: SUM-SQUARES
m-c-H c-U m-% replace some occurrences of: X with: MEAN
s-<end> Finish editing the function MEAN-AND-DEVIATION. <end>
c-shift-C [Compiling MEAN-AND-DEVIATION]
```

```
(DEFUN MEAN-AND-DEVIATION (TIMINGS)
  (LET* ((COUNT 0)
         (LIST TIMINGS)
         (MEAN)
         (SUM 0)
         (SUM-SQUARES 0)
         (TIMING))
    (LOOP
      (IF (NULL LIST) (RETURN))
      (SETQ TIMING (CAR LIST))
      (SETQ SUM-SQUARES (+ SUM-SQUARES (EXPT TIMING 2)))
      (SETQ COUNT (+ COUNT 1))
      (SETQ LIST (CDR LIST))
      (SETQ SUM (+ SUM TIMING)))
    (SETQ MEAN (/ SUM COUNT))
    (LIST MEAN (SQRT (- (/ SUM-SQUARES COUNT) (EXPT MEAN 2))))))
```

KBEmacs (LISP) <KBE.DEMO>TIMINGS.LISP

Screen 7.15 Renaming variables.

```
(DEFUN MEAN-AND-DEVIATION (TIMINGS)
  (LIST (/ {a sum of a cdr-enumeration of TIMINGS}
          {a count of a cdr-enumeration of TIMINGS})
        (SQRT (- (/ {a sum of a squaring of a cdr-enumeration
                        of TIMINGS}
                    {a count of a cdr-enumeration of TIMINGS})
                 (EXPT {the return-value of the first /} 2)))))
```

Figure 7.10 Command summary.


```
<select> L
```

```
(DEFUN TEST-REPORT-TIMINGS ()
  (REPORT-TIMINGS '(10041 9315 10722 11473 10834 11076
                    10447 10658 9529 9041 10452 11137
                    10351 10384 10474 11706 9592 10685
                    9987 10891))
  (DISPLAY-REPORT))
TEST-REPORT-TIMINGS

(TEST-REPORT-TIMINGS)
<5 blank lines>
          Report of Reaction Timings (in msec.)

                    5/27/89 12:16:39
<page>
Page:  1    Report of Reaction Timings (in msec.)    5/27/89 12:16:39

        10041
         9315
        10722
        11473
        10834
        11076
        10447
        10658
         9529
         9041
        10452
        11137
        10351
        10384
        10474
        11706
         9592
        10685
         9987
        10891

mean:   10439.75    (deviation: 680.24)
▯
```

```
Lisp Listener
```

Screen 7.16 Testing.

7.4   Modification and Documentation

Although KBEmacs focuses primarily on program construction, the basic
capabilities of the system also provide considerable assistance in program
modification and documentation.

Replacing a Role Filler

Looking at the test output produced in Screen 7.16, the programmer decides
that the report would look better if the timings were printed in tabular form
rather than one to a line. To perform this modification, the programmer
first switches back into the editor (using the command <select> E) and
then uses the standard Emacs command m-. (go to definition) to move the
cursor to the definition of REPORT-TIMINGS (see Screen 7.17).

The programmer then uses the knowledge-based command Replace to
change the filler of the print-item role to an instance of a tabular-print-out
instead of a print-out. The Replace command removes the code currently
filling a role and replaces it with the new computation specified. This replacement is possible because the plan for the program contains a record

```
<select> E
m-. Edit definition of REPORT-TIMINGS
s-X Replace the print-item with a tabular-print-out of "~9D". <end>
s-<end> Finish editing the function REPORT-TIMINGS. <end>
c-shift-C Compiling REPORT-TIMINGS
```

```
(DEFUN REPORT-TIMINGS (TIMINGS)
  (WITH-OPEN-FILE (REPORT "report.txt" :DIRECTION :OUTPUT)
    (LET* ((DATE (TIME:PRINT-CURRENT-TIME NIL))
           (LINE 66)
           (LIST TIMINGS)
           (PAGE 0)
           (TITLE "Report of Reaction Timings (in msec.)"))
      (FORMAT REPORT "~5%~60:@<~A~>~2%~60:@<~A~>~%" TITLE DATE)
      (LOOP
        (IF (NULL LIST) (RETURN))
        (WHEN (> LINE 62)
          (SETQ PAGE (+ PAGE 1))
          (FORMAT REPORT "~|~%Page:~3D~44:@<~A~>~17A~2%"
                         PAGE TITLE DATE)
          (SETQ LINE 3))
        (WHEN (> (CHARPOS REPORT) 59)
          (FORMAT REPORT "~&")
          (SETQ LINE (+ LINE 1)))
        (FORMAT REPORT "~9D" (CAR LIST))
        (SETQ LIST (CDR LIST)))
      (FORMAT REPORT "~2&~{mean:~11,2F   (deviation: ~,2F)~}"
              (MEAN-AND-DEVIATION TIMINGS)))))
```

KBEmacs (LISP) <KBE.DEMO>TIMINGS.LISP

Screen 7.17 Replacing a role filler.

```
(DEFINE-PLAN TABULAR-PRINT-OUT
    (PRIMARY-ROLES (FORMAT-STRING ITEM)
    DESCRIBED-ROLES (FORMAT-STRING ITEM NUMBER-OF-COLUMNS)
    COMMENT "prints {the item} in columns"
    CONSTRAINTS
      ((DEFAULT {the format-string} "~15A")
       (DERIVED {the maximum-charpos}
              (- 68 (SIZE-IN-CHARACTERS
                        {the format-string})))))
    (WHEN (> (CHARPOS REPORT) {the maximum-charpos})
      (FORMAT REPORT "~&")
      (SETQ LINE (+ LINE 1)))
    (FORMAT REPORT {the format-string} {the input item}))
```

Figure 7.11 A cliché for tabular printing.

of what subplan fills each role. (After recompiling REPORT-TIMINGS, the programmer returns to the Lisp execution environment and retests the program in Screen 7.18.)

The tabular-print-out cliché (Figure 7.11) is similar to print-out (Figure 7.4 on page 92) in that it has two primary roles: a format-string and an input item to print. However, unlike print-out, tabular-print-out assumes that the format-string will not force a newline and prints as many items as possible on each line. Before printing an item, the cliché tests to see whether there is enough room at the end of the current line to print it. If there is not enough room, then a newline is inserted (and the line number is incremented). The special function CHARPOS returns the output character position on the current line. The role maximum-charpos is derived by a constraint based on the assumption that only 68 characters can be printed on a line. The function SIZE-IN-CHARACTERS is capable of analyzing simple

```
<select> L
```

```
(TEST-REPORT-TIMINGS)
<5 blank lines>
            Report of Reaction Timings (in msec.)

                    5/27/89 12:18:07
<page>
Page:  1    Report of Reaction Timings (in msec.)   5/27/89 12:18:07

    10041    9315   10722   11473   10834   11076   10447
    10658    9529    9041   10452   11137   10351   10384
    10474   11706    9592   10685    9987   10891

mean:   10439.75   (deviation: 680.24)
□
```

```
Lisp Listener
```

Screen 7.18 Retesting.

format control strings and determining the maximum number of characters that will be printed.

In Screen 7.17, the format-string specified prints nine characters. As a result, the maximum-charpos is set at 59. The line-limit role of simple-report remains fixed at 62 because tabular-print-out can print at most one output line at a time.

Documentation Generation

In Screen 7.19, the programmer goes back to the editor and asks KBEmacs to generate a comment for REPORT-TIMINGS. This illustrates another way KBEmacs can use the information it maintains about a program to assist a programmer. If a program is constructed using KBEmacs, the Comment command (here triggered by the abbreviated command s-;) can be used to create a summary comment describing the program and insert it into the editor buffer.

The comment is in the form of a two-level outline. The first line specifies the top-level cliché in the program. The subsequent entries describe how the major roles in this cliché are filled. The comment is based on the clichés that were used to construct the program. The DESCRIBED-ROLES declaration in the definition of the top-level cliché (see Figure 7.3 on page 90) specifies which roles to describe and what order to describe them in.

Each role is described in one of four ways. If the role has been removed, then it is reported as missing (e.g., the column-headings). If the role is filled by a cliché, then this cliché is named (e.g., cdr-enumeration). Further, a brief description showing how the roles of this nested cliché are filled is included. (This description is generated from the COMMENT declaration in the definition of the nested cliché.) If a role is filled with nonclichéd computation that is short enough to fit on a single line, then the corresponding code is displayed (e.g., the title). Otherwise, the computation is simply reported to be idiosyncratic (e.g., the summary). The individual lines of the comment are written in the same style as the knowledge-based commands. In particular, variable names and code fragments are rendered in uppercase.

The comment generation capability currently supported by KBEmacs is intended only as an illustration of the kind of comments that are possible. There are many other kinds of comments containing either more or less information that could just as well have been produced. For example, KBEmacs could easily include a description of the inputs and outputs of the program in the comment. The form of comment shown was chosen because it contains a significant amount of high-level information that is not explicit in the program code. As a result, it could be of genuine assistance to a person who is trying to understand the program.

A key benefit of the comments produced by KBEmacs is that, since each comment is generated directly from the plan underlying a program, it is guaranteed to be correct. In contrast, much of the program documentation one typically encounters is of little value due to inaccuracies.

Highlighting a Role Filler

Another way in which KBEmacs can assist a programmer in understanding a program is to point out various logical parts of the program. In Screen 7.19, the programmer asks to see the summary role. The `Highlight` command uses standard editor highlighting (rendered in Screen 7.19 as underlining) to show the programmer a particular part of a program. To support this command, KBEmacs maintains a mapping showing which pieces of program text correspond to each part of the plan.

```
<select> E
s-; Comment the function REPORT-TIMINGS. <end>
s-X Highlight the summary. <end>
```

```
;;; The function REPORT-TIMINGS is a simple-report.
;;;     The file-name is "report.txt".
;;;     The title is "Report of Reaction Timings (in msec.)".
;;;     The enumerator is a cdr-enumeration.
;;;         It enumerates the elements of TIMINGS.
;;;     There are no column-headings.
;;;     The print-item is a tabular-print-out.
;;;         It prints (CAR LIST) in columns.
;;;     The summary is an idiosyncratic computation.

(DEFUN REPORT-TIMINGS (TIMINGS)
  (WITH-OPEN-FILE (REPORT "report.txt" :DIRECTION :OUTPUT)
    (LET* ((DATE (TIME:PRINT-CURRENT-TIME NIL))
           (LINE 66)
           (LIST TIMINGS)
           (PAGE 0)
           (TITLE "Report of Reaction Timings (in msec.)"))
      (FORMAT REPORT "~5%~60:@<~A~>~2%~60:@<~A~>~%" TITLE DATE)
      (LOOP
        (IF (NULL LIST) (RETURN))
        (WHEN (> LINE 62)
          (SETQ PAGE (+ PAGE 1))
          (FORMAT REPORT "~|~%Page:~3D~44:@<~A~>~17A~2%"
                         PAGE TITLE DATE)
          (SETQ LINE 3))
        (WHEN (> (CHARPOS REPORT) 59)
          (FORMAT REPORT "~&")
          (SETQ LINE (+ LINE 1)))
        (FORMAT REPORT "~9D" (CAR LIST))
        (SETQ LIST (CDR LIST)))
      (FORMAT REPORT "~2&~{mean:~11,2F    (deviation: ~,2F)~}"
              (MEAN-AND-DEVIATION TIMINGS)))))
```

KBEmacs (LISP) <KBE.DEMO>TIMINGS.LISP

Screen 7.19 Documentation generation.

Chapter 8

Implementing an Ada Program

This chapter demonstrates the language independence of KBEmacs by show-ing the construction of programs written in Ada [155]. Another purpose of the chapter is to show that KBEmacs can be used to operate on programs of moderate size and complexity. The examples up to this point have been subroutines that are only 10 to 20 lines long. The last section of this chap-ter shows the construction of a 57-line Ada procedure. The construction of an even larger procedure (110 lines) is shown in [21]. It could be argued that individual subroutines should never be larger than that.

The transcript in this chapter also demonstrates a number of capabilities of KBEmacs that are illustrated better in Ada than in Lisp. For example, unlike Lisp, data declarations are an important part of any Ada program. These declarations are used in at least three ways: They state key pieces of information that cannot be determined by looking at the rest of the pro-gram. They enhance reliability by redundantly specifying information that is evident in the rest of the program. They summarize information in a place where it is conveniently accessible to the reader (and the compiler). From the perspective of the first two uses, declarations need to be specified separately from the rest of the program. However, from the perspective of their third use, it is convenient to have a tool that generates declarations automatically. KBEmacs can automatically generate most of the data dec-larations in an Ada program that are in fact redundant with the rest of the program. This is particularly appropriate during prototyping.

8.1 Ada Clichés

In the transcript below, as in the Lisp transcript in Chapter 7, clichés are central to the communication between the programmer and KBEmacs.

```
plan SQUARING is
  primary roles NUMBER;
  described roles NUMBER;
  comment "computes the square of {the number}";
begin
  return {the input number}**2;
end SQUARING;
```

Figure 8.1 Ada version of Figure 7.1.

This section presents several Ada clichés and contrasts them with their Lisp counterparts.

Lisp clichés and Ada clichés differ in the same way that the Lisp and Ada languages differ. Many corresponding clichés in the two languages are, apart from syntax, identical. In this situation, the Plan Calculus makes it possible for the same cliché definition to be used for both languages. However, there are a number of semantic differences between the languages (and their run-time environments) that can lead to significant differences between corresponding clichés.

The squaring cliché (Figure 7.1 on page 88) is an example of a cliché that is the same in Lisp and Ada. This cliché can be used when constructing an Ada program without having to be explicitly defined in Ada. However, if defined in Ada, squaring would appear as shown in Figure 8.1.

To support the definition of plans for clichés, Ada syntax is extended in two ways. Role annotation is supported in analogy with the way it is supported in Lisp. This annotation can appear either in the form of a function call (e.g., {the operation}(DATA)) or as a value (e.g., {the input number}).

A new defining form **plan** is introduced in close analogy with Ada **procedure** definitions. As can be seen in Figure 8.1, the Ada definition of squaring is simply a transliteration of the Lisp definition into Ada-like syntax. The keywords **primary roles**, **described roles**, and **comment** correspond to the Lisp cliché declarations PRIMARY-ROLES, DESCRIBED-ROLES, and COMMENT. (This book uses the standard Ada orthographic convention of rendering reserved words in lowercase.) The remainder of the **plan** definition specifies the computation corresponding to the cliché and is the same as the body of an Ada **procedure** definition.

The File-Enumeration Cliché

The cliché file-enumeration shown in Figure 8.2 enumerates the records in a file, reading them sequentially. Since it is a type of enumeration cliché, it has the same basic structure and roles as cdr-enumeration. The input role *file* is the file to enumerate. The *empty* role (END_OF_FILE) tests whether the end of the file has been reached. The *rest* role steps from one record in the file to the next. The *current* role returns the individual records. (READ returns the record read via the variable specified as its second argument,

```
cliche FILE_ENUMERATION is
   primary roles FILE;
   described roles FILE;
   comment "enumerates the records in {the file}";
   constraints
      RENAME("DATA_RECORD", SINGULAR_FORM({the file}));
      DEFAULT({the file_name}, CORRESPONDING_FILE_NAME({the file}));
   end constraints;
   FILE: {};
   DATA_RECORD: {};
begin
   FILE := {the input file};
   OPEN(FILE, IN_FILE, {the file_name});
   while not {END_OF_FILE, the empty}(FILE) loop
      {{READ, the current}, the rest}(FILE, DATA_RECORD);
      {DATA_RECORD, the output data_record};
   end loop;
   CLOSE(FILE);
exception
   when DEVICE_ERROR | END_ERROR | NAME_ERROR | STATUS_ERROR =>
      CLOSE(FILE); PUT("Data Base Inconsistent");
   when others => CLOSE(FILE); raise;
end FILE_ENUMERATION;
```

Figure 8.2 A cliché for enumerating a file.

here DATA_RECORD, and steps from one record to the next.) The output role *data-record* is a temporal sequence of the records in the file.

Two syntactic features of Figure 8.2 are worthy of note. First, in Ada, identifiers cannot contain hyphens. To accommodate this, KBEmacs renders hyphenated cliché and role names in Ada code using underscores in place of the hyphens. Second, role annotation of the form {} is used to indicate a role that is not important enough to be given a name—e.g., the data types of the variables FILE and DATA_RECORD.

In addition to enumerating records, file-enumeration takes care of opening and closing the file. The exception handlers at the end of the body specify that, no matter what happens, the file should be closed. (This is equivalent to the support provided by the Lisp function WITH-OPEN-FILE.) In addition, the exception handlers specify that if an exception is raised while accessing a file, an error message should be printed and the exception suppressed. Other exceptions are passed on to be handled at a higher level.

In the transcript shown in the screens in this chapter, it is assumed that the procedures being written conform to a number of stylistic conventions. Three of these conventions are evident in Figure 8.2.

The first convention facilitates the use of input/output functions. Strong typing in Ada requires that there be different input/output functions for each type of file. It is assumed that overloading will always be used so that the input/output functions can be referred to as just OPEN, CLOSE, READ, etc., rather than DATA_FILE.OPEN, TEXT_FILE.OPEN, DATA_FILE.CLOSE, etc.

Another convention concerns the handling of exceptions. While clichés must check for other kinds of abnormal conditions relevant to them, they can assume that the database files will be in a consistent state. For example, file-enumeration does not have to check that the file actually exists before opening it. To deal with the fact that, in extraordinary circumstances, a file might not exist, a single blanket exception handler (shown at the bottom of Figure 8.2) is included as part of the outermost block of every procedure that accesses files.

A final convention concerns the way files and variables are named. File variables have plural names, and record variables have corresponding singular names. For instance, the names INVOICES and INVOICE could be used for a file of invoices and a variable holding records from this file.

The first of the two constraints in the definition of file-enumeration suggests a name to use for the variables associated with the file. A RENAME constraint is textual in nature. Its first argument is a target string, and its second argument is an expression that evaluates to a replacement string. The target string is replaced by the replacement string everywhere in the cliché instance. This causes renaming of variable names and function names. It also changes the values of string literals. As illustrated at the end of this paragraph, the renaming applies not only to the exact target string, but also to compound forms of the target string. In particular, the plural form of the target string is replaced by the plural form of the replacement string, and renaming is applied to multiword identifiers containing the target string. However, renaming is not applied to names that merely contain the target string as a substring. For instance, if "DATA_RECORD" is renamed to "INVOICE" then:

DATA_RECORD	becomes	INVOICE
DATA_RECORDS	becomes	INVOICES
DATA_RECORD_TYPE	becomes	INVOICE_TYPE
"The DATA_RECORD key"	becomes	"The INVOICE key"
DATA_RECORDING	remains	DATA_RECORDING

The second constraint on file-enumeration specifies a default value for the external name of the file. This constraint makes use of the function CORRESPONDING_FILE_NAME, which is discussed in the subsection after next.

A Data Structure Cliché

A concept central to the Ada transcript in this chapter is that of a *chain file*—a file in which each record has a field pointing to the next logical record in a chain. The chains in a chain file are typically pointed to by records in some other file. As an example Figure 8.3 shows a main file of student records, each of which points to a chain of records indicating the classes that the student has taken. Each main record contains the index of a chain record in its *classes* field. Each chain record contains the index of

Main File

Student	Year	Classes
H.B. Bonner	90	1
R.W. Hawk	91	0
T.E. Johnson	90	3

Chain File

Index	Course	Date	Grade	Next
1	Physics 101	Fall 88	A	2
2	English 204	Fall 88	C	0
3	Physics 101	Fall 88	C	4
4	English 320	Fall 88	C	0

Figure 8.3 An example of a chain file.

the subsequent chain record in its *next* field. The index value 0 is used to represent the end of a chain.

The cliché chain-file-definition (Figure 8.4) captures the stereotyped aspects of the definition of a chain file. The cliché has two roles: the external name of the file being defined and the data fields in the chain record. A renaming constraint is used to give aesthetic names to the identifiers used. The function FILE_NAME_ROOT computes a reasonable name to use based on the external name of the file.

The body of the cliché consists of five declarations. A variable is defined that holds a string containing the external name. A type is defined for index values pointing to the chain records. The type of the chain records

```
with FUNCTIONS; use FUNCTIONS;
plan CHAIN_FILE_DEFINITION is
  primary roles FILE_NAME;
  described roles FILE_NAME;
  comment "defines a file named {the file_name} of chain records";
  constraints
    RENAME("DATA_RECORD", FILE_NAME_ROOT({the file_name}));
  end constraints;
  DATA_RECORDS_NAME: constant STRING := {the file_name};
  subtype DATA_RECORD_INDEX_TYPE is INDEX_TYPE;
  type DATA_RECORD_TYPE is
    record
      {the data};
      NEXT: DATA_RECORD_INDEX_TYPE;
    end record;
  package DATA_RECORD_IO is
    new CHAINED_IO(DATA_RECORD_TYPE, DATA_RECORD_INDEX_TYPE);
  DATA_RECORDS: DATA_RECORD_IO.FILE_TYPE;
end CHAIN_FILE_DEFINITION;
```

Figure 8.4 A cliché for defining a chain file.

themselves is defined. (The only record field specified in the cliché is the
NEXT field, which points from one chain record to the next.) A package is
created that defines the input and output functions operating on the chain
file. A variable that can contain an instance of the chain file is defined.

Much of the content of the chain-file-definition cliché is contained in the
generic package CHAINED_IO, which is contained in the package FUNCTIONS
(shown in [21]). CHAINED_IO defines the functions needed for accessing chain
files. Using standard constructs such as subroutines and packages whenever
possible to facilitate the definition of clichés is part of the basic philosophy
behind the Programmer's Apprentice.

A Suite of Clichés Operating on Files

Like the Lisp clichés simple-report, print-out, and tabular-print-out, the
various Ada clichés for operating on files are designed as a tightly interacting group. In addition to passively embodying a number of shared conventions, these clichés have constraints that actively share information. In
particular, constraints in an Ada cliché that operates on a file often utilize
information obtained from the definition of the file. For example, the second constraint in the cliché file-enumeration (Figure 8.2) uses the function
CORRESPONDING_FILE_NAME to determine how to refer to the external name
of the file being operated on. This function works by locating and analyzing the definition of the file. It depends on the fact that the file was
defined in accordance with one of the standard clichés for defining a file
(e.g., chain-file-definition).

As a further example of how clichés that operate on files refer to the
definition of those files, consider the chain-enumeration cliché shown in
Figure 8.5. This cliché specifies how to enumerate a chain of records in a
chain file starting from a record in a main file.

Chain-enumeration is similar to file-enumeration. In particular, it shares
the basic structure of enumeration and the code associated with opening
and closing files. (Since two files have to be closed, a helping function
that closes both files, called CLEAN_UP, is defined. This function contains
an exception handler that deals with the situation in which the files have
not been successfully opened.) However, chain-enumeration embodies an
entirely different method for reading records from a file.

Instead of reading records sequentially, chain-enumeration uses explicit
indices to read successive records in a chain. The input role *main-file-key*
is the key of a record in a main file that points to a chain of records in
a chain file. The *empty* role (NULL_INDEX) tests whether the end of the
chain has been reached. The *rest* role steps from one record in the chain
to the next by accessing the appropriate field. The *current* role reads the
appropriate record from the chain file. (The third argument to READ specifies
the index/key of the record to read.) The output role *chain-record* is a
temporal sequence of the records in the chain.

```
plan CHAIN_ENUMERATION is
  primary roles MAIN_FILE, CHAIN_FILE, MAIN_FILE_KEY;
  described roles MAIN_FILE, CHAIN_FILE, MAIN_FILE_KEY;
  comment "enumerates the records in {the chain_file} starting
          from the header record indexed by {the main_file_key}";
  constraints
    RENAME("MAIN_RECORD", SINGULAR_FORM({the main_file}));
    RENAME("CHAIN_RECORD", SINGULAR_FORM({the chain_file}));
    DEFAULT({the main_file_name},
            CORRESPONDING_FILE_NAME({the main_file}));
    DEFAULT({the chain_file_name},
            CORRESPONDING_FILE_NAME({the chain_file}));
    DEFAULT({the main_file_chain_field},
            CHAIN_FIELD({the main_file}, {the chain_file}));
    DEFAULT({the rest},
            CHAIN_FIELD({the chain_file}, {the chain_file}));
  end constraints;
  CHAIN_FILE: {};
  CHAIN_RECORD: {};
  CHAIN_RECORD_INDEX: {};
  MAIN_FILE: {};
  MAIN_RECORD: {};
  procedure CLEAN_UP is
  begin
    CLOSE(CHAIN_FILE); CLOSE(MAIN_FILE);
  exception when STATUS_ERROR => return;
  end CLEAN_UP;
begin
  CHAIN_FILE := {the chain_file};
  MAIN_FILE := {the main_file};
  OPEN(CHAIN_FILE, IN_FILE, {the chain_file_name});
  OPEN(MAIN_FILE, IN_FILE, {the main_file_name});
  READ(MAIN_FILE, MAIN_RECORD, {the input main_file_key});
  CHAIN_RECORD_INDEX := MAIN_RECORD.{the main_file_chain_field};
  while not {NULL_INDEX, the empty}(CHAIN_RECORD_INDEX) loop
    {READ, the current}(CHAIN_FILE,
                        CHAIN_RECORD,
                        CHAIN_RECORD_INDEX);
    {CHAIN_RECORD, the output chain_record};
    CHAIN_RECORD_INDEX := CHAIN_RECORD.{the rest};
  end loop;
  CLEAN_UP;
exception
  when DEVICE_ERROR | END_ERROR | NAME_ERROR | STATUS_ERROR =>
    CLEAN_UP; PUT("Database Inconsistent");
  when others => CLEAN_UP; raise;
end CHAIN_ENUMERATION;
```

Figure 8.5 A cliché for enumerating a chain.

The most interesting aspect of the chain-enumeration cliché is its constraints. The first four of the six constraints are analogous to the constraints on the file-enumeration cliché. The first and second constraints suggest mnemonic identifiers for the variables associated with the main-file

and chain-file. The third and fourth constraints specify default values for
the external names of the two files.

The fifth and sixth constraints on chain-enumeration specify how to follow the chain. The function CHAIN_FIELD looks at the definitions of two
files and determines which field of the record in the first file contains an
index into the second file. The fifth constraint on chain-enumeration specifies how to get the index of the first record in the chain from the main file
record. The sixth constraint specifies how to step from one chain record to
the next.

Simple Reports in Ada

As a final example of an Ada cliché, consider the Ada version of simple-
report (Figure 8.6) in comparison with the Lisp version (Figure 7.3 on
page 90). Many of the differences between these clichés are merely syntactic.
However, there are several computational differences as well.

The textual input and output functions available in Ada are quite different from the ones in Lisp. In particular, there is nothing corresponding to
the Lisp function FORMAT. Instead, combinations of more primitive functions
(e.g., NEW_LINE, SET_COL, PUT, etc.) have to be used.

The Lisp expression (TIME:PRINT-CURRENT-TIME NIL) is replaced by the
equivalent Ada expression FORMAT_DATE(CLOCK). The function CLOCK, which
returns the current date and time, is part of the standard Ada package
CALENDAR. (In Ada, calls on zero-argument functions are identical in ap-
pearance to variable references.) The function FORMAT_DATE (defined in the
package FUNCTIONS) converts a date into a character string.

Ada does not contain a construct like WITH-OPEN-FILE. In Figure 8.6, the
same effect is obtained by explicitly opening and closing the file and using
exception handlers to make sure that the file will always be closed.

Another difference between the Lisp and Ada versions of simple-report
stems from the fact that Ada automatically keeps track of the line number
and the page number in an output file. This leads to significant simplifications in the Ada version. However, it also leads to a slight complication. To
trigger a page break after the title page is printed, the Ada version has to
print 60 blank lines to force the line counter to be incremented sufficiently.
(Note that, while the Lisp version of simple-report follows the standard
Lisp style of counting things starting with zero, Ada counts lines and pages
starting with one.)

A final difference between the two versions is that the Ada version takes
advantage of the strong typing enforced by Ada to add two powerful constraints. The function CORRESPONDING_PRINTING determines what should be
used to fill the print-item role based on the type of object that is being
enumerated. The function CORRESPONDING_HEADINGS determines what headings should be used based on how the print-item is filled. Given these
constraints, the print-item and the column-headings can be automatically

```
with CALENDAR, FUNCTIONS, TEXT_IO; use CALENDAR, FUNCTIONS, TEXT_IO;
plan SIMPLE_REPORT is
  primary roles ENUMERATOR, PRINT_ITEM, SUMMARY;
  described roles FILE_NAME, TITLE,
                  ENUMERATOR, COLUMN_HEADINGS,
                  PRINT_ITEM, SUMMARY;
  comment "prints a report of {the input data of the enumerator}";
  constraints
    DEFAULT({the file_name},
            "report.txt");
    DERIVED({the line_limit},
            66-SIZE_IN_LINES({the print_item})
              -SIZE_IN_LINES({the summary}));
    DEFAULT({the print_item},
            CORRESPONDING_PRINTING({the enumerator}));
    DEFAULT({the column_headings},
            CORRESPONDING_HEADINGS({the print_item}));
  end constraints;
  use INT_IO;
  CURRENT_DATE: constant STRING := FORMAT_DATE(CLOCK);
  DATA: {};
  REPORT: TEXT_IO.FILE_TYPE;
  TITLE: STRING(1..{});
  procedure CLEAN_UP is
  begin
    SET_OUTPUT(STANDARD_OUTPUT); CLOSE(REPORT);
  exception when STATUS_ERROR => return;
  end CLEAN_UP;
begin
  CREATE(REPORT, OUT_FILE, {the file_name});
  DATA := {the input data of the enumerator};
  SET_OUTPUT(REPORT);
  TITLE := {the title};
  NEW_LINE(4); SET_COL(20); PUT(CURRENT_DATE); NEW_LINE(2);
  SET_COL(13); PUT(TITLE); NEW_LINE(60);
  while not {the empty of the enumerator}(DATA) loop
    if LINE > {the line_limit} then
        NEW_PAGE; NEW_LINE; PUT("Page: "); PUT(INTEGER(PAGE-1), 3);
        SET_COL(13); PUT(TITLE);
        SET_COL(61); PUT(CURRENT_DATE); NEW_LINE(2);
        {the column_headings}({CURRENT_OUTPUT, modified});
    end if;
    {the print_item}({CURRENT_OUTPUT, modified},
                     {the current of the enumerator}(DATA));
    DATA := {the rest of the enumerator}(DATA);
  end loop;
  {the summary}({CURRENT_OUTPUT, modified});
  CLEAN_UP;
exception
  when DEVICE_ERROR | END_ERROR | NAME_ERROR | STATUS_ERROR =>
    CLEAN_UP; PUT("Database Inconsistent");
  when others => CLEAN_UP; raise;
end SIMPLE_REPORT;
```

Figure 8.6 A cliché for printing a simple-report.

filled as soon as the type of object being enumerated is known.

The functions CORRESPONDING_PRINTING and CORRESPONDING_HEADINGS operate in one of two modes. Typically, a number of clichés will have been defined for printing types of objects in reports and the corresponding headings. If appropriate clichés exist, the functions CORRESPONDING_PRINTING and CORRESPONDING_HEADINGS simply retrieve them from the library. However, if there are no such clichés, a simple program generator is used to construct appropriate code based on the definition of the type of object in question.

Their differences notwithstanding, the two versions of simple-report are actually most notable for their similarities. The two clichés have the same purpose and the same roles and perform basically the same computation. At a high enough level of abstraction, these similarities could be captured in an abstract simple-report cliché identical in Lisp and Ada. The two more specific clichés shown are specializations of that abstract cliché. For example, the abstract cliché would require only that some method be employed to keep track of line numbers and page numbers. The Lisp and Ada versions differ in the way this is achieved because Lisp and Ada differ in the support they provide.

Limits to the Power of Constraints

In KBEmacs, the power of a constraint follows directly from the power of the functions used in the constraint expression. Constraint expressions can utilize any of the standard functions and operators in the target language. In addition, the programmer is free to write additional functions (e.g., SIZE_IN_LINES). As a result, there is no theoretical limit to what a constraint can do.

However, as a practical matter, the power of constraints is limited by the difficulty of writing new functions to use in constraints. Each instance of {...} annotation in a constraint expression evaluates to a pointer into the current plan. Constraint functions such as SIZE_IN_LINES have to operate on these pointers. This allows for great flexibility but requires the constraint-function writer to be conversant with plans. In contrast, when defining the body of a cliché, the programmer need not understand anything other than the target language and role annotation.

The typical programmer is unlikely to write new functions to use in constraints, but rather will write expressions that only use predefined constraint functions. Thus, as a practical matter, the power of constraints is limited by the constraint functions provided by the designer of the basic cliché library.

Viewed from this perspective, the constraints in the example clichés in the previous discussion fall into two categories. Simple constraints such as the one deriving the line-limit role in simple-report are quite common. They depend only on standard functions and a few general-purpose constraint functions such as SIZE_IN_LINES. There is no reason why such con-

Models File

Key	Name	Maker
OS1	Opal Sorter	Perth Mining
GA2	Gas Analyzer	Benson Labs

Defects File

Key	Name	Model
OS-03	Power supply thermistor blown	OS1
GA-11	Control board cold solder joint	GA2
GA-32	Clogged gas injection port	GA2

Units File

Key	Model	Repair
OS1-271	OS1	3
GA2-342	GA2	4

Repairs File

Index	Date	Defect	Comment	Next
1	9/14/87	GA-32	Probably caused by humidity.	0
2	1/23/89	GA-11	Took two days to find.	1
3	2/25/89	OS-03	Sorter arm got stuck.	0
4	3/19/89	GA-32	Port diameter seems below specs.	2

Figure 8.7 The example database.

straints could not be included as part of special-purpose clichés defined by programmers.

Constraint functions such as CORRESPONDING_FILE_NAME, CHAIN_FIELD, and CORRESPONDING_PRINTING are at a level of significantly greater complexity. Such functions are typically defined in conjunction with a suite of clichés. A programmer might use these functions when defining a new cliché to add to the suite. However, the constraint functions are of no use outside of the suite.

8.2   Defining Data Structures

In the first part of the transcript in this chapter, the programmer constructs an Ada package MAINTENANCE_FILES, which defines the files in a database. The database contains information about repairs performed on instruments sold by an imaginary company that sells and maintains the instruments but does not build them.

As illustrated in Figure 8.7, the database is composed of four files: a file specifying the name and maker of each model of instrument the company sells, a file specifying the kinds of defects that can occur on each model, a main file describing each unit sold, and a chain file describing each repair performed on these units. In addition to illustrating the structure of the database, Figure 8.7 shows an example of the kind of data that might be in the database.

(In the interest of brevity, the database has been simplified to its barest essentials. A real database would contain more files and have many more fields in each record. However, these simplifications do not alter the basic nature of the example.)

Switching to Ada Mode

To shorten the transcript, the programmer is assumed to have already begun the implementation of the package MAINTENANCE_FILES by defining the files MODELS and DEFECTS. In Screen 8.1, the programmer picks up the implementation at that point. Before doing anything else, the programmer uses the knowledge-based command "Use language" to tell KBEmacs to use the language Ada (see Screen 8.1). The standard Symbolics Lisp Machine editor has been extended by adding an Ada mode. This mode enables several of the program-oriented Emacs commands, e.g., m-. (goto definition) and c-shift-C (compile definition), to operate properly on Ada procedures.

```
s-X Use language ADA. <end>
c-X c-F Find file <KBE.DEMO>MAINTENANCE_FILES.ADA
  cursor motion
```

```
with FUNCTIONS; use FUNCTIONS;
package MAINTENANCE_FILES is
  MODELS_NAME: constant STRING := "models.data";
  type MODEL_KEY_TYPE is STRING(1..3);
  type MODEL_TYPE is
    record
      NAME: STRING(1..16);
      MAKER: STRING(1..16);
    end record;
  package MODEL_IO is new KEYED_IO(MODEL_TYPE, MODEL_KEY_TYPE);
  MODELS: MODEL_IO.FILE_TYPE;
  DEFECTS_NAME: constant STRING := "defects.data";
  type DEFECT_KEY_TYPE is STRING(1..5);
  type DEFECT_TYPE is
    record
      NAME: STRING(1..32);
      MODEL: MODEL_KEY_TYPE;
    end record;
  package DEFECT_IO is new KEYED_IO(DEFECT_TYPE, DEFECT_KEY_TYPE);
  DEFECTS: DEFECT_IO.FILE_TYPE;
  []
end MAINTENANCE_FILES;
```

KBEmacs (ADA) <KBE.DEMO>MAINTENANCE_FILES.ADA

Screen 8.1 Switching to Ada mode.

Defining a File

In Screen 8.2, the programmer begins to define the file REPAIRS by inserting an instance of chain-file-definition. Note the way renaming has been applied to the various identifiers in the cliché. In Screen 8.3, the programmer moves to the data role and uses direct editing to specify the fields of a repair record.

Having finished the definition of the file REPAIRS, the programmer tells KBEmacs that, for the moment, the editing of the package MAINTENANCE_FILES is complete (see Screen 8.4). KBEmacs then proceeds to analyze the editing done by the programmer.

To understand the change that occurs on the first line of Screen 8.4, one must consider the interaction between naming scopes and packages in Ada. The names defined in a package are local to that package. To refer to one of these names in another package, you must ensure that the packages are

```
s-X Insert a chain_file_definition of "repairs.data". <end>
```

```
with FUNCTIONS; use FUNCTIONS;
package MAINTENANCE_FILES is
  MODELS_NAME: constant STRING := "models.data";
  type MODEL_KEY_TYPE is STRING(1..3);
  type MODEL_TYPE is
    record
      NAME: STRING(1..16);
      MAKER: STRING(1..16);
    end record;
  package MODEL_IO is new KEYED_IO(MODEL_TYPE, MODEL_KEY_TYPE);
  MODELS: MODEL_IO.FILE_TYPE;
  DEFECTS_NAME: constant STRING := "defects.data";
  type DEFECT_KEY_TYPE is STRING(1..5);
  type DEFECT_TYPE is
    record
      NAME: STRING(1..32);
      MODEL: MODEL_KEY_TYPE;
    end record;
  package DEFECT_IO is new KEYED_IO(DEFECT_TYPE, DEFECT_KEY_TYPE);
  DEFECTS: DEFECT_IO.FILE_TYPE;
  REPAIRS_NAME: constant STRING := "repairs.data";
  subtype REPAIR_INDEX_TYPE is INDEX_TYPE;
  type REPAIR_TYPE is
    record
      {the data};
      NEXT: REPAIR_INDEX_TYPE;
    end record;
  package REPAIR_IO is
    new CHAINED_IO(REPAIR_TYPE, REPAIR_INDEX_TYPE);
  REPAIRS: REPAIR_IO.FILE_TYPE;
end MAINTENANCE_FILES;
```

KBEmacs (ADA) <KBE.DEMO>MAINTENANCE_FILES.ADA

Screen 8.2 Inserting a file definition cliché.

known to each other and unambiguously refer to the name.

If the source package is not defined within the destination package, Ada must be told to compile the destination package **with** the source package. (The beginning of the first line of Screen 8.3 specifies that the package MAINTENANCE_FILES is to be compiled with the package FUNCTIONS.)

The basic way to refer to a name in another package is to use a compound reference of the form *package-name.object-name*. For example, the second to last line of Screen 8.3 refers to the data type FILE_TYPE defined in the package REPAIR_IO as REPAIR_IO.FILE_TYPE.

Alternatively, one can specify that the destination package should **use** the source package (see the end of the first line of Screen 8.3) and then refer to the object by its simple name, if this is not ambiguous. For example,

s-N *direct editing*

```
with FUNCTIONS; use FUNCTIONS;
package MAINTENANCE_FILES is
  MODELS_NAME: constant STRING := "models.data";
  type MODEL_KEY_TYPE is STRING(1..3);
  type MODEL_TYPE is
    record
      NAME: STRING(1..16);
      MAKER: STRING(1..16);
    end record;
  package MODEL_IO is new KEYED_IO(MODEL_TYPE, MODEL_KEY_TYPE);
  MODELS: MODEL_IO.FILE_TYPE;
  DEFECTS_NAME: constant STRING := "defects.data";
  type DEFECT_KEY_TYPE is STRING(1..5);
  type DEFECT_TYPE is
    record
      NAME: STRING(1..32);
      MODEL: MODEL_KEY_TYPE;
    end record;
  package DEFECT_IO is new KEYED_IO(DEFECT_TYPE, DEFECT_KEY_TYPE);
  DEFECTS: DEFECT_IO.FILE_TYPE;
  REPAIRS_NAME: constant STRING := "repairs.data";
  subtype REPAIR_INDEX_TYPE is INDEX_TYPE;
  type REPAIR_TYPE is
    record
      DATE: TIME;
      DEFECT: DEFECT_KEY_TYPE;
      COMMENT: STRING(1..32);▯
      NEXT: REPAIR_INDEX_TYPE;
    end record;
  package REPAIR_IO is
   new CHAINED_IO(REPAIR_TYPE, REPAIR_INDEX_TYPE);
  REPAIRS: REPAIR_IO.FILE_TYPE;
end MAINTENANCE_FILES;
```

KBEmacs (ADA) <KBE.DEMO>MAINTENANCE_FILES.ADA

Screen 8.3 Defining the fields of a record with direct editing.

the third to last line of Screen 8.3 refers to the generic package CHAINED_IO, which is defined in the package FUNCTIONS.

In Screen 8.3, the programmer failed to obey these rules. The DATE field of a repair record is defined as having the data type TIME; however, this identifier is not defined in any of the packages used by MAINTENANCE_FILES in Screen 8.2.

When KBEmacs analyzes the direct editing in Screen 8.3, it notices that an unknown data type TIME is being referred to. It searches the various packages it knows about and discovers that there is only one package (the standard package CALENDAR) that contains a definition of TIME. Given that this is the case, KBEmacs assumes that the programmer was trying to refer

```
s-<end> Finish editing the package MAINTENANCE_FILES. <end>
    The cliches PRINT_REPAIR_HEADINGS and PRINT_REPAIR defined.
```

```
with CALENDAR, FUNCTIONS; use CALENDAR, FUNCTIONS;
package MAINTENANCE_FILES is
  MODELS_NAME: constant STRING := "models.data";
  type MODEL_KEY_TYPE is STRING(1..3);
  type MODEL_TYPE is
    record
      NAME: STRING(1..16);
      MAKER: STRING(1..16);
    end record;
  package MODEL_IO is new KEYED_IO(MODEL_TYPE, MODEL_KEY_TYPE);
  MODELS: MODEL_IO.FILE_TYPE;
  DEFECTS_NAME: constant STRING := "defects.data";
  type DEFECT_KEY_TYPE is STRING(1..5);
  type DEFECT_TYPE is
    record
      NAME: STRING(1..32);
      MODEL: MODEL_KEY_TYPE;
    end record;
  package DEFECT_IO is new KEYED_IO(DEFECT_TYPE, DEFECT_KEY_TYPE);
  DEFECTS: DEFECT_IO.FILE_TYPE;
  REPAIRS_NAME: constant STRING := "repairs.data";
  subtype REPAIR_INDEX_TYPE is INDEX_TYPE;
  type REPAIR_TYPE is
    record
      DATE: TIME;
      DEFECT: DEFECT_KEY_TYPE;
      COMMENT: STRING(1..32);
      NEXT: REPAIR_INDEX_TYPE;
    end record;
  package REPAIR_IO is
    new CHAINED_IO(REPAIR_TYPE, REPAIR_INDEX_TYPE);
  REPAIRS: REPAIR_IO.FILE_TYPE;
end MAINTENANCE_FILES;
```

KBEmacs (ADA) <KBE.DEMO>MAINTENANCE_FILES.ADA

Screen 8.4 Analyzing direct editing.

to `CALENDAR.TIME` and fixes things up by adding the package `CALENDAR` to the
with and **use** clauses of the package `MAINTENANCE_FILES` as can be seen in
Screen 8.4.

In Screen 8.4, the only thing that remains to be done to finish the
definition of the package `MAINTENANCE_FILES` is to define the file `UNITS`. This
can be done using commands like the ones in the Screens 8.2 and 8.3, using
the cliché *keyed-file-definition* (which defines random-access files) instead
of chain-file-definition. However, in the interest of brevity, the definition of
the `UNITS` file is not shown here.

8.3   Defining a Cliché

This section illustrates how new clichés can be defined in KBEmacs. In the
transcript in Screens 8.5–8.7, the programmer modifies clichés whose initial
definitions have been automatically generated by KBEmacs. Clichés can
also be defined entirely from scratch.

As part of the basis for the example in this chapter, a special procedure
that automatically defines clichés for printing data records was added to
KBEmacs. This procedure monitors the programs being written. Whenever
it detects the definition of a new data file, it generates a pair of clichés
that are appropriate for printing the records in the file. The names of
these clichés are stored so that they can be retrieved by the functions

m-. Edit definition of PRINT_REPAIR_HEADINGS

```
with TEXT_IO;
use TEXT_IO;
plan PRINT_REPAIR_HEADINGS is
  comment "prints headings for printing repair records";
begin
  PUT(" Date      Defect                Comment");
  NEW_LINE(2);
end PRINT_REPAIR_HEADINGS;

with FUNCTIONS, TEXT_IO; use FUNCTIONS, TEXT_IO;
plan PRINT_REPAIR is
  primary roles REPAIR;
  described roles REPAIR;
  comment "prints the fields of {the repair}";
  REPAIR: REPAIR_TYPE;
begin
  REPAIR := {the input repair};
  PUT(FORMAT_DATE(REPAIR.DATE)); SET_COL(13); PUT(REPAIR.DEFECT);
  SET_COL(20); PUT(REPAIR.COMMENT); NEW_LINE;
end PRINT_REPAIR;
```

KBEmacs (ADA) <KBE.DEMO>CLICHE-LIBRARY.ADA

Screen 8.5 Automatically defined clichés.

CORRESPONDING_PRINTING and CORRESPONDING_HEADINGS (used as constraints in the simple-report cliché).

The action of the special cliché-defining procedure is reflected in the response of KBEmacs to the s-<end> command in Screen 8.4. In Screen 8.5, the programmer examines the two clichés defined by KBEmacs in Screen 8.4: *print-repair*, which prints a repair record and *print-repair-headings*, which prints the appropriate column headings.

These clichés were created by the same special-purpose program generator used by the functions CORRESPONDING_PRINTING and CORRESPONDING_HEAD-INGS and were added to the file containing the library of Ada clichés. Each field is printed in a standardized way based on its data type. For example, any field whose data type is CALENDAR.TIME is printed using the function FORMAT_DATE.

Actual cliché definitions are created (as opposed to simply generating the corresponding code at the moment the user desires to print a repair) to allow the programmer to modify the clichés. This would be desirable even if the program generator were a great deal better than the one used because opinions about the aesthetics of printing data objects differ widely between programers.

In Screen 8.6, the programmer modifies print-repair so that, in addition to printing the key of the defect repaired, it reads the corresponding defect record and prints the full name of the defect. Print-repair-headings is modified analogously.

direct editing

```
with TEXT_IO; use TEXT_IO;
plan PRINT_REPAIR_HEADINGS is
  comment "prints headings for printing repair records";
begin
  PUT("   Date     Defect    Description/Comment"); NEW_LINE(2);
end PRINT_REPAIR_HEADINGS;

with FUNCTIONS, TEXT_IO; use FUNCTIONS, TEXT_IO;
plan PRINT_REPAIR is
  primary roles REPAIR;
  described roles REPAIR;
  comment "prints the fields of {the repair}";
  REPAIR: REPAIR_TYPE;
begin
  REPAIR := {the input repair};
  PUT(FORMAT_DATE(REPAIR.DATE)); SET_COL(13); PUT(REPAIR.DEFECT);
  SET_COL(20); PUT({a read of DEFECTS and (REPAIR.DEFECT)}.NAME);
  NEW_LINE; SET_COL(22); PUT(REPAIR.COMMENT); NEW_LINE;
end PRINT_REPAIR;
```

KBEmacs (ADA) <KBE.DEMO>CLICHE-LIBRARY.ADA

Screen 8.6 Modifying cliché definitions.

When editing print-repair, the programmer uses an in-line reference to the cliché *read*. This cliché has two roles: the file to be read and the key of the desired record. Using this in-line reference, the read operation is specified as if it were a function call even though the Ada read operation is a procedure call. Beyond this, note in Screen 8.6 that .NAME is used after the cliché annotation to select the NAME field of the record read just as if the annotation were a variable reference. Together these two features enable the desired computation to be represented as a simple expression.

Having finished editing print-repair and print-repair-headings, the programmer tells KBEmacs that they are completed (see Screen 8.7). In ad-

---

s-<end> Finish editing the cliche PRINT_REPAIR. <end>
c-shift-C Compiling PRINT_REPAIR
cursor motion
s-<end> Finish editing the cliche PRINT_REPAIR_HEADINGS. <end>
c-shift-C Compiling PRINT_REPAIR_HEADINGS

```
with TEXT_IO;
use TEXT_IO;
plan PRINT_REPAIR_HEADINGS is
  comment "prints headings for printing repair records";
begin
  PUT("   Date     Defect   Description/Comment"); NEW_LINE(2);
end PRINT_REPAIR_HEADINGS;

with FUNCTIONS, MAINTENANCE_FILES, TEXT_IO;
use FUNCTIONS, MAINTENANCE_FILES, TEXT_IO;
plan PRINT_REPAIR is
  primary roles REPAIR;
  described roles REPAIR;
  comment "prints the fields of {the repair}";
  use DEFECT_IO;
  DEFECT: DEFECT_TYPE;
  REPAIR: REPAIR_TYPE;
begin
  OPEN(DEFECTS, IN_FILE, DEFECTS_NAME);
  REPAIR := {the input repair};
  READ(DEFECTS, DEFECT, REPAIR.DEFECT);
  PUT(FORMAT_DATE(REPAIR.DATE)); SET_COL(13); PUT(REPAIR.DEFECT);
  SET_COL(20); PUT(DEFECT.NAME); NEW_LINE;
  SET_COL(22); PUT(REPAIR.COMMENT); NEW_LINE;
  CLOSE(DEFECTS);
exception
  when DEVICE_ERROR | END_ERROR | NAME_ERROR | STATUS_ERROR =>
    CLOSE(DEFECTS); PUT("Database Inconsistent");
  when others => CLOSE(DEFECTS); raise;
end PRINT_REPAIR;
```

KBEmacs (ADA) <KBE.DEMO>CLICHE-LIBRARY.ADA

Screen 8.7 Analyzing direct editing.

dition, the programmer compiles the clichés. This causes the clichés to be entered into the cliché library so that they are available for later use.

When it analyzes the editing done by the programmer in Screen 8.6, KBEmacs replaces the embedded cliché instance phrase specifying a read with the corresponding Ada code. As can be seen in Screen 8.7, this leads to extensive changes in print-repair. The package MAINTENANCE_FILES is added to the with and use clauses, in order to to render the reference to the identifier DEFECTS meaningful. A use clause for the package DEFECT_IO is added to the declarations to make the appropriate input and output procedures for the file DEFECTS available. A variable DEFECT is added to hold the record read along with code that opens and closes the file DEFECTS and code that handles any error conditions that might arise.

8.4 Propagation of Design Decisions

In the following part of the Ada transcript, the programmer constructs a procedure named UNIT_REPAIR_REPORT, which prints a report of the repairs performed on a given unit. In this program, the user is queried to obtain the key UNIT_KEY of a unit record from which to start. The title ("Repairs on Unit " & UNIT_KEY) is printed. The chain of repairs associated with the unit record are enumerated and a description of each one is printed. There is no summary.

Like REPORT-TIMINGS, UNIT_REPAIR_REPORT is constructed in a top-down fashion, starting with the cliché simple-report. However, the construction of UNIT_REPAIR_REPORT illustrates a number of features of KBEmacs not shown in the earlier transcript. In particular, a large portion of the procedure is implemented due to the action of constraints.

In Screen 8.8, the programmer begins the construction of the procedure UNIT_REPAIR_REPORT by creating a file to hold the procedure and creating an instance of simple-report. This is done in one step by using an extended form of the Define command.

The central design decision in any report program is deciding what values are to be reported. When using the simple-report cliché, this decision is specified by selecting an appropriate enumerator. In Screen 8.9, the programmer specifies that the enumerator should be a chain-enumeration, which enumerates a chain of records in the file REPAIRS pointed to from a record in the file UNITS. Several parts of the code produced are specified by the constraints in the cliché chain-enumeration (see Figure 8.5). In particular, the REPAIR field is used to get the initial index into the chain file, and the NEXT field is used to get the index of each successive repair record. Appropiate renaming of variables is also applied. (In Screen 8.9, KBEmacs positions the cursor on the read of the file UNITS on the theory that changes to the body of a procedure are more interesting than changes to the declarations or to the code that opens files.)

Once the enumerator has been specified, the constraints in the cliché simple-report fill out most of the rest of the procedure UNIT_REPAIR_REPORT. In particular, the print-repair cliché is used to fill the print-item role and the print-repair-headings cliché is used to fill the column-headings role.

```
c-X c-F Find file <KBE.DEMO>UNIT_REPAIR_REPORT.ADA
(New File)
s-X Define a simple_report procedure UNIT_REPAIR_REPORT. <end>
```

```
with CALENDAR, FUNCTIONS, TEXT_IO;
use CALENDAR, FUNCTIONS, TEXT_IO;
procedure UNIT_REPAIR_REPORT is
  use INT_IO;
  CURRENT_DATE: constant STRING := FORMAT_DATE(CLOCK);
  DATA: {};
  REPORT: TEXT_IO.FILE_TYPE;
  TITLE: STRING(1..{});
  procedure CLEAN_UP is
    begin
      SET_OUTPUT(STANDARD_OUTPUT); CLOSE(REPORT);
    exception when STATUS_ERROR => return;
    end CLEAN_UP;
begin
  CREATE(REPORT, OUT_FILE, "report.txt");
  TITLE := {the title};
  SET_OUTPUT(REPORT);
  NEW_LINE(4); SET_COL(20); PUT(CURRENT_DATE); NEW_LINE(2);
  SET_COL(13); PUT(TITLE); NEW_LINE(60);
  DATA := {the input data of the enumerator};
  while not {the empty of the enumerator}(DATA) loop
    if LINE > 64 then
      NEW_PAGE; NEW_LINE; PUT("Page: "); PUT(INTEGER(PAGE-1), 3);
      SET_COL(13); PUT(TITLE);
      SET_COL(61); PUT(CURRENT_DATE); NEW_LINE(2);
      {the column_headings}({CURRENT_OUTPUT, modified});
    end if;
    {the print_item}({CURRENT_OUTPUT, modified},
                     {the current of the enumerator}(DATA));
    DATA := {the rest of the enumerator}(DATA);
  end loop;
  {the summary}({CURRENT_OUTPUT, modified});
  CLEAN_UP;
exception
  when DEVICE_ERROR | END_ERROR | NAME_ERROR | STATUS_ERROR =>
    CLEAN_UP; PUT("Database Inconsistent");
  when others => CLEAN_UP; raise;
end UNIT_REPAIR_REPORT;
```

KBEmacs (ADA) <KBE.DEMO>UNIT_REPAIR_REPORT.ADA

Screen 8.8 Defining a program using a cliché.

s-X Fill the enumerator with a chain_enumeration of UNITS and
    REPAIRS. <end>

```
with CALENDAR, FUNCTIONS, MAINTENANCE_FILES, TEXT_IO;
use CALENDAR, FUNCTIONS, MAINTENANCE_FILES, TEXT_IO;
procedure UNIT_REPAIR_REPORT is
  use DEFECT_IO, REPAIR_IO, UNIT_IO, INT_IO;
  CURRENT_DATE: constant STRING := FORMAT_DATE(CLOCK);
  DEFECT: DEFECT_TYPE;
  REPAIR: REPAIR_TYPE;
  REPAIR_INDEX: REPAIR_INDEX_TYPE;
  REPORT: TEXT_IO.FILE_TYPE;
  TITLE: STRING(1..{});
  UNIT: UNIT_TYPE;
  procedure CLEAN_UP is
    begin
      SET_OUTPUT(STANDARD_OUTPUT); CLOSE(DEFECTS);
      CLOSE(REPAIRS); CLOSE(UNITS); CLOSE(REPORT);
    exception when STATUS_ERROR => return;
    end CLEAN_UP;
begin
  OPEN(DEFECTS, IN_FILE, DEFECTS_NAME);
  OPEN(REPAIRS, IN_FILE, REPAIRS_NAME);
  OPEN(UNITS, IN_FILE, UNITS_NAME);
  CREATE(REPORT, OUT_FILE, "report.txt");
  TITLE := {the title};
  SET_OUTPUT(REPORT);
  NEW_LINE(4); SET_COL(20); PUT(CURRENT_DATE); NEW_LINE(2);
  SET_COL(13); PUT(TITLE); NEW_LINE(60);
  READ(UNITS, UNIT, {the main_file_key});
  REPAIR_INDEX := UNIT.REPAIR;
  while not NULL_INDEX(REPAIR_INDEX) loop
    READ(REPAIRS, REPAIR, REPAIR_INDEX);
    if LINE > 63 then
        NEW_PAGE; NEW_LINE; PUT("Page: "); PUT(INTEGER(PAGE-1), 3);
        SET_COL(13); PUT(TITLE);
        SET_COL(61); PUT(CURRENT_DATE); NEW_LINE(2);
        PUT("  Date      Defect    Description/Comment"); NEW_LINE(2);
    end if;
    READ(DEFECTS, DEFECT, REPAIR.DEFECT);
    PUT(FORMAT_DATE(REPAIR.DATE)); SET_COL(13); PUT(REPAIR.DEFECT);
    SET_COL(20); PUT(DEFECT.NAME); NEW_LINE;
    SET_COL(22); PUT(REPAIR.COMMENT); NEW_LINE;
    REPAIR_INDEX := REPAIR.NEXT;
  end loop;
  {the summary}({CURRENT_OUTPUT, modified});
  CLEAN_UP;
exception
  when DEVICE_ERROR | END_ERROR | NAME_ERROR | STATUS_ERROR =>
    CLEAN_UP; PUT("Database Inconsistent");
  when others => CLEAN_UP; raise;
end UNIT_REPAIR_REPORT;
```

KBEmacs (ADA) <KBE.DEMO>UNIT_REPAIR_REPORT.ADA

Screen 8.9 The propagation of design decisions.

s-F Fill the main_file_key with a query_user_for_key of UNITS. <end>

```
with CALENDAR, FUNCTIONS, MAINTENANCE_FILES, TEXT_IO;
use CALENDAR, FUNCTIONS, MAINTENANCE_FILES, TEXT_IO;
procedure UNIT_REPAIR_REPORT is
  use DEFECT_IO, REPAIR_IO, UNIT_IO, INT_IO;
  CURRENT_DATE: constant STRING := FORMAT_DATE(CLOCK);
  DEFECT: DEFECT_TYPE;
  REPAIR: REPAIR_TYPE;
  REPAIR_INDEX: REPAIR_INDEX_TYPE;
  REPORT: TEXT_IO.FILE_TYPE;
  TITLE: STRING(1..{});
  UNIT: UNIT_TYPE;
  UNIT_KEY: UNIT_KEY_TYPE;
  procedure CLEAN_UP is
    begin
      SET_OUTPUT(STANDARD_OUTPUT); CLOSE(DEFECTS);
      CLOSE(REPAIRS); CLOSE(UNITS); CLOSE(REPORT);
    exception when STATUS_ERROR => return;
    end CLEAN_UP;
begin
  OPEN(DEFECTS, IN_FILE, DEFECTS_NAME);
  OPEN(REPAIRS, IN_FILE, REPAIRS_NAME);
  OPEN(UNITS, IN_FILE, UNITS_NAME);
  CREATE(REPORT, OUT_FILE, "report.txt");
  TITLE := {the title};
  SET_OUTPUT(REPORT);
  NEW_LINE(4); SET_COL(20); PUT(CURRENT_DATE); NEW_LINE(2);
  SET_COL(13); PUT(TITLE); NEW_LINE(60);
  loop
    begin
      NEW_LINE; PUT("Enter UNIT Key: "); GET(UNIT_KEY);
      READ(UNITS, UNIT, UNIT_KEY);
      exit;
    exception
      when END_ERROR => PUT("Invalid UNIT Key"); NEW_LINE;
    end;
  end loop;
  READ(UNITS, UNIT, UNIT_KEY);
  REPAIR_INDEX := UNIT.REPAIR;
  while not NULL_INDEX(REPAIR_INDEX) loop
    READ(REPAIRS, REPAIR, REPAIR_INDEX);
    if LINE > 63 then
      NEW_PAGE; NEW_LINE; PUT("Page: "); PUT(INTEGER(PAGE-1), 3);
      SET_COL(13); PUT(TITLE);
      SET_COL(61); PUT(CURRENT_DATE); NEW_LINE(2);
      PUT("  Date    Defect   Description/Comment"); NEW_LINE(2);
    end if;
    READ(DEFECTS, DEFECT, REPAIR.DEFECT);
    PUT(FORMAT_DATE(REPAIR.DATE)); SET_COL(13); PUT(REPAIR.DEFECT);
    SET_COL(20); PUT(DEFECT.NAME); NEW_LINE;              ⇓ more below ⇓
```

KBEmacs (ADA) <KBE.DEMO>UNIT_REPAIR_REPORT.ADA

Screen 8.10 Filling a role with a cliché.

```
with TEXT_IO; use TEXT_IO;
plan QUERY_USER_FOR_KEY is
  primary roles FILE;
  described roles FILE;
  comment "queries the user for a key to a record in {the file}";
  constraints
    RENAME("DATA_RECORD", SINGULAR_FORM({the file}));
    DEFAULT({the file_name}, CORRESPONDING_FILE_NAME({the file}));
  end constraints;
  DATA_RECORD: {};
  DATA_RECORD_KEY: {};
  FILE: {};
begin
  FILE := {the file};
  OPEN(FILE, IN_FILE, {the file_name});
  loop
    begin
      NEW_LINE; PUT("Enter DATA_RECORD Key: ");
      GET(DATA_RECORD_KEY);
      READ(FILE, DATA_RECORD, DATA_RECORD_KEY);
      exit;
    exception
      when END_ERROR => PUT("Invalid DATA_RECORD Key"); NEW_LINE;
    end;
  end loop;
  CLOSE(FILE);
  return DATA_RECORD_KEY;
exception
  when DEVICE_ERROR | END_ERROR | NAME_ERROR | STATUS_ERROR =>
    CLOSE(FILE); PUT("Database Inconsistent");
  when others => CLOSE(FILE); raise;
end QUERY_USER_FOR_KEY;
```

Figure 8.8 A cliché for querying the user.

The use of these three clichés leads to the introduction of a number of
new declarations. In addition, the line-limit is changed from **64** to **63**, since
print-repair prints two lines of output, whereas the default assumption used
by SIZE_IN_LINES in Screen 8.8 was that it would print one line of output.

The Query-User-for-Key Cliché

In Screen 8.9, the only roles that are left unfilled are the title, the main-file-
key, and the summary. In Screen 8.10, the programmer specifies that the
user of the procedure UNIT_REPAIR_REPORT should be queried to determine
what main file key to use. This is done with the cliché *query-user-for-key*
(Figure 8.8).

Besides getting a key from the user, query-user-for-key checks the key
to make sure it is valid. To check the key, the cliché attempts to read the

corresponding record from the file. If the read fails, the user is asked for a different key.

Both the code in Screen 8.9 and the cliché query-user-for-key specify that the file UNITS should be opened and closed. If nothing more were said this would cause the file UNITS to be opened twice and closed twice in Screen 8.10. To prevent this from happening, KBEmacs determines which files are required to be open and makes sure that each file is opened only once and closed only once. Special provision is made for the opening and closing of files because this is an important efficiency issue in file-oriented input and output.

Sharing Computations

The code in Screen 8.10 is inefficient because it reads the same record in the file UNITS twice. The record is read for two different reasons by two different clichés. Query-user-for-key reads the record to determine whether the key is valid, and chain-enumeration reads the record to obtain the index of the first repair record.

The existence of this problem illustrates that, while KBEmacs is capable of automatically sharing multiple opens and closes on a file, it is not capable of automatically sharing redundant code in general. However, KBEmacs provides a command Share that can assist a programmer in sharing code.

From the point of view of KBEmacs, the most difficult thing about sharing is guessing where sharing might be useful. Checking that sharing is possible in a given situation and modifying the code to effect the sharing are both relatively easy.

From the point of view of a programmer, the situation is reversed. The most difficult thing is verifying that two computations are in fact identical and can therefore really be shared.

This divergence in abilities between the programmer and KBEmacs provides an opportunity for a useful division of labor. In Screen 8.11, the programmer asks KBEmacs to change the procedure so that the two calls on READ for the file UNITS are shared. KBEmacs checks that the two calls are in fact reading the same record and that they can be shared. It then modifies the procedure to achieve the sharing.

The sharing shown in Screen 8.11 is a simple example. There are two ways things can be more complex. First, if side effects are involved, it can be much harder to determine whether the two computations to be shared can indeed be shared. KBEmacs is able to deal with many kinds of side effects by representing their net effect in terms of data flow in the plan.

Second, sharing two computations can require more extensive changes in the program text. In particular, a variable usually has to be introduced so that one value can be used in two places. Here a single line merely

s-X Share the first READ and the second READ. <end>
direct editing

```
with CALENDAR, FUNCTIONS, MAINTENANCE_FILES, TEXT_IO;
use CALENDAR, FUNCTIONS, MAINTENANCE_FILES, TEXT_IO;
procedure UNIT_REPAIR_REPORT is
  use DEFECT_IO, REPAIR_IO, UNIT_IO, INT_IO;
  CURRENT_DATE: constant STRING := FORMAT_DATE(CLOCK);
  DEFECT: DEFECT_TYPE;
  REPAIR: REPAIR_TYPE;
  REPAIR_INDEX: REPAIR_INDEX_TYPE;
  REPORT: TEXT_IO.FILE_TYPE;
  TITLE: STRING(1..{});
  UNIT: UNIT_TYPE;
  UNIT_KEY: UNIT_KEY_TYPE;
  procedure CLEAN_UP is
    begin
      SET_OUTPUT(STANDARD_OUTPUT); CLOSE(DEFECTS);
      CLOSE(REPAIRS); CLOSE(UNITS); CLOSE(REPORT);
    exception when STATUS_ERROR => return;
    end CLEAN_UP;
begin
  OPEN(DEFECTS, IN_FILE, DEFECTS_NAME);
  OPEN(REPAIRS, IN_FILE, REPAIRS_NAME);
  OPEN(UNITS, IN_FILE, UNITS_NAME);
  CREATE(REPORT, OUT_FILE, "report.txt");
  TITLE := "Repairs on Unit " & UNIT_KEY;
  SET_OUTPUT(REPORT);
  NEW_LINE(4); SET_COL(20); PUT(CURRENT_DATE); NEW_LINE(2);
  SET_COL(13); PUT(TITLE); NEW_LINE(60);
  loop
    begin
      NEW_LINE; PUT("Enter UNIT Key: "); GET(UNIT_KEY);
      READ(UNITS, UNIT, UNIT_KEY);
      exit;
    exception
      when END_ERROR => PUT("Invalid UNIT Key"); NEW_LINE;
    end;
  end loop;
  REPAIR_INDEX := UNIT.REPAIR;
  while not NULL_INDEX(REPAIR_INDEX) loop
    READ(REPAIRS, REPAIR, REPAIR_INDEX);
    if LINE > 63 then
      NEW_PAGE; NEW_LINE; PUT("Page: "); PUT(INTEGER(PAGE-1), 3);
      SET_COL(13); PUT(TITLE);
      SET_COL(61); PUT(CURRENT_DATE); NEW_LINE(2);
      PUT("  Date     Defect   Description/Comment"); NEW_LINE(2);
    end if;
    READ(DEFECTS, DEFECT, REPAIR.DEFECT);
    PUT(FORMAT_DATE(REPAIR.DATE)); SET_COL(13); PUT(REPAIR.DEFECT);
    SET_COL(20); PUT(DEFECT.NAME); NEW_LINE;
    SET_COL(22); PUT(REPAIR.COMMENT); NEW_LINE;          ⇓ more below ⇓
```

KBEmacs (ADA) <KBE.DEMO>UNIT_REPAIR_REPORT.ADA

Screen 8.11 Sharing computations.

has to be removed because the same variable was already being used in conjunction with the two calls on READ. (KBEmacs tries to reuse variable names in logically related contexts to reduce the number of variables in a program.)

Using Common Sense

Once the sharing has been completed, the programmer uses direct editing in Screen 8.11, to fill the title role. In Screen 8.12, the programmer completes UNIT_REPAIR_REPORT by removing the summary role. This is done with the abbreviated command s-R, which offers to remove the first unfilled role following the current position of the cursor. The line-limit is changed from 63 to 64 since it is now known that zero lines are required for the summary. (Because the program is too large to fit on a single page, the position where the summary line used to be is not visible in Screen 8.11. This position was last visible in Screen 8.9.)

Before doing the remove requested by the programmer in Screen 8.12, KBEmacs analyzes the direct editing in Screen 8.11. This leads to two interesting changes in the program.

The code in Screen 8.11 is malformed because the expression used to fill the title role refers to the variable UNIT_KEY before it has been given a value. This problem arose because in Screen 8.10, the title role happens to precede the GET of the UNIT_KEY.

However, while the title role is first in Screen 8.10, there is no reason why this has to be so. The two computations are not ordered by control flow or data flow. KBEmacs tries to forestall problems in situations like this by not taking the exact order of program statements too literally. When the programmer writes an expression, KBEmacs interprets each variable reference as a request to reference the associated value. If a variable does not have a value at the exact place where the expression was placed, KBEmacs rearranges the procedure (within the limits of data flow and control flow) to make an appropriate value available. In Screen 8.12, the GET of the UNIT_KEY is moved before the title.

Another change in Screen 8.12 is that the length of the variable TITLE is now declared. This is automatically generated by KBEmacs based on the expression specified by the programmer. (The length of a UNIT_KEY is determined by looking at the definition of the file UNITS in the package MAINTENANCE_FILES.)

The fact that KBEmacs can determine the appropriate declaration for the variable TITLE shields the programmer from an irritating detail of Ada. Since there is no varying-length string data type in standard Ada, the declaration of a string variable (e.g., TITLE) must always include the exact length, unless the string is a constant (cf., CURRENT_DATE).

s-R Remove the summary. <end>
s-<end> Finish editing the procedure UNIT_REPAIR_REPORT. <end>
c-shift-C Compiling UNIT_REPAIR_REPORT

```
with CALENDAR, FUNCTIONS, MAINTENANCE_FILES, TEXT_IO;
use CALENDAR, FUNCTIONS, MAINTENANCE_FILES, TEXT_IO;
procedure UNIT_REPAIR_REPORT is
  use DEFECT_IO, REPAIR_IO, UNIT_IO, INT_IO;
  CURRENT_DATE: constant STRING := FORMAT_DATE(CLOCK);
  DEFECT: DEFECT_TYPE;
  REPAIR: REPAIR_TYPE;
  REPAIR_INDEX: REPAIR_INDEX_TYPE;
  REPORT: TEXT_IO.FILE_TYPE;
  TITLE: STRING(1..33);
  UNIT: UNIT_TYPE;
  UNIT_KEY: UNIT_KEY_TYPE;
  procedure CLEAN_UP is
    begin
      SET_OUTPUT(STANDARD_OUTPUT); CLOSE(DEFECTS);
      CLOSE(REPAIRS); CLOSE(UNITS); CLOSE(REPORT);
    exception when STATUS_ERROR => return;
    end CLEAN_UP;
begin
  OPEN(DEFECTS, IN_FILE, DEFECTS_NAME);
  OPEN(REPAIRS, IN_FILE, REPAIRS_NAME);
  OPEN(UNITS, IN_FILE, UNITS_NAME);
  CREATE(REPORT, OUT_FILE, "report.txt");
  loop
    begin
      NEW_LINE; PUT("Enter UNIT Key: "); GET(UNIT_KEY);
      READ(UNITS, UNIT, UNIT_KEY);
      exit;
    exception
      when END_ERROR => PUT("Invalid UNIT Key"); NEW_LINE;
    end;
  end loop;
  TITLE := "Repairs on Unit " & UNIT_KEY;
  SET_OUTPUT(REPORT);
  NEW_LINE(4); SET_COL(20); PUT(CURRENT_DATE); NEW_LINE(2);
  SET_COL(13); PUT(TITLE); NEW_LINE(60);
  REPAIR_INDEX := UNIT.REPAIR;
  while not NULL_INDEX(REPAIR_INDEX) loop
    READ(REPAIRS, REPAIR, REPAIR_INDEX);
    if LINE > 64 then
      NEW_PAGE; NEW_LINE; PUT("Page: "); PUT(INTEGER(PAGE-1), 3);
      SET_COL(13); PUT(TITLE);
      SET_COL(61); PUT(CURRENT_DATE); NEW_LINE(2);
      PUT("   Date      Defect   Description/Comment"); NEW_LINE(2);
    end if;
    READ(DEFECTS, DEFECT, REPAIR.DEFECT);
    PUT(FORMAT_DATE(REPAIR.DATE)); SET_COL(13);          ⇓ more below ⇓
```

KBEmacs (ADA) <KBE.DEMO>UNIT_REPAIR_REPORT.ADA

Screen 8.12 Using common sense.

```
Define a simple_report procedure UNIT_REPAIR_REPORT.
Fill the enumerator with a chain_enumeration of UNITS and REPAIRS.
Fill the main_file_key with a query_user_for_key of UNITS.
Share the first READ and the second READ.
Fill the title with ("Repairs on Unit " & UNIT_KEY).
Remove the summary.
```

Figure 8.9 Command summary.

Evaluation of the Commands Used

The set of knowledge-based commands used to implement the procedure
UNIT_REPAIR_REPORT is summarized in Figure 8.9. These 6 commands suffice
to construct a 57-line procedure.

It is interesting to compare the commands in Figure 8.9 with the commands used to create the Lisp function REPORT-TIMINGS (Figure 7.5 on
page 93). The commands for UNIT_REPAIR_REPORT are simpler due to the
action of the constraints in the Ada version of simple-report and the existence of the clichés print-repair and print-repair-headings.

The language independence of KBEmacs is illustrated by the fact that
the two sets of commands are otherwise very similar. If it were not for the
inclusion of a few literal pieces of program code, there would be no way to
know that the programs produced by the two sets of commands were coded
in two different programming languages.

```
s-; Comment the procedure UNIT_REPAIR_REPORT. <end>

-- The procedure UNIT_REPAIR_REPORT is a simple_report:
--    The file_name is "report.txt".
--    The title is ("Repairs on Unit " & UNIT_KEY).
--    The enumerator is a chain_enumeration.
--       It enumerates the records in REPAIRS starting from the
--       the header record indexed by UNIT_KEY.
--    The column_headings are a print_repair_headings.
--       It prints headings for printing repair records.
--    The print_item is a print_repair.
--       It prints the fields of REPAIR.
--    There is no summary.
□
with CALENDAR, FUNCTIONS, MAINTENANCE_FILES, TEXT_IO;
use CALENDAR, FUNCTIONS, MAINTENANCE_FILES, TEXT_IO;
procedure UNIT_REPAIR_REPORT is
  use DEFECT_IO, REPAIR_IO, UNIT_IO, INT_IO;        ⇓ more below ⇓
```

KBEmacs (ADA) <KBE.DEMO>UNIT_REPAIR_REPORT.ADA

Screen 8.13 An automatically generated comment.

Documentation

In Screen 8.13, the programmer asks KBEmacs to create a comment for the procedure UNIT_REPAIR_REPORT. This comment is created in exactly the same way as the comment for a Lisp program. The only difference is that the Ada comment delimiter is used and literal pieces of code in the comment are rendered in Ada.

Testing

As an adjunct to KBEmacs, a minimal interpreter for a subset of Ada has been implemented so that Ada procedures can be tested. In Screen 8.14, the programmer tests UNIT_REPAIR_REPORT. The programmer first uses a procedure CREATE_TEST_RECORDS to create a test database containing the records shown in Figure 8.7 and then runs the procedure UNIT_REPAIR_REPORT. In addition to creating a report, the programmer tests what happens when the user inputs an invalid key. Finally, the programmer uses the procedure DISPLAY_REPORT to display the report produced.

```
<select> A
```

```
CREATE_TEST_RECORDS;
UNIT_REPAIR_REPORT;
Enter Unit Key: GA2-341
Invalid Unit Key

Enter Unit Key: GA2-342

DISPLAY_REPORT;
<4 blank lines>
                        5/27/1989


           Repairs on Unit GA2-342
<59 blank lines>
<page>
Page:   1    Repairs on Unit GA2-342                    5/27/1989

   Date     Defect   Description/Comment

 3/19/1989  GA-32   Clogged gas injection port
                      Port Diameter seems below specs.
 1/23/1989  GA-11   Control board cold solder joint
                      Took two days to find.
 9/14/1987  GA-32   Clogged gas injection port
                      Probably caused by humidity.
□
```

```
Ada Listener
```

Screen 8.14 Testing.

Chapter 9

Architecture of KBEmacs

Figure 9.1 shows the architecture of KBEmacs. Discussion of the architecture begins with a description of the general facilities in KBEmacs supporting plans and clichés. This is followed by a description of each of the four modules in Figure 9.1, paying particular attention to their high-level design and how they could be improved. The last section of this chapter describes an experiment indicating that KBEmacs could be sped up by an order of magnitude.

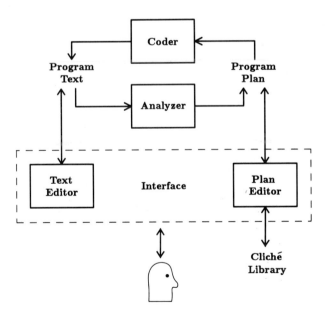

Figure 9.1 Architecture of KBEmacs.

147

empty unnamed role	`{}`
empty named role	`{input file-key}`
empty compound role	`{input data of the enumerator}`
empty role with arguments	`({operation} A (CAR L))`
filled role	`{(LIST A (CAR L)), operation}`
alternate syntax for filled role	`({LIST, operation} A (CAR L))`
modified argument	`{REPORT, modified}`
embedded cliché instance phrase	`{a squaring of X}`

```
(DEFINE-PLAN EQUALITY-WITHIN-EPSILON
   (PRIMARY-ROLES (X Y)
   DESCRIBED-ROLES (X Y EPSILON)
   COMMENT "determines whether {the x} and {the y}
            differ by less than {the epsilon}"
   CONSTRAINTS ((DEFAULT {the epsilon} 0.00001)))
  (< (ABS (- {the input x} {the input y})) {the epsilon}))
```

Figure 9.2 Syntax of machine-understandable annotation in Lisp and an example
of a Lisp cliché definition.

9.1   Clichés

In KBEmacs, the definition of clichés is supported by two mechanisms. First,
a textual syntax is provided for representing roles. Second, special forms
(in Lisp and Ada) are provided for defining the plan for a cliché. Since the
details of these mechanisms are presented at the beginnings of Chapters 7
and 8, they are merely summarized here.

Machine-Understandable Annotation

The various kinds of machine-understandable Lisp and Ada annotation supported by KBEmacs are illustrated in the top halves of Figures 9.2 and 9.3.
The annotation is the same in both languages except that, when the annotation is in the form of a function call, it uses the syntax appropriate
for the language. Annotation can appear anywhere a syntactic unit of the
language can appear—in place of a function call, statement, data value,
record field name, type, etc.

Annotation describing a role is supported by the analyzer module (see
Section 9.3), which converts it into an appropriate plan box. Annotation
specifying the arguments of roles and whether or not an argument is modified is also supported by the analyzer. This information is needed so that
KBEmacs can correctly analyze the data flow in the definition of a plan
without knowing what will eventually fill the roles. Annotation specifying
an embedded cliché instance phrase is converted into equivalent program
code by the plan editor module (see Section 9.5).

an empty unnamed role	`{}`
an empty named role	`{input file_key}`
an empty role with arguments	`{operation}(A, CAR(L))`
empty compound role	`{input data of the enumerator}`
a filled role	`{LIST(A, CAR(L)), operation}`
alternate syntax for a filled role	`{LIST, operation}(A, CAR(L))`
modified argument	`{REPORT, modified}`
embedded cliché instance phrase	`{a squaring of X}`

```
plan EQUALITY_WITHIN_EPSILON is
   primary roles X, Y;
   described roles X, Y, EPSILON;
   comment "determines whether {the x} and {the y}
           differ by less than {the epsilon}";
   constraints
      DEFAULT({the epsilon}, 0.00001);
   end constraints;
begin
   return abs({the input x} - {the input y}) < {the epsilon};
end EQUALITY_WITHIN_EPSILON;
```

Figure 9.3 Syntax of machine-understandable annotation in Ada and an example of an Ada cliché definition.

Defining Plans For Clichés

The bottom halves of Figures 9.2 and 9.3 show how the plan for a cliché can be defined using Lisp and Ada. In each case, the form is analogous to the way a subroutine is defined. In Lisp, the defining form is implemented as a macro. In Ada, the syntax of the language has to be extended, adding several keywords. In addition, when using Ada, KBEmacs renders multiword names using underscores rather than hyphens.

In both Lisp and Ada, the main body of the plan definition is ordinary program text (containing role annotation), which specifies a computation. This text is converted into a plan by the analyzer module. Further information about the cliché is provided by the declarations shown in Figure 9.4. The way the PRIMARY-ROLES, COMMENT and DESCRIBED-ROLES declarations are used is discussed in Section 9.5.

PRIMARY-ROLES	roles fillable in an instance phrase
COMMENT	template for short comment
DESCRIBED-ROLES	roles to describe in a long comment
CONSTRAINTS	constraints on the plan

Figure 9.4 Plan definition declarations.

DEFAULT   constraints specifying default values
DERIVED   continuously enforced constraints
RENAME   textual renaming constraints

Figure 9.5 Constraint types.

Constraints

The various kinds of constraints (see Figure 9.5) are supported by converting them into procedures that ensure that the constraints are satisfied. For example, the constraint

```
(DERIVED {the limit} (- 65 (SIZE-IN-LINES {the summary})))
```

is converted into a procedure ensuring that the line-limit role is always filled with a number equal to 65 minus the number of lines printed by the summary role. The key step of the conversion is replacing all instances of role annotation with function calls that return pointers to the appropriate role boxes in the plan under consideration. The functions used in constraints directly manipulate these pointers. For instance, the function SIZE-IN-LINES determines how many lines are printed by the subplan filling a box in a plan. The function DERIVED fills the box pointed to by its first argument with the value of its second.

When a plan representing an instance of a cliché is initially created, all of the constraints on the cliché are applied to it. Subsequently, the DERIVED constraints are reapplied every time the contents of a role changes. (While it is logical that DEFAULT constraints are run only once, it is a defect of KBEmacs that RENAME constraints are not run as often as DERIVED ones. This could and should be fixed.)

Language Independence

Comparison of the way plans for clichés are defined in Lisp and Ada shows the language independence of the ideas involved. It is easy to extend the syntax of almost any language to support the definition of plans for clichés. Role annotation is supported using the notation {...} in analogy with the way function calls are rendered in the language's syntax. Similarly, cliché definition is rendered in analogy with subroutine definition.

9.2   Plans

The implementation of KBEmacs began before the design of the Plan Calculus was completed. Because of this, and because KBEmacs does not contain a general-purpose reasoning module, KBEmacs does not support the full Plan Calculus described in Chapters 3–5. In particular, it does not support data plans, arbitrary logical constraints, or arbitrarily complex overlays.

The heart of KBEmacs's support for plans is an explicit representation of plan diagrams as directed graphs. Boxes in a plan are represented as nodes in the graph, with data and control flow represented as arcs. The graph is hierarchical in that a box can contain a subgraph representing a subplan. Recursive plan diagrams are rendered finite by using a special link indicating that the contents of a box are identical to the contents of a containing box.

There is no support for data plans—every box is required to correspond to a computation. Boxes corresponding to constant data items are viewed as computations without inputs that return the appropriate value.

A plan is stored as a set of facts in a database. These facts record various pieces of information about the plan—e.g., that there is a box A and a box B, and B is inside A, and B corresponds to calling some particular function, and there is a flow of data from the first input of A to the second input of B, and so on. The database is indexed based on every field of every fact. This makes it possible to answer a wide variety of queries without the need for a general-purpose reasoning component. For instance, one can ask, What box contains B? or Where does the data flow to the second input of B come from?

The database supports a chronological context mechanism for rapidly switching back to prior states of the data. This can be used to support limited kinds of hypothetical reasoning. It is also useful for creating checkpoints during debugging.

The various modules of KBEmacs manipulate plans by directly manipulating the state of the plan database. For instance, a constraint is represented as a procedure that checks the plan database and modifies it as necessary to ensure that the constraint is satisfied.

As an adjunct to the plan for a program, the database contains a number of links between the plan and the corresponding program text. In particular, links exist between each box and the part or parts of the code that implement the box and between data-flow arcs and the program variables (if any) that implement them. These links are used in a number of situations—e.g., when selecting pieces of code to include in an automatically generated comment.

KBEmacs makes use of two kinds of plans: *surface* plans and *grouped* plans. Surface plans are "flat" in the sense that every box is a terminal box—a box that does not contain any other boxes. Grouped plans contain boxes nested within boxes. The nesting encodes information about the use of overlays and clichés.

All roles, including input and output roles, are represented as boxes. The act of filling a role with a cliché is a use of an overlay and sets up correspondences between the role box and the plan for the cliché. In KBEmacs, the correspondences are represented by inserting the cliché plan *inside* the role box and connecting the ports of the role box to the appropriate ports of the plan. (KBEmacs supports only overlays in which the right hand side is a single box.) A sequence of role-filling acts yields a grouped plan. In this plan, the terminal boxes correspond to function calls and empty roles, and the nonterminal boxes record the clichés used.

9.3   Analyzer

The analyzer is used in two situations. First, whenever the programmer textually modifies the program being worked on, the analyzer creates a new plan for the program so that knowledge-based editing can continue. Second, the analyzer is used to process cliché definitions to create plans that are stored in the cliché library. An important feature of the analyzer in both situations is the ability to understand role annotation.

The analyzer operates in six stages: parsing, semantic processing, surface plan creation, grouping, temporal abstraction, and role location. The first three stages are similar to operations performed by an optimizing compiler and are only sketched out briefly here. Each stage is described in full in [70].

Parsing

The analyzer begins by parsing the program in question. For Lisp, this parsing is performed by the Lisp reader. The only direct support that has to be supplied by the analyzer is the parsing of role annotation. This is done by defining a reader macro for the character {. For other languages, such as Ada, a parser has to be implemented along traditional lines.

Semantic Processing

The parse tree created for the program being analyzed is translated into an equivalent parse tree in a simple intermediate language. The purpose of this translation is to convert all complex control constructs and data constructs in the source language into simple operations. All of the control constructs are converted to simple conditional and unconditional branches. All of the data constructs are converted into bindings of and assignments to variables holding simple atomic values.

The translation is done through a process of macro expansion. When analyzing a Lisp program, any macro calls in the source program are expanded. When analyzing a program in any language, macrolike definitions are then used to expand each complex construct in the source into an expression involving simpler forms. The set of macrolike definitions used acts as a semantic definition for the complex constructs.

Surface Plan Creation

Once complex constructs have been removed, a surface plan is created using a symbolic evaluator that follows every control path in the program, creating boxes, data flow, and control flow as it goes. Each time a function call or role is encountered, an appropriate box is created. In addition, data flow is created that links this box with the appropriate arguments, if any. Each time a conditional branch is encountered, a split box is created, and the symbolic evaluator proceeds along both paths indicated by the conditional branch. Each time a branch steers the symbolic evaluator onto a path that has already been processed, a join is created and the symbolic evaluator is prevented from reprocessing the path.

Grouping

The surface plan is converted into a grouped plan by inserting appropriate intermediate boxes. This is done by parsing the surface plan in terms of four primitive clichés: *expression, conditional, predicate,* and *single-self-recursion.*

The expression cliché corresponds to the basic notion of straight-line computation. An instance of an expression contains n subboxes connected by data flow. The only restriction is that there cannot be any splits, joins, or control flow.

The conditional cliché corresponds to the basic notion of conditional computation. It contains a predicate, which selects between n subboxes, and a join, which merges the control flow coming from the computations. Each time the conditional is evaluated, exactly one of the subboxes is evaluated.

The predicate cliché is used to build complex splits out of simpler ones. It can contain one or more subsplits and boxes that compute values used by these splits.

The single-self-recursion cliché corresponds to the basic notion of single recursion. This covers both singly self-recursive programs (e.g., the traditional implementation of factorial) and loops. Loops are covered because any loop can be transformed into a tail-recursive program. Representing loops in this fashion eliminates the need for cycles in the data and control flow in grouped plans.

These four primitive clichés are sufficient to group any program that does not contain a multiple entry loop or an instance of multiple recursion. Grouping proceeds in a bottom-up fashion. Each time a group of boxes is located that interacts in accordance with one of the four primitive clichés, these boxes are gathered together into a single intermediate box.

A priori, one might think that grouping in terms of the four primitive clichés might be a difficult task requiring significant backtracking. However, this is not the case. In fact, grouping is relatively straightforward, and no backtracking is ever required. This is so because the four primitive clichés are so different from each other that it is very difficult to make a mistake about which one is applicable where.

The grouping process is driven primarily by the control flow in the surface plan. After grouping is completed, the grouped plan is adjusted based on the data flow in the plan. In particular, each box that creates a value is moved as close as possible (within the constraints of control flow) to the place where the value is used. This adjustment is done to keep closely related boxes close together and unrelated boxes far apart.

Temporal Abstraction

Once a grouped plan has been obtained, temporal abstraction (see Section 5.5) is used to view individual single-self-recursions as combinations of functions operating on sequences. For instance, a loop computing the sum of the elements in a Lisp list is viewed as an expression composed of two operations: an enumeration computing a sequence of the elements of the list and an accumulation computing the sum of the elements in this sequence.

As discussed in [71], the decomposition of single-self-recursions in terms of temporal abstraction is done based on the data flow in the loop. The main goal is to locate fragments of the loop that can be understood in isolation. The key requirement is that all the feedback of information from the fragment to itself must be contained within the fragment.

A significant weakness of the current support for temporal abstraction is that it works only for tail-recursive programs (i.e., loops). The discussion in [70] indicates how support could be extended to singly recursive programs that are not tail-recursive. Extending temporal abstraction to cover multiply recursive programs is a topic of current research.

Locating Roles

Up to this point in analysis, instances of {...} annotation are treated just like function calls. However, after grouping has been completed, the boxes corresponding to {...} annotation are flagged specially as roles. In addition, the analyzer identifies intermediate boxes that correspond to compound roles by observing where the various subroles appear in the plan. This cannot be done until after the other stages of analysis have identified what grouping is appropriate.

Language Independence

The analyzer is largely programming-language independent. To support a new language, only the first two stages have to be modified. One must provide a parser for the language and a set of macrolike definitions that specify the semantics of the constructs in the language in terms of the intermediate language used by the analyzer. In addition to Lisp and Ada, this has been done, at least to some extent, for the languages Fortran (see [70]), Cobol (see [67]), and PL/I (see [19]).

It should be noted that KBEmacs's support for Ada is much less extensive than its support for Lisp. Basically, it supports the features of Ada that are equivalent to Lisp, and little else.

In particular, data declarations are treated in a minimal way. They are essentially processed as literals. The analyzer does nothing with them other than save them. Note, however, that even this minimal support allows KBEmacs to have clichés for data declarations by simply having clichés that contain the appropriate declaration literals.

The only parts of KBEmacs that do anything with Ada declarations are special-purpose procedures in the coder module and in constraints. To provide better support for declarations, the support for plan would have to be extended to support data plans as well as computational plans.

A good example of the limits to KBEmacs's understanding of declarations is demonstrated by its support for generic packages. On one hand, it understands almost nothing about them. On the other hand, it succeeds in making use of them in Screens 8.1–8.14. KBEmacs contains an Ada interpreter that correctly interprets generic packages. In addition, there are several generic packages (shown in [21]) that are assumed to have been written before the transcript begins. All of this is basically outside of the understanding of KBEmacs. Within the understanding of KBEmacs, there are several clichés that refer to generic packages (e.g., CHAIN_FILE_DEFINITION). These clichés make it possible for KBEmacs to create programs that use generic packages.

Another problematical aspect of the analyzer's support for Ada is the support for exception handlers. In Lisp, the analyzer does not handle interrupt processing code at all since it cannot be represented in the Plan Calculus. In Lisp, this weakness is easy to avoid since relatively few Lisp programs use interrupts. However, interrupts cannot be so easily ignored in Ada programs. The analyzer provides minimal support for Ada exception handlers by converting them into special conditionals that are semantically incorrect but representable in the Plan Calculus. A reverse conversion is then performed by the coder module.

The analyzer's support for Ada should be looked at only as illustrative. There is, however, no fundamental reason why more complete support could not be provided.

Possible Improvements

The analyzer is the oldest and most robust part of KBEmacs. It is well tested and relatively bug free. Nevertheless, there are many ways it could be improved.

There are several limitations on the kinds of programs the analyzer can handle. Most of these limitations stem from limitations of the Plan Calculus (e.g. the Plan Calculus cannot represent nonlocal control flow). Other limitations stem from weaknesses of the analyzer itself (e.g., temporal abstraction can only be applied to loops).

Little attempt has been made to make the analyzer efficient. It should be possible to speed it up considerably by using some of the efficient graph algorithms that are employed by optimizing compilers.

The analyzer does not attempt to recognize which clichés from the library could have been used to construct a program. It recognizes only how the program could have been constructed using the four primitive clichés.

When a program is constructed by means of knowledge-based editing, the construction process groups the plan according to the clichés used to construct it. This grouping is an essential underpinning of knowledge-based commands such as **Replace** and **Comment**. Since analysis is not able to recover the full grouping in terms of library clichés, these commands cannot be used after a program has been modified textually.

There is one situation where KBEmacs can avoid this problem. If the only effect of a textual modification is to fill a role, KBEmacs converts the textual modification into an equivalent **Fill** command and is thereby able to maintain its knowledge of how the program was built out of clichés.

As discussed in Chapter 10, a module (called the recognizer) has been constructed that is capable of performing an analysis of a program in terms of library clichés. However, this module is based on a different implementation of the Plan Calculus and has not been integrated with KBEmacs.

9.4   Coder

The coder is used to create new program text whenever the plan for the program being edited is changed. The coder operates in six stages: temporal composition, grouping, data-flow implementation, basic coding, code transformation, and pretty printing. Like the analyzer stages, most of the coder stages are programming-language independent.

Temporal Composition

The process of temporal composition reverses the process of temporal abstraction. Computations on sequences are converted back into single-self-recursions. Where several single-self-recursions are composed together, they are combined into one single-self-recursion. This process is relatively straightforward and is described in detail in [70] and [77].

Grouping

The coder uses the same grouping stage as the analyzer. Each box in the plan is processed to ensure that it is fully grouped in terms of the four primitive clichés. For the most part, this does not entail anything more than a rapid check that the contents of the box are grouped because grouping is generally guaranteed by the way plans are constructed. In particular, whenever the analyzer makes a plan for a program or for a cliché, it groups the plan. Further, whenever the plan editor combines plans together, it makes sure that the result is appropriately grouped. The only place where the coder has to explicitly apply grouping is the bodies of the single-self-recursions created by temporal composition.

Grouping is an essential part of coding for several reasons. The primitive clichés conditional and single-self-recursion indicate the basic control-flow structure of the plan—i.e., where conditional statements and loops will appear in the code produced. Further, the fact that each box is moved as close as possible to the place where its value is used is important because it makes it easier to detect where nesting of expressions can be used to implement data flow.

Data-Flow Implementation

At least a third of the coder's effort goes towards determining how the data flow in the plan should be implemented. Doing a good job is important because it has a large impact on the readability of the resulting program. It is difficult because a large number of competing requirements have to be balanced against each other.

The data-flow stage of the coder proceeds in several steps. The data flow in the plan is divided into sections such that all of the data flow in each individual section can be implemented in the same way.

The data-flow stage then identifies which data-flow sections can be implemented using nesting of expressions. Each time a nesting decision is made, additional ordering constraints have to be introduced into the plan. These have to be recorded so that they will not be contradicted later.

Variable names are then chosen for the remaining data-flow sections. These names must satisfy the constraint that sections whose execution overlaps cannot use the same variable name.

Advice on mnemonic names is obtained by consulting links in the plan database between data-flow arcs and variable names. Each of these links comes either from a cliché or from something typed in by the programmer.

If more than one variable name is suggested for a given section, various heuristics are used to pick the best name. For instance, informative names such as UNIT and SUM are preferred over uninformative names such as DATA and RESULT.

If no variable names are suggested for a section, the data-flow stage attempts to use the same name as a preceding or following section that appears to correspond to the same logical object. If this is not helpful, the coder attempts to generate a variable name based on the name of the function that creates the value being transmitted. If all else fails, an uninformative variable name such as X, Y, or Z is used.

At the current time, the constraints and heuristics just discussed are supported by an ad hoc procedure that makes the necessary choices serially without backtracking. This is relatively fast but has a number of problems. In particular, this approach is quite sensitive to the exact order that data-flow sections come up for consideration. It would probably be better to use a constraint propagation approach that arrives at a simultaneous consensus on all of the choices that have to be made.

Basic Coding

Once decisions have been made about how to implement the data flow in a plan, actual program code is produced. This is done recursively one box at a time. For each terminal box, code representing the appropriate function call, constant, or role annotation is generated. For each nonterminal box, code is created for the control construct that corresponds to the primitive cliché associated with the box. Data-flow constructs (nesting of expressions, assignments, and variable bindings) are introduced following the decisions of the data-flow stage.

The result of basic coding is a more or less language-independent parse tree for the program. It is language independent in that it relies only on a few basic constructs (such as variable binding, conditionals, simple loops, variable assignments, and function calls) that most languages support. In this parse tree, roles are expressed as a special kind of function call. Links in the plan database are created that record the correspondence between the plan and the parse tree.

Code Transformation

The aesthetic quality of the language-independent parse tree is improved by applying a number of language-dependent transformations to it. For example, in Lisp, transformations introduce uses of the special forms IF, WHEN, LET*, and LOOP.

In Ada, much more extensive transformations are supported. In particular, transformations reverse the processing that the analyzer uses to encode Ada declarations and exception handlers. Going beyond this, a special procedure inspects the program and creates variable declarations for any variables that do not have explicitly specified declarations.

A significant complexity in the transformation stage is that the transformations must be careful to maintain the links between the plan and the parse tree so that KBEmacs can keep track of what parts of the plan correspond to what parts of the code.

Pretty Printing

The final stage of the coder creates program text corresponding to the transformed parse tree. This is done using a pretty printer (see [29, 30]), which takes care of aesthetically laying out the program text.

Language Independence

Like the analyzer, the coder is largely programming-language independent. Only the last two stages are language dependent. To support a new language, one has to define an appropriate set of transformations that introduce language-specific forms into the language-independent parse tree created by the first four stages of the coder. In addition, one has to provide an unparser for the language. This latter task is facilitated by the existence of the pretty printer. One merely has to define a set of pretty printing functions corresponding to the various kinds of nodes in the parse tree.

In addition to Lisp, the coder supports all of the aspects of Ada that the analyzer supports. The coder also provides basic support for PL/I (see [19]).

Possible Improvements

As can be seen in the screens in Chapters 7 and 8, the coder produces reasonable results for completed programs, partial programs containing empty roles, and clichés. However, experimentation has shown that the coder has a number of weaknesses.

The biggest problem stems from defects in the data-flow implementation stage. This stage does a good job of creating correct programs. However, it has a tendency to produce programs that, while correct, are unreadable because they make use of too many uninformative variables. As noted above, a constraint propagation approach would probably yield better results. However, it is not clear that that would be a complete solution to the problem. The fundamental difficulty is that the coder does not have any real understanding of what makes data flow aesthetic.

Another problem is that the transformational stage is not supported in a general way. Each transformation is implemented as a procedure that operates directly on parse trees. It would have been better to provide a general-purpose pattern-based transformational system. This would make it easier to state the individual transformations and to control the order of application of transformations.

An interesting problem with the coder is that it is not able to make good use of macros in the Lisp code it produces. A few macros are introduced by transformations that are specifically designed to introduce them; however, there is no general mechanism for ensuring that user-defined macros will be used. It is probably not possible to use macros effectively in the absence of a general-recognition mechanism that can reliably detect where computation corresponding to a macro exists in the plan for a program.

A final issue is that of *stability*. When a programmer modifies the algorithm being used in a program, it is desirable for the code to change neither more nor less than necessary to express the new algorithm well. Programmers tend to err on the side of excess stability. Rather than totally revamping a program after a major change, they often settle for patches. This leads to awkward code that looks like one algorithm but actually implements another. The coder avoids this problem by always recoding the program completely. However, this leaves the coder open to the reverse problem—it sometimes makes changes in parts of the program that should be left alone. This happens because the coder contains almost nothing that explicitly provides for stability. Rather, stability is merely implicit in the fact that the coder processes similar plans in similar ways. Unfortunately, the coder's implicit definition of similarity is not the same as a typical programmer's notion of similarity.

A related problem is that the programmer cannot, in general, control the style of the code produced. If the programmer makes some purely stylistic (as opposed to semantic) change in the program text, the coder will simply restore the text to its old form the next time it codes the plan. The only exception to this is variable names, which are the only place where the coder explicitly takes advice from the programmer.

9.5   Plan Editor

The knowledge-based plan editor supports fourteen commands that operate on plans. These commands are specified using a simple English-like command language. Figure 9.6 shows the grammar for this command language. Numerous examples of commands are shown in Chapters 7 and 8.

References

A central concept in the command language is referring to a role or function call. This is done by using the same kind of phrase that is used in `{the ...}` annotation. For example, one might say "`the rest of the enumerator`" or "`the FORMAT.`"

The cursor position in the Emacs buffer is an implicit part of each command. It is used to disambiguate references. The phrase "`the rest of the enumerator`" is interpreted to mean the rest of the enumerator in the program containing the cursor.

Alternately, the program the reference is in can be stated explicitly in a reference phrase. For example, one might say "`the enumerator in the program REPORT-TIMINGS.`"

If there is more than one role or function of the same name in a given program, a reference can be disambiguated with respect to the execution order of the forms in the program. For example, one might say "`the last FORMAT`" to refer to the last call on `FORMAT` (in execution order) in the program containing the cursor.

One can refer to both empty roles and filled roles. However, the ability to refer to a filled role depends on the fact that the role is represented in the plan. If textual editing forces a new plan to be created by analyzing the program text, information about filled roles will be lost.

```
<command> ::= Define a {<plan>} <def> {with <param-list>}.
            | Add a parameter <SYMBOL> {to <def>}.
            | Fill <ref> with <instance>.
            | Replace <ref> with <instance>.
            | Insert <instance>.
            | Copy <def> {to <def>}.
            | Remove <ref>.
            | Share <ref> and <ref>.
            | Highlight <ref>.
            | Comment {<def>}.
            | What needs to be done {in <def>}?
            | Analyze {<def>}.
            | Finish editing {<def>}.
            | Use language <SYMBOL>.

        <def> ::= <def-type> <SYMBOL>
   <def-type> ::= program | function | procedure | package | plan

 <param-list> ::= a parameter <SYMBOL> | parameters <SYMBOLS>
    <SYMBOLS> ::= <SYMBOL> and <SYMBOL>
                | <SYMBOL>, {<SYMBOL>,}* and <SYMBOL>
     <SYMBOL> ::= a name rendered in upper case

        <ref> ::= <role-ref> {of <role-ref>}* {in the <def>}
                | {the return-value of} <fn-ref> {in the <def>}
   <role-ref> ::= the {<ordinal>} <role-name>
     <fn-ref> ::= the {<ordinal>} <FN-NAME>
    <ordinal> ::= first | second | third | fourth | ... | last
  <role-name> ::= the name of a role rendered in lower case
    <FN-NAME> ::= the name of a function rendered in upper case

   <instance> ::= <CODE>
                | <ref>
                | <a-or-an> <plan> {of <instances>}
   <a-or-an> ::= a | an
  <instances> ::= <instance>
                | <instance> and <instance>
                | <instance>, {<instance>,}* and <instance>
       <CODE> ::= code in the current language rendered in upper case
       <plan> ::= the name of a cliché plan rendered in lower case
```

Figure 9.6 The knowledge-based command language.

Instances

Another basic part of the command language is the ability to create plans
corresponding to instances of clichés and pieces of code. There are three
kinds of instances. An instance can specify a literal piece of code, in which
case the code is analyzed to create an equivalent plan. An instance can be
a role reference, in which case the instance is converted into a trivial plan
that represents data flow from the indicated plan box. An instance can be
an instance of a cliché, in which case the plan for the cliché is copied out
of the library.

In addition to the name of the cliché, a cliché instance phrase can specify subinstances to be used to fill roles of the cliché. The PRIMARY-ROLES declaration of the cliché definition specifies which subinstance is used to fill which role of the cliché. The Fill command is called to fill the appropriate roles in the instance.

When an instance of a cliché is created, the constraints for the cliché are run. (This is the only time that DEFAULT and RENAME constraints are run.) The constraints can access any subinstances that are specified as part of the instance phrase.

For the most part, the grammar in Figure 9.6 is trivial in nature and can be parsed with no lookahead. However, there are two areas of complexity involving instances.

First, an instance of a cliché can contain an instance of a cliché as one of its subinstances. The grammar in Figure 8.7 is ambiguous if such a subinstance contains further subinstances. Consider parsing the phrase

```
"a list of X, a list of Y, Z, and W"
```

This could be parsed either as

```
(LIST X (LIST Y Z W))
```

or

```
(LIST X (LIST Y) Z W)
```

This problem is arbitrarily resolved by making the lowest level cliché instance contain as much of the command as possible (e.g., choosing the first alternative above).

Second, parsing the nonterminal <CODE> can be very difficult because it requires the ability to parse whatever language KBEmacs is currently operating on. To decouple the command parser from the program text parser, restrictions are placed on the kinds of code that can be typed in a command. Code is required to be a string literal, a number, a symbol, an expression surrounded by parentheses, or a quoted instance of any of the above. This restriction allows the command parser to delimit a piece of code without having to actually parse it. (Fortunately, although this restriction is not as natural for Ada as it is for Lisp, it is still palatable.)

Knowledge-Based Commands

The following subsections describe how each of the commands in Figure 9.6 is implemented. Each command is supported by a special-purpose procedure that operates directly on the plan database. Most of these procedures are straightforward—the representation shift to the Plan Calculus does most of the work.

Before any command is run, the plan editor checks to see whether the program containing the editing cursor has been textually modified. If it has, the program text is analyzed to create an up-to-date plan.

Typically, running a command modifies the plan for the program being worked on. When this is the case, the plan is recoded, and the cursor is positioned before the first *interesting* change in the program text. This position is determined by comparing the program text before and after the command, under the assumption that changes to the body of a program are more interesting than changes to declarations.

Defining

The basic action of the `Define` command is to create a plan corresponding to an empty program definition. This plan is then coded, creating program text corresponding to an empty program definition. This text is inserted in the editor buffer at the position of the cursor.

The `Define` command specifies the name of the definition and the type of the definition—i.e., whether it is a function, procedure, cliché plan, etc. This information is entered into the plan. The command checks whether there is already a program defined with the same name and complains if there is.

A `Define` command can specify a list of parameter names, in which case they are made inputs of the plan as a whole. A `Define` command can also specify the name of a cliché that is to be instantiated as the body of the program being defined. This form of the `Define` command is an abbreviation for a simple `Define` command followed by an `Insert` command.

Adding a Parameter

The "`Add a parameter`" command makes it possible to add additional parameters to a program definition. This is done by adding more inputs to the plan as a whole. If no destination definition is specified, the destination defaults to the program containing the cursor.

Filling Roles

The `Fill` command is the central knowledge-based command. It fills a role with an instance after checking that the role is empty. A role is filled by replacing the role box with the plan for the instance. If a compound role is being filled, the prior contents of the role box (the subroles and any computation connecting them) are removed before inserting the instance. Thus, the computation connecting the subroles in the instance replaces the computation connecting the subroles of the compound role.

As discussed in Section 7.2, a number of heuristics are used to decide how to connect the inputs and outputs of the instance plan with the surrounding program plan. Once the instance plan is connected into the larger plan, any `DERIVED` constraints specified for the cliché that contains the filled role are rerun. This may result in further filling of roles. (Both `DEFAULT` and `DERIVED` constraints call the `Fill` command to perform their actions.)

Replacing the Contents of a Role

The `Replace` command is used to replace a filled role or function call with an instance. It first checks to see that the reference to be replaced is not an empty role. It then removes the contents of the role or function call box and uses the `Fill` command to insert the plan for the instance into the box.

Inserting a Cliché in a Program

The `Insert` command inserts an instance into a plan at a place corresponding to the position of the editor cursor. To do this, KBEmacs inserts a special role marker at the position of the cursor and analyzes the program to get a plan containing that role. It then calls the `Fill` command to fill this special role with the specified instance.

Embedded instances of {a ...} annotation are handled exactly the same way. They are converted into `Insert` commands at the time when the program text is analyzed.

Copying a Cliché

As shown in Screens 8.5–8.7, KBEmacs can be used to edit clichés as well as programs. When editing a cliché, it is sometimes convenient to start from some preexisting cliché and then modify it into the desired cliché. (An example of this is shown in [21].) To use this style of editing, it is necessary to obtain a copy of a cliché rather than an instance of it.

The `Copy` command is similar to an `Insert` command except that, instead of instantiating the cliché specified as its first argument, it copies the whole cliché verbatim, including the cliché declarations. All of this is then inserted into the appropriate plan without running any constraints. If no destination definition is specified, it defaults to the definition containing the cursor.

Removing a Role

The `Remove` command deletes the indicated role or function call. In addition, it deletes every box that exists solely to provide data to the deleted box. This is done on the theory that all such boxes have become useless.

Sharing Two Parts of a Program

The `Share` command takes two references and eliminates one of them, by using the other twice. The references are first resolved to boxes in the plan. Then the plan is checked to see that the two boxes compute the same thing. This is relatively straightforward to do by simply comparing the boxes and the sources of the data flow to them. The locality of information in the Plan Calculus greatly facilitates this comparison.

If the two boxes do compute the same thing, then whichever box comes later in the plan is removed and data flow is routed from the first box to all of the places where the value of the second box was used.

Highlighting the Contents of a Role

The `Highlight` command uses the standard editor highlighting mechanism (underlining) to highlight a role or a function call. This command depends on the plan database maintaining links showing the correspondence between boxes and the code that implements them.

There are two basic limitations to this command. First, there are situations where the plan database fails to keep an adequate record of what program text corresponds to a role. Second, the standard editor highlighting mechanism is not capable of highlighting anything other than a single contiguous portion of program text. Thus, if a role corresponds to several separate pieces of program text (e.g., an enumerator), it cannot be fully highlighted. The latter difficulty would be easy to overcome. The former might not be.

Generating a Comment

The `Comment` command creates a comment for a program in the form of an outline. An example of this is shown in Figure 9.7, which reproduces the comment generated for the program `REPORT-TIMINGS` (Screen 7.19 on page 115). If no particular definition is specified as part of the command, a comment is constructed for the program containing the cursor. The comment is created by following the hierarchical structure of the plan and using the `DESCRIBED-ROLES` and `COMMENT` declarations for the relevant clichés.

The first line of the comment specifies the name of the function or procedure being described and the top-level cliché in its plan. The subsequent lines in the comment describe the `DESCRIBED-ROLES` of the top-level cliché in order. Each role is described in one of four ways. If the role is missing, this fact is reported. If the role is filled with a cliché, the name of the filling cliché is given, and a one-line description of the filling cliché is

```
;;; The function REPORT-TIMINGS is a simple-report.
;;;    The file-name is "report.txt".
;;;    The title is "Report of Reaction Timings (in msec.)".
;;;    The enumerator is a list-enumeration.
;;;        It enumerates the elements of TIMINGS.
;;;    There are no column-headings.
;;;    The print-item is a tabular-print-out.
;;;        It prints out (CAR LIST) in columns.
;;;    The summary is an idiosyncratic computation.
```

Figure 9.7 An automatically generated comment.

created based on the COMMENT declaration for the filling cliché. If the role is filled with a simple nonclichéd piece of code, this piece of code is exhibited. Finally, if the role is filled with a complex piece of nonclichéd code, the phrase "idiosyncratic computation" is used to describe the role.

Asking What Needs To Be Done

This command looks at the plan for the specified definition and determines what roles still need to be filled and what output roles still need to be used. A report of this information is displayed to the programmer in a temporary window at the top of the screen. If no definition is specified as part of the command, a report is displayed of what needs to be done for every program for which a plan exists.

Analyzing a Program

The Analyze command triggers the analysis of the named definition if it has been textually modified since it was last analyzed. If no definition is specified, the definition containing the cursor is analyzed.

Finishing the Editing of a Program

The "Finish editing" command calls the "What needs to be done" command to check that the program is indeed finished and removes any output role annotation from the program text so that it can be processed by a standard interpreter or compiler.

There is also a procedural hook that is part of the "Finish editing" command. This hook checks to see whether any additional actions should be performed based on the program just completed. This is how the creation of printing clichés after the definition of the package MAINTENANCE_FILES is triggered (see Screen 8.4).

Selecting the Programming Language

The "Use language" command sets an internal variable that controls what language is being used for output to the programmer. It is assumed that the programmer will use this same language when typing literal pieces of code in commands.

Language Independence

Since it operates almost exclusively in the domain of plans, the plan editor is almost completely programming-language independent. The only exceptions to this are the Comment and Highlight commands, which have to interact with the actual language being used. Even these commands are largely programming-language independent. They both depend on the fact that the coder has already created program text in the appropriate language.

Possible Improvements

The plan editor is one of the most experimental parts of KBEmacs. We expected that the interface to the Design Apprentice (see Section 11.2) will be very different. However, as demonstrated by the screens in Chapters 7 and 8, the current commands are quite useful.

9.6   Text Editor and Interface

Editing of program text is supported by the Symbolics Lisp Machine's standard Emacs-style editor. This editor supports both text- and syntax-based editing. The KBEmacs interface (see [25]) unifies ordinary program editing and knowledge-based plan editing so that they can both be conveniently accessed through the standard editor.

A number of KBEmacs commands are supported directly in the interface rather than in the plan editor. In particular, the extended commands such as s-<end>, s-F, and s-R operate on a purely textual basis, generating full knowledge-based commands that are sent to the plan editor.

The commands s-N (move to the next empty role) and s-P (move to the previous empty role) are implemented as user-defined commands in Emacs without using the plan editor at all. They operate in a textual manner simply searching for the next (or previous) occurrence of empty role annotation respectively.

Language Independence

The interface itself is totally language independent. However, it relies on the fact that the standard editor has a basic understanding of the language being edited. If this is not the case, the standard editor has to be extended.

For example, Version 4 of the Symbolics Lisp Machine editor does not support Ada. To make the interface work for Ada, a few basic extensions had to be made to provide minimal support for Ada. In particular, the editor was given the ability to locate Ada programs in a buffer. This provides support for the standard Emacs commands m-. (goto definition) and c-shift-C (compile definition).

However, the Symbolics editor was not extended to support syntax-based editing of Ada programs. As a result, only text-based editing can be applied.

A simple Ada interpreter was implemented so that the programmer could test Ada programs on the Symbolics Lisp machine. This interpreter is capable of running the programs in Chapter 8. However, it supports only part of the language and is intended only as an illustration.

9.7   From Demonstration to Prototype

It is useful to distinguish three levels of systems: *demonstrations, prototypes,* and *fully operational systems.* A demonstration system illustrates some general principles of operation, but is not expected to work on anything other than a few selected examples. A prototype typically has many defects, but operates (more or less) in a fairly wide range of situations. A fully operational system operates correctly (almost) all of the time.

Using this categorization, one must realize that KBEmacs is a demonstration system. The transcripts in this book show approximately a third of the test cases KBEmacs has ever been applied to. In addition, KBEmacs is slow. The commands in Chapter 8 take from one to five minutes each to execute.

To convert KBEmacs from a demonstration system to a prototype, the system needs to be reimplemented with special attention to speed, robustness, and completeness. This section suggests several changes that should be made when KBEmacs is reimplemented. It also describes an experiment showing that KBEmacs can be straightforwardly sped up by more than an order of magnitude.

A More Efficient Representation for Plans

Storing plans in a fully indexed database is convenient for a number of reasons, but is extraordinarily slow. An experiment was performed showing that plan diagrams can be implemented much more efficiently than they currently are in KBEmacs.

The experimental implementation encodes basically the same information as the implementation discussed in Section 9.2, but much more compactly, using record structures that point directly to each other. Retrieval is done by following pointers instead of by means of patterns and indexing. For example, each box points to its containing box and to each of its subboxes. Following pointers directly speeds up retrieval by many orders of magnitude. In addition, since all the information about a box is contained in a single structure, only one retrieval has to be performed to get all this information. In the current database, several retrievals are needed.

Parts of the plan editor were reimplemented in terms of the experimental plan representation. When tested on the task of instantiating a relatively complex cliché and inserting it into a plan, the reimplemented plan editor was 30 times faster than the current implementation of KBEmacs. Although other parts of KBEmacs might not speed up as much as the plan editor, there is reason to believe that the experimental plan representation would lead to at least an order of magnitude increase in speed in KBEmacs as a whole.

Moving Temporal Abstraction Out of the System

Use of the improved plan representation just discussed would speed up KBEmacs without fundamentally changing the way it operates. Further speedups could be obtained by making more fundamental changes.

A key step would be to remove temporal abstraction from the analyzer and temporal composition from the coder. This would simplify these modules and approximately double their speed.

This is possible without losing the benefits of temporal abstraction by incorporating the idea of temporal composition into the target language. This could be done by using a compiler extension (such as the one presented in [78, 79, 80]) that directly supports computations in terms of sequences. KBEmacs could then manipulate these computations as simple expressions, while the compiler extension handled the problem of temporal composition.

Deemphasizing Primitive Grouping

Another way in which KBEmacs could be fundamentally simplified would be to downplay the importance of grouping in terms of the four primitive clichés. It turns out that the only place where this grouping is important is in the coder. As it is now, a fair amount of effort is expended in the analyzer and plan editor to continually maintain proper grouping in terms of the primitive clichés even though this grouping is not used by these modules. A significant amount of time would be saved if this grouping were used only in the coder.

It should be noted that grouping in terms of the primitive clichés is quite separate from grouping in terms of other clichés. Grouping induced by the filling of roles with clichés is essential for the operation of the plan editor. However, it comes more or less for free and does not depend on grouping in terms of the four primitive clichés.

Knowledge About Data Structures

To become a true prototype, KBEmacs would have to be extended so that it had a better understanding of data types. To do this, its implementation of the Plan Calculus would have to incorporate significant support for data types and data plans. KBEmacs currently records a little data type information in Ada plans and no data information in Lisp plans. To fully support a language (such as Ada) that allows extensive user definition of new data structures, plans would have to contain information about how complex data structures are built out of simple ones.

Defining a Realistic Cliché Library

A final step in converting KBEmacs into a true prototype would be the construction of a more complete cliché library. This might require the definition of as many as a thousand clichés. Although this would not be an easy task, there is no theoretical reason why it could not be done. (It should be noted that the speed of KBEmacs is independent of the size of the cliché library.) If a large body of clichés were defined, then it would be beneficial to add some kind of indexing facility to facilitate the retrieval of clichés.

Chapter 10

Automated Cliché Recognition

Experienced programmers can often reconstruct a program's design by recognizing the clichés used. Section 2.2 presented an imagined scenario of a programmer recognizing the clichés in a simple hash-table program. This chapter describes a system, called the Recognizer (see [40, 41, 42]), that demonstrates the feasibility of automated cliché recognition. Given a program and a library of algorithmic clichés, the Recognizer finds occurrences of the clichés in the program and builds a hierarchical description of the program in terms of the clichés found and the overlays between them.

There are both practical and theoretical motivations for automating cliché recognition. On the practical side, understanding existing programs is an important activity in software-engineering practice. A large percentage of many organizations's software budgets is currently spent maintaining, documenting, enhancing, and debugging existing systems, often without adequate documentation of the original design. Automated cliché recognition can facilitate these tasks by reconstructing design information.

In general, design reconstruction is not necessary for software produced using the Programmer's Apprentice because (as illustrated by KBEmacs) the Apprentice keeps track of the clichés used in the development process and uses this record to support maintenance and evolution. Nevertheless, there are situations in which automated cliché recognition can be helpful even when using the Apprentice. For example, if a programmer using KBEmacs chooses to edit the source code of a program at the textual level, automated recognition can identify any new clichés used.

Another potential use for automated cliché recognition, even when there is a complete design record, is to facilitate program optimization. A software system can often be decomposed into clichés in several different ways. Finding alternative decompositions to the one used in the actual design may suggest additional optimizations.

From a theoretical standpoint, demonstrating the feasibility of automated cliché recognition lends support to the theory of clichés and inspection methods in software engineering. Furthermore, the use of the Plan Calculus in the Recognizer strengthens the case for this formalization of clichés, since it shows that the same formalism can be used for both synthesis and analysis.

An Example

Figure 10.1 shows the result of applying the Recognizer to the TABLE-LOOKUP program of Figure 2.3 on page 15. Given the Common Lisp code shown at the top of the figure (and an appropriate cliché library), the Recognizer automatically produces the documentation shown at the bottom of the figure. Uppercase words in the documentation, e.g., TABLE, indicate relevant identifiers in the program.

The Recognizer's main output is a graph-grammar derivation tree such as the one in Figure 10.8 (page 181). The documentation shown in Figure 10.1 is produced by knitting together schematized textual fragments associated with the plans and overlays mentioned in the derivation tree and filling in slots in the fragments using identifiers taken from the program text (e.g., TABLE, BUCKET, and KEY in Figure 10.1). The documentation that results sounds stilted, but describes the important design decisions in the program and can help a programmer locate relevant objects in the code.

```
(DEFUN TABLE-LOOKUP (TABLE INPUT)
  (LET ((BUCKET (AREF TABLE (HASH INPUT TABLE))))
    (LOOP
      (IF (NULL BUCKET) (RETURN NIL))
      (LET ((ENTRY (CAR BUCKET)))
        (IF (EQUAL (KEY ENTRY) INPUT) (RETURN ENTRY)))
      (SETQ BUCKET (CDR BUCKET)))))
```

$$\Downarrow$$

```
TABLE-LOOKUP is an associative retrieval operation.
  If there is an element of the set TABLE with key INPUT,
  then that element is returned; otherwise NIL is returned.
  The key function is KEY.
The set TABLE is implemented as a hash table.
  The hashing function is HASH.
A bucket BUCKET of the hash table TABLE is implemented
as a list.
  The elements of the list BUCKET are enumerated.
  Linear search is used to find the first element of the
  list BUCKET whose key is equal to INPUT.
```

Figure 10.1 Documentation generated by the Recognizer.

One way to evaluate the potential practical benefit of automated cliché recognition is to imagine using automatically produced documentation such as shown in Figure 10.1 for the maintenance of poorly documented or undocumented programs. An advantage of automatically produced documentation is that it can be automatically updated whenever the corresponding source code is changed, thereby avoiding the pernicious problem of misleading out-of-date documentation.

Difficulties in Automating Cliché Recognition

Although it often seems effortless for people to recognize clichés in source code, this task is difficult to automate. The main difficulties are:

- *Syntactic variation* — The same net flow of data and control can typically be achieved in many different ways. For example, the program in Figure 10.1 could have had more temporary variables or used DO instead of LOOP.

- *Unrecognizable code* — Not all programs are constructed completely of clichés. The recognition process must be able to ignore an indeterminate amount of idiosyncratic code.

- *Implementation variation* — A given abstraction can typically be implemented in many different ways. For example, the hash-table buckets in Figure 10.1 could have been implemented using sorted lists.

- *Noncontiguousness* — A cliché's parts can be scattered throughout the text of a program, rather than appearing in adjacent lines or expressions. For example, the CAR, CDR, and NULL parts of the cdr-enumeration cliché in Figure 10.1 are separated by unrelated expressions.

- *Overlapping implementations* — Program optimization often merges the implementations of two or more distinct abstractions. Therefore portions of a program may need to be recognized as part of more than one cliché.

The following sections describe the algorithms and representations used in the Recognizer to deal with these difficulties.

10.1   Architecture of the Recognizer

The heart of the Recognizer is a flow-graph parser developed by Brotsky [43], which is a generalization of Earley's algorithm [99] for string parsing. As shown in Figure 10.2, the source code for a program is analyzed to extract a surface plan (see Section 9.3), translated into an attributed flow

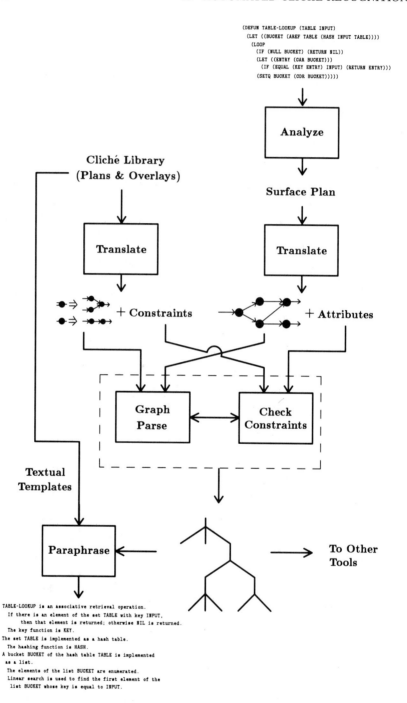

Figure 10.2 Architecture of the automated cliché recognition system.

graph, and then parsed against a grammar and a set of constraints derived from the cliché library. (If the grammar is ambiguous, as is typically the case, the parser produces all possible derivations. Constraint checking is interleaved with parsing for efficiency.) The primary output of the recognition process is a derivation tree, which represents a design for the program. This tree can be used by a paraphraser that generates documentation or by other tools.

Flow Graphs and Grammars

A *flow graph* is a labeled, directed, acyclic graph, in which edges connect labeled input and output ports of nodes. Figure 10.3 shows an example flow graph, in which the edges have been labeled with subscripted e's and the ports with subscripted p's. Note that each node type (e.g., a, b, d, g, and h) has a fixed number of input and output ports and that fan-in (e.g., e_3 and e_6) and fan-out (e.g., e_1 and e_2) are allowed.

A flow graph is derived from a context-free flow-graph grammar in much the same way that a string is derived from a context-free string grammar. A context-free flow-graph grammar is a set of rewrite rules, each specifying how a node in a graph may be replaced by a subgraph. The left side of each rule is a nonterminal node; the graph on the right side may contain both terminal and nonterminal nodes. (Nonterminals are denoted by capital letters and terminals are denoted by lowercase letters.) Figure 10.4 is a simple flow-graph grammar that derives the graph in Figure 10.3 by the sequence of steps shown in Figure 10.5. As with string grammars, it is convenient to represent graph grammar derivations as parse trees, as shown in Figure 10.6.

Note that, unlike string grammars, each rule in a flow-graph grammar specifies a mapping (shown in Figure 10.4 by corresponding numbers) between the unconnected input and output ports on the left side and unconnected input and output ports on the right side. This mapping determines how the subgraph is connected to the surrounding nodes when it replaces a nonterminal node in a derivation. When two or more edges on the right side of a rule are mapped to the same port on the left side, this leads to fan-in or fan-out in the flow graph being derived. This is illustrated in the second step of the derivation in Figure 10.5. (For more information on graph grammars in general, see [100].)

Translating the Plan Calculus to Flow Graphs

Returning to Figure 10.2, recall that the flow graph to be parsed by the Recognizer is computed by first analyzing the source code to extract a surface plan (as described in Section 9.3) and then translating this surface plan to a flow graph. Also, the cliché library is translated to an attributed

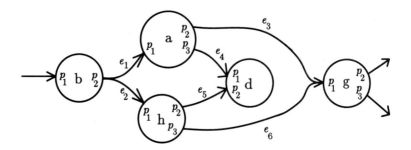

Figure 10.3 An example flow graph.

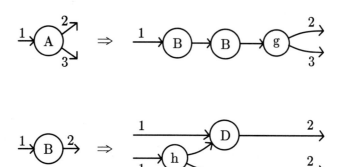

Figure 10.4 A flow-graph grammar.

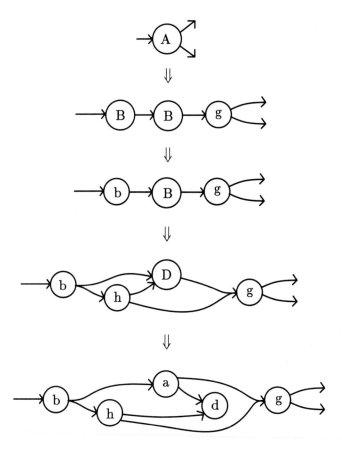

Figure 10.5 Derivation sequence for the graph of Figure 10.3 using the grammar of Figure 10.4 with starting type A.

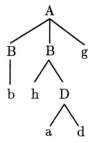

Figure 10.6 Derivation tree corresponding to the derivation in Figure 10.5.

flow-graph grammar. Figure 10.7 illustrates the basic features of the latter two translations (further details can be found in [42]).

In translating a plan to a flow graph, each operation and test box in the plan becomes a node of the corresponding type and number of ports in the flow graph. Data-flow arcs are translated directly to edges in the graph. Control-flow arcs, however, are not translated to edges in the graph, due to their lack of canonical form (see the discussion in Section 3.4). Instead, control information is encoded in the attributes of the graph. In particular, each node has a *control environment* attribute, whose value specifies when it is executed in relation to when other nodes are executed. Nodes translated from test boxes also specify a pair of subenvironments corresponding to the truth and falsity of their test condition.

Join boxes in plans are not translated to nodes in the graph. Instead, data-flow edges are allowed to fan-in. The information encoded in join specifications, namely, which data flow is used in which control environment, is translated into attributes of the fan-in node.

The cliché library is translated into a graph grammar in two conceptual steps. First, each plan definition is translated into a rule in which the node on the left side has the plan's name as its type and the right side is the plan's graph translation. For example, the first rule in Figure 10.7 is the translation of the hash-table-retrieve plan. Using this rule when parsing a flow graph amounts to recognizing the hash-table-retrieve cliché in a program.

Second, each overlay in the library is translated into a simple grammar rule with single nodes on both the left and right sides. (Note that the left side of the overlay becomes the right side of the rule and the right side of the overlay becomes the left side of the rule.) The mapping between the input and output ports of the nodes on the two sides of the grammar rule is derived from the overlay's correspondence links. For example, the second rule in Figure 10.7 is the translation of the overlay at the top. Using this rule when parsing a flow graph amounts to reconstructing a design decision.

Plans are encoded as individual grammar rules (instead of having a single rule for each overlay) for two reasons. First, there can be plans in the library that are not used in any overlay. Second, some overlays, such as optimizations, have plans on both sides, whereas a grammar rule must have a single node on one side. (Additional mechanisms in the Recognizer handle such overlays by interleaving expansion steps with reduction steps during the parsing process.)

Flow-Graph Parsing

The parsing algorithm used in the Recognizer is a generalization of context-free string parsing. The following is a simplified description of the algorithm (see [43] for more details).

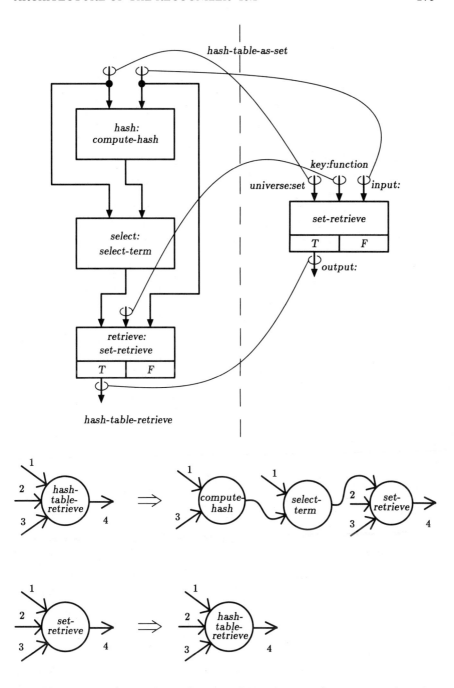

Figure 10.7 An overlay and its translation into graph grammar rules.

The parsing algorithm deterministically simulates the behavior of a non-deterministic stack-based parser. The simulation essentially allows several graph parsers to run in parallel, each eventually coming up with a different guess as to the derivation of the input. All possible parses of the input are obtained by passing a *read head* over the input graph in one pass—scanning each node and edge exactly once. When a node is scanned by the read head, the algorithm generates all reachable configurations of all parsers. The reachable configurations are recorded in lists of *items*. Each item represents a parser that is attempting to match the right side of some grammar rule to some portion of the input graph. As the read head is stepped ahead in the input graph, the corresponding read heads are stepped ahead in the items. When a nonterminal is reached, a separate subitem is activated for each grammar rule that derives that nonterminal. Each item keeps a list of pending calls to subitems and a list of items to return to when its own parser finishes.

Because this algorithm is agenda-based (it works by consulting and updating item lists), its behavior can be controlled by altering the item lists. We intend to take advantage of this architecture to extend the parser in two ways. Recognition of code that nearly matches a cliché can be supported by restarting failed items. Users can guide the recognition process by pruning unpromising items off of item lists.

The parsing algorithm just described is polynomial in the size of the input and the grammar. Therefore, cliché recognition is possible in polynomial time. However, in the simple form presented, the algorithm can parse a program *only* if it is completely derivable from the given grammar. Unfortunately, most programs contain nonclichéd computation in addition to clichéd computation.

What is needed is an algorithm that will recognize all of the subparts of a program that are clichéd. This can be done by extending the basic algorithm in the following two ways. However, it must be realized that the extended algorithm essentially has to solve the subgraph isomorphism problem. Since this problem is known to be NP-complete, it comes as no surprise that the extended algorithm no longer runs in polynomial time.

First, to recognize clichés in the midst of unrecognizable code, the parser must be able to ignore indeterminate amounts of both leading and trailing input that is unparsable. To allow for unparsable leading input, a read head is started not only at the leftmost edge of the input graph, but also at every possible intermediate read head position in the graph. Unparsable trailing input is trivially handled by allowing items to finish before the input graph is totally scanned.

Second, every nonterminal in the grammar is considered as a possible starting type for a derivation. This allows for the possibility of partially reconstructing the design of a program, i.e., recognizing only the lower-level clichés, but not how they are being used together.

10.2   Examples of the Recognizer's Abilities

The preceding sections have described the algorithms and representations used by the Recognizer. In this section, we present several examples of the current Recognizer in action. These examples illustrate how the algorithms and representations address the difficulties in automating cliché recognition described in the bulleted list on page 173.

To begin, Figure 10.8 shows the derivation produced by the Recognizer for the TABLE-LOOKUP program in Figure 10.1. The full grammar used in this example is too large to be shown here. However, most of the clichés used have been introduced earlier (see the List of Clichés on page 231).

The root of the derivation is the set-retrieve specification, which is the highest-level description of the program. The first step in the derivation corresponds to the overlay of Figure 10.7. In this step, the set is implemented as a hash table (a sequence of sets, called *buckets*). The nonterminals below hash-table-retrieve are the types of the parts of the hash-table-retrieve plan: compute-hash (given a hash table and a key, compute the index of

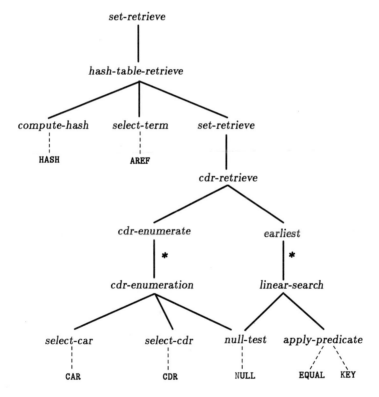

Figure 10.8 Derivation produced by the Recognizer for the programs in Figures 10.1 and 10.9.

the corresponding bucket set), select-term (select the term of a sequence corresponding to a given index), and the recursive set-retrieve operation on the selected bucket.

The next level in the derivation represents the decision to implement the buckets of the hash table as Lisp lists. This means that the recursive set-retrieve specification is implemented by the cdr-retrieve plan. The nonterminals below cdr-retrieve are the types of the parts of this plan: cdr-enumerate (produce the sequence of elements of a Lisp list) and earliest (find the first term in a sequence satisfying a given predicate). These two input/output specifications are the temporal abstractions, respectively, of cdr-enumeration and linear-search. (Steps in a derivation involving temporal abstraction are marked with an asterisk.) Cdr-enumeration and linear-search are then expanded into nonterminals for their respective parts. Note the sharing of the null-test.

Finally, the dashed lines at the fringe of the derivation tree are links to identifiers in the source code, created during the translation process to facilitate documentation generation.

Syntactic Variation

Figure 10.9 illustrates the Recognizer's ability to deal with syntactic variation in the input program. A detailed comparison of the program in this

```
(DEFUN R (L X &AUX B)
  (SETQ B (AREF L (H X L)))
  (PROG (E)
LP (WHEN (NULL B) (RETURN NIL))
   (SETQ E (CAR B))
   (COND ((EQUAL (K E) X) (RETURN E))
         (T (SETQ B (CDR B))
            (GO LP)))))
```

⇓

```
R is an associative retrieval operation.
   If there is an element of the set L with key X,
     then that element is returned; otherwise NIL is returned.
   The key function is K.
The set L is implemented as a hash table.
   The hashing function is H.
A bucket B of the hash table L is implemented as a list.
   The elements of the list B are enumerated.
   Linear search is used to find the first element of the
     list B whose key is equal to X.
```

Figure 10.9 A syntactic variation of the program in Figure 10.1 and the corresponding documentation produced by the Recognizer.

figure with the original TABLE-LOOKUP program in Figure 10.1 (page 172) shows many syntactic differences, such as different variable names (L versus TABLE), different control primitives (PROG and GO versus LOOP), and radically different syntactic trees. Nevertheless, due to the fact that both of these programs have the same surface plan, the Recognizer produces the identical derivation (Figure 10.8) and therefore the identical documentation (except identifiers) in both cases.

Unrecognizable Code

Figure 10.10 illustrates the Recognizer's ability to deal with unrecognizable code. RIGHTP is a somewhat contrived program, which checks if its three arguments could be the lengths of the sides of a right triangle within some tolerance. This program contains occurrences of two clichés defined earlier—equality-within-epsilon (Figure 4.2) and squaring (Figure 7.1)—in the midst of other unrecognizable code.

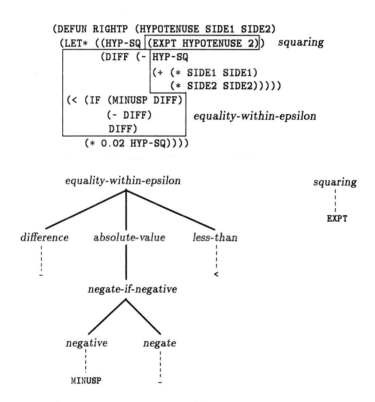

Figure 10.10 Recognizing occurrences of the equality-within-epsilon and squaring clichés amidst other unrecognizable code.

The derivation produced by the Recognizer for this example (see Figure 10.10) consists of two disjoint trees, with nonterminals corresponding to the recognized clichés at the roots. The addition and multiplication operations in the code for RIGHTP are not part of any recognized cliché.

Implementation Variation

Figure 10.11 illustrates the Recognizer's ability to deal with implementation variation in the input program. The program in Figure 10.11 is similar to the original TABLE-LOOKUP program, except that the buckets of the hash table are sorted Lisp lists. Given the same grammar as used in Figure 10.8, with additional rules describing the implementation of set-retrieve on sorted Lisp lists (using a plan named sorted-cdr-retrieve), the Recognizer produces the derivation shown in Figure 10.12 for the version of TABLE-LOOKUP in Figure 10.11. Note that the top three levels of this derivation are the same as in Figure 10.8. This causes the first seven lines of the documentation generated in Figure 10.11 to be the same as in Figure 10.1.

```
(DEFUN TABLE-LOOKUP (TABLE INPUT)
  (LET ((BUCKET (AREF TABLE (HASH INPUT TABLE))))
    (LOOP
      (IF (NULL BUCKET) (RETURN NIL))
      (LET* ((ENTRY (CAR BUCKET)))
            ((Y (KEY ENTRY))))
        (COND ((STRING> Y INPUT) (RETURN NIL))
              ((EQUAL Y INPUT) (RETURN ENTRY)))
        (SETQ BUCKET (CDR BUCKET)))))
```

$$\Downarrow$$

```
TABLE-LOOKUP is an associative retrieval operation.
  If there is an element of the set TABLE with key INPUT,
    then that element is returned; otherwise NIL is returned.
  The key function is KEY.
The set TABLE is implemented as a hash table.
  The hashing function is HASH.
A bucket BUCKET of the hash table TABLE is implemented
as a sorted list.
  The elements of the sorted list BUCKET are enumerated.
  The iteration is terminated when an element of the sorted
    list BUCKET is found whose key Y is greater than INPUT.
  Linear search is used to find the first element of the
    sorted list BUCKET whose key Y is equal to INPUT.
  The sorting relation on keys is STRING>.
```

Figure 10.11 An implementation variation of the program in Figure 10.1, in which the buckets of the hash table are sorted lists.

Noncontiguousness

The use of the Plan Calculus in the Recognizer also addresses the difficulty of noncontiguousness, i.e., parts of a cliché being scattered throughout the text of a program. For example, even though the CAR, CDR, and NULL steps of the cdr-enumeration cliché are separated by unrelated expressions in the source code in Figure 10.11, they become neighboring nodes in the flow-graph representation.

Other systems that recognize clichés in programs (e.g., PROUST [116] and PUDSY [126]) typically operate directly on the programming-language syntax. This limits the variability and complexity of the clichés that can be recognized because these systems must wrestle directly with syntactic variations, typically performing source-to-source transformations to twist the code into a recognizable form. Most of these systems's effort is therefore expended dealing with the syntax of the program, rather than concentrating on its semantic content. In addition, noncontiguousness poses a serious problem for text-based approaches.

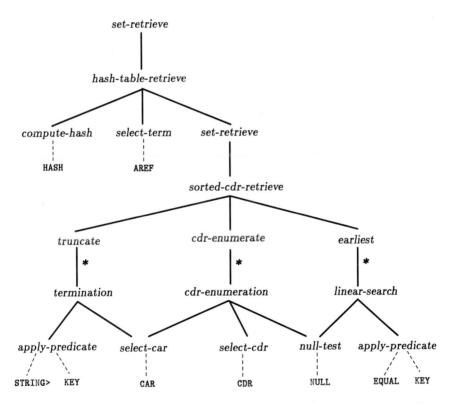

Figure 10.12 Derivation produced by the Recognizer for the program in Figure 10.11.

Overlapping Implementations

Figures 10.13 and 10.14 illustrate the Recognizer's ability to deal with over-lapping implementations in the input program. The grammar for this example includes rules for implementing the list-max (and list-min) specifications by enumerating the elements of the list and accumulating the maximum (or minimum) element seen thus far.

The MAX-MIN program in Figure 10.13 is a simple inefficient program for computing both the maximum and minimum elements of a given list, which could be straightforwardly generated from the cliché library by implementing the list-max and list-min specifications separately. It is inefficient because it enumerates the given list twice.

The optimized version of this program in Figure 10.14 enumerates the given list only once, i.e., there is an overlap between the implementations of list-max and list-min. This overlap is evident in the derivation produced by the Recognizer for this program, wherein the cdr-enumerate nonterminal is shared between the two subtrees below list-max and list-min.

Note that min-accumulate and max-accumulate used in this example are specializations of the accumulate specification defined in Section 5.5, wherein the op input is a function that returns, respectively, the greater or lesser of its two arguments. Min-accumulation and max-accumulation are the corresponding specializations of the accumulation plan.

The derivation in Figure 10.14 also illustrates a kind of partial recog-nition, in which a derivation does not have a single root. Since there is no single specification in the cliché library for computing both the maxi-

```
(DEFUN MAX-MIN (L)
  (VALUES (LIST-MAX L) (LIST-MIN L)))

(DEFUN LIST-MAX (L)
  (LET ((MAX MOST-NEGATIVE-FIXNUM))
    (LOOP
      (IF (NULL L) (RETURN MAX))
      (LET ((N (CAR L)))
        (IF (> N MAX) (SETQ MAX N)))
      (SETQ L (CDR L)))))

(DEFUN LIST-MIN (L)
  (LET ((MIN MOST-POSITIVE-FIXNUM))
    (LOOP
      (IF (NULL L) (RETURN MIN))
      (LET ((N (CAR L)))
        (IF (< N MIN) (SETQ MIN N)))
      (SETQ L (CDR L)))))
```

Figure 10.13 Unoptimized Common Lisp program that computes the maximum and minimum elements of a nonempty list of integers.

mum and minimum elements of a given list, there is no nonterminal in the grammar than can be the root of the derivation. It seems reasonable in this example that the library need not include such trivial combinations of specifications. In general, a derivation with multiple roots indicates either that the top-level structure of the program is idiosyncratic or just that the relevant cliché is not in the library.

Finally, note that this is not an example of unrecognizable code. All of the code in the example program (exclusive of connective tissue primitives, as usual) is accounted for in one of the derivation's two parts.

```
(DEFUN MAX-MIN (L)
  (LET ((MAX MOST-NEGATIVE-FIXNUM)
        (MIN MOST-POSITIVE-FIXNUM))
    (LOOP
      (IF (NULL L) (RETURN (VALUES MAX MIN)))
      (LET ((N (CAR L)))
        (IF (> N MAX) (SETQ MAX N))
        (IF (< N MIN) (SETQ MIN N)))
      (SETQ L (CDR L)))))
```

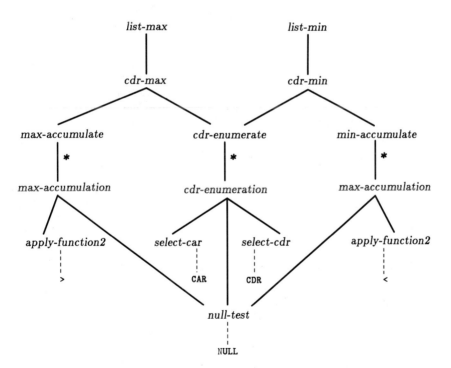

Figure 10.14 Optimized version of program in Figure 10.13 with derivation produced by the Recognizer.

10.3   Limitations and Future Work

The Recognizer system is still under development. In order for it to be a practical aid for software maintenance, the Recognizer will need to be improved and extended in a number of ways (see [45]).

First, the Recognizer (like KBEmacs) has been developed in parallel with—and lagging slightly behind—the evolution of the Plan Calculus. In particular, the Recognizer does not currently handle data plans or data overlays. Also, its treatment of destructive operations is not adequate. These deficiencies should be relatively straightforward to correct. We also plan to connect the Recognizer with the logical reasoning system (Cake), described in Section 11.1, for checking constraints and reasoning about attributes in the grammar.

Second, it is already clear from our experiments that the exhaustive, purely code-driven recognition approach used by the Recognizer will not be directly applicable to programs of commercial size and complexity. An exhaustive algorithmic search for clichés is too expensive.

A possible source of guidance to reduce this search is the many forms of existing documentation, such as comments and the mnemonic identifiers used for variables and procedures. (The PUDSY system discussed in [126], for example, uses variables names as hints to the clichés that might be present.) This kind of information is not currently used by the Recognizer because it is often incomplete and inaccurate. However, it could provide an important independent source of expectations about the purpose of a program and how it was designed. These expectations could then be confirmed, amended, and completed by checking them against the code.

In addition to a program and the cliché library, many other recognition systems are given a third input in the form of a specification (see PUDSY [126]), a set of goals (see PROUST [116]), or a model program that performs the same task (see TALUS [139]).

We envisage a hybrid approach to cliché recognition in the future, with two complementary processes: one documentation- and/or specification-driven (top-down) and the other code-driven (bottom-up). The heuristic top-down process will use the available documentation information to guide the code-driven process by generating expectations. The algorithmic bottom-up process will fill in the gaps in the documentation and verify or reject the expectations.

Learning New Clichés

Finally, and in the more distant future, we hope to explore how the Recognizer can be used to help automate the task of knowledge acquisition in the Programmer's Apprentice—in particular, how the Apprentice might automatically learn new clichés.

One idea is to have the Apprentice look at programs that implement familiar specifications using some parts that are unfamiliar. First, the Recognizer would be used to identify what specifications are being implemented by those parts of the program that are familiar. Working generatively from the given top-level specification of the program, it should also be possible to identify some lower-level specifications that are not accounted for by the recognized parts of the program. A learning procedure could then reasonably hypothesize that the unrecognizable part of the program is a new cliché for implementing the remaining specifications.

For example, consider how the Apprentice might learn a new way of deleting an association pair from an a-list (list of dotted pairs) in Lisp. The most abstract plan for implementing this operation has two steps, roughly, "find it" and "remove it." The "find it" step can be implemented by a combination of trailing-cdr-enumeration and linear-search, as in the BUCKET-DELETE program of Figure 2.6 on page 17. The only implementation of the "remove it" step in the initial library is splice-out, which uses RPLACD.

Now suppose that the Apprentice is presented with the program in Figure 10.15. After locating a pair with the "find it" step, this program uses RPLACA to change the car of the pair to NIL. Assuming that NIL is not a valid key, this causes the associated datum to be ignored in subsequent retrieval operations. (In certain special circumstances, this can be a very efficient method of removal.)

The Recognizer should be able to recognize all but the underlined RPLACA as part of the standard implementation of the "find it" step using cdr-enumeration and linear-search. Being told that FUNNY-DELETE correctly implements deletion from an a-list, the learning procedure could then hypothesize that the underlined portion of the program is a new way to implement the missing "remove it" step. (Once the focus of attention has been narrowed to this small part of the program, it might even be practical to formally prove that the new cliché is a correct implementation of the specifications of the "remove it" step.) Finally, the new cliché would need to be generalized somewhat from this example and installed at the appropriate place in the library.

```
(DEFUN FUNNY-DELETE (KEY ALIST)
  (LET ((L ALIST))
    (LOOP
      (IF (NULL L) (RETURN ALIST))
      (LET ((ENTRY (CAR L)))
        (WHEN (EQUAL (CAR ENTRY) KEY)
          (RPLACA ENTRY NIL)
          (RETURN ALIST)))
      (SETQ L (CDR L)))))
```

Figure 10.15 A version of DELETE that uses RPLACA for its "remove it" step.

Chapter 11

Requirements and Design

This chapter describes two demonstration systems we are developing that illustrate the capabilities of the Programmer's Apprentice in the areas of requirements and design. Before presenting target scenarios that define our research in these areas, we briefly review the automated reasoning system we are using as the basis for these demonstration systems.

Research Strategy

Viewed most simply (see Figure 11.1), the software-development process has, at one end, the desires of an end-user and, at the other end, a program that can be executed on a machine. The part of the software process closest to the user is typically called requirements acquisition; the part of the process nearest the machine is typically called implementation; the area in the middle is generally described as design. To achieve dramatic productivity improvements, the Programmer's Apprentice must eventually span this entire process. However, since this is a very large undertaking, we have adopted the strategy of building demonstrations of parts of the Apprentice, working inward from the two ends of Figure 11.1.

KBEmacs supports the right end of Figure 11.1. The Design Apprentice demonstration will extend this support into the realm of low-level design. The Requirements Apprentice demonstration will support the left end of the figure, in which the user's informal desires are captured and formalized.

Requirements   Design   Implementation

Figure 11.1 Incremental approach to the Programmer's Apprentice.

Because each demonstration effort is rooted at an external boundary, it could lead to a system that is useful by itself. The Design Apprentice will produce code, albeit not from as high-level a specification as ultimately desirable. The Requirements Apprentice will produce a complete and consistent requirements document, even if the rest of the software process is not yet machine-mediated. We want to emphasize, however, that this division into two efforts is purely a research strategy. We intend to connect the two demonstrations in the future to build a complete Apprentice.

General Issues in the Target Scenarios

Understanding what the Apprentice does and does not know is important when considering the upcoming scenarios. In each scenario, the Apprentice is assumed to have an intermediate level of prior knowledge.

On one hand, we assume that it is not practical for the Apprentice to have complete knowledge of an engineer's exact problem. In those few restricted application areas where complete knowledge is possible, you can construct a fully automatic program generator and dispense with the need for an assistant system. A key strength of the Apprentice is that it is applicable to a broad range of applications.

On the other hand, an essential goal of the Apprentice is to have a significant amount of knowledge in the problem domain. The productivity and reliability benefits of the Apprentice follow directly from the use of predefined and preverified clichés. Without such knowledge, the Apprentice cannot provide much leverage. A major focus of our research is ensuring that the Apprentice knows enough about a given area to be useful.

A second issue in the two target scenarios is the user interface. Considerably more work has to be done before a firm design for the Apprentice's interface can be developed. The interactions in the scenarios are intended to illustrate the major features of this interface, without being overly specific.

For example, the engineer's input in the scenarios in this chapter is shown in simple English. The Apprentice will not, however, support arbitrary English input. The most important feature of the interface language in the scenarios is not the degree of syntactic flexibility, but the use of a large vocabulary of clichés. Because the Apprentice is targeted at expert software engineers, we can assume that the engineer is conceptually familiar with the appropriate clichés. We expect that some combination of training, synonyms, spelling correction, and browsing the cliché library will get around the problem of needing to know the exact names of clichés.

Finally, note that several errors have intentionally been introduced into what the engineer says in each scenario. The errors chosen may not appear plausible to all readers. However, large numbers of errors are made during the software process—many of which look implausibly stupid in hindsight. The errors introduced in the scenarios were chosen to illustrate the ability of the Apprentice to detect and help correct errors.

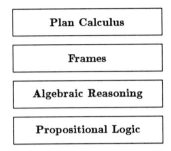

Figure 11.2 The layered architecture of Cake.

11.1   A Hybrid Reasoning System

The degree of automation that the Programmer's Apprentice can provide depends ultimately on its ability to reason about structured objects (programs, specifications, requirements) and their properties. As discussed in Section 6.3, the greatest limitation of KBEmacs is that it is not capable of general-purpose reasoning. In parallel with the completion of KBEmacs, we have worked intensively to rectify this problem by constructing a hybrid knowledge-representation and reasoning system called Cake (see [49]). Cake is nearly completed and will be an important basis for all our future work on the Apprentice.

Cake supports reasoning through a combination of special-purpose techniques and general-purpose logical reasoning. Special-purpose representations and algorithms are essential to avoid the combinatorial explosions that typically occur in general-purpose logical reasoning systems. On the other hand, logic-based reasoning is very valuable when used, under tight control, as the glue between inferences made in different special-purpose representations.

Figure 11.2 shows the architecture of Cake. Note that Cake combines special-purpose representations, such as frames and the Plan Calculus, with general-purpose logical and mathematical reasoning. Each layer of Cake builds on facilities provided by the more primitive layers. The facilities in these layers are motivated by the desired characteristics of the Apprentice. The following scenarios show specific examples of these facilities in action.

The propositional layer of Cake provides three principal facilities. First, it automatically performs simple one-step logical deductions (technically, unit propositional resolution). Placing tight limits on the kinds of deductions that are performed is essential to avoid combinatorial explosions.

Second, the propositional layer acts as a recording medium for dependencies (what is often called a truth-maintenance system; see [98]) and thus supports explanation (using the dependency records as a trace of the system's reasoning) and retraction (nonmonotonic reasoning). These facilities are motivated by the observation that when you delegate work to an assistant, you need to have accountability and the ability to recover from mistakes, in case it does not do what you expected.

Third, the propositional layer detects a certain class of shallow contradictions. Importantly, contradictions are represented explicitly in such a way that reasoning can continue with other information not involved in the contradiction. This feature is motivated by the desire for the Apprentice to support an evolutionary software process. In this kind of process, the engineer's knowledge is very often in an inconsistent state, particularly during the requirements acquisition phase.

The algebraic layer of Cake contains special-purpose decision procedures for equality (congruence closure), common algebraic properties of operators (such as commutativity, associativity, and transitivity), partial functions, and the algebra of sets. For example, the congruence closure algorithm determines whether or not terms are equal by substitution of equal subterms. The decision procedure for transitivity determines when elements of a binary relation follow by transitivity from other elements. The algebra of sets involves the theory of membership, subset, union, intersection, and complements. The algebraic layer of Cake also extends the basic propositional logic with the addition of typing (sorts) and limited quantificational facilities.

Equality reasoning is particularly important for the Apprentice because the formal semantics of the Plan Calculus makes heavy use of equality. Data-flow arcs in plans denote equalities between terms representing the source and destination points; correspondences in overlays also denote equalities. Other algebraic properties, such as transitivity, commutativity, etc., and type structures appear everywhere in the formal modeling of data structures.

The frames layer of Cake supports the standard frame notions of inheritance, slots, and instantiation. In the future, frame inheritance will be the primary organizing principle in the Apprentice's cliché library. A notable feature of Cake's frame system is that constraints between the slots of a frame can be reasoned about in a general way. This will help support the Apprentice's ability to incrementally acquire information in any order.

The Plan Calculus layer of Cake supports graph-theoretic manipulations of plan diagrams and overlay diagrams, such as tracing arcs. It also implements the formal semantics of the Plan Calculus, so that hybrid reasoning can take place involving both the structural properties of plans (as expressed in plan diagrams) and their associated logical properties (as expressed in preconditions, postconditions, and other logical annotations). In the semantics of the Plan Calculus, names of plans become predicate symbols, names of roles and overlays become function symbols, correspondences become equalities, data flow becomes a combination of equalities and a partial order, and control flow becomes a combination of an equivalence relation and a partial order.

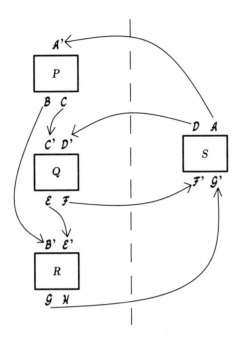

Figure 11.3 An overlay diagram illustrating teleological structure.

Teleological Structure

The implementation of the Plan Calculus in Cake will make it possible to make use of an important new kind of structure in plans: The *teleological structure* of a plan is the set of dependencies between the preconditions and postconditions of the specifications for its parts.

Figure 11.3 illustrates the concept of teleological structure with an abstract example. The figure shows an implementation overlay between a plan with three parts, P, Q, R, and an input/output specification, S. $\mathcal{A}$, $\mathcal{A}'$, $\mathcal{B}$, $\mathcal{B}'$, etc., are formulas in the preconditions and postconditions of the various specifications, as shown. Data- and control-flow arcs between P, Q, and R are omitted.

For the overlay in Figure 11.3 to be valid, each postcondition of S must be derivable from some postcondition of P, Q, or R; and each precondition of P, Q, and R must be derivable from either a postcondition of a preceding step or a precondition of S. (The possibility that a postcondition achieved by one step may be undone by a subsequent step is taken care of inside the logic through the use of situations.)

The pattern of these logical dependencies in Figure 11.3 provides a deeper characterization of each step's purpose than is provided by data- and control-flow structure alone. For example, we can see that P is essentially a preparatory step—all of its postconditions are prerequisites for later steps. Q and R, on the other hand, are main steps—each contributes to accomplishing part of the overall postconditions of S. (This vocabulary for describing steps of a plan in terms of their purpose is due to Goldstein; see [107].)

Exploring the use of teleological structure in analysis and synthesis is an important area for our work. For example, the teleological structure in Figure 11.3 suggests that step R could be replaced by a weaker specification, since postcondition $\mathcal{H}$ is not needed to accomplish any part of S.

11.2 Toward a Design Apprentice

The Design Apprentice demonstration will illustrate the key capabilities of the Apprentice in the realm of low-level design. It will go beyond KBEmacs by demonstrating the following capabilities:

- support for a declarative (specification-like) input language,

- detection of errors made by the engineer,

- automatic selection of low-level clichés.

The target design scenario concerns the detailed design of a device driver system. This application area was chosen for two reasons. First, device drivers are of significant practical importance. Second, they are a good example of the kind of application area in which the assistant approach is most appropriate—applications in which there are many similar programs, but in which each program is likely to have some unanticipated idiosyncrasy.

Design Clichés

The Apprentice's design knowledge (see Figure 11.4) will be composed of clichés for typical specifications, typical designs, typical hardware, and the links between these clichés. Examples of specification clichés in the device driver domain include *reading*, *writing*, *initializing*, *opening*, and *closing* a device. Each cliché is annotated with information about what parts and constraints are mandatory, likely, or possible.

Examples of design clichés in the device driver domain include *device driver* and its specializations, such as *printer driver* and *interactive display driver*. The device driver cliché is an abstract cliché, containing information that is common to all drivers. The printer driver cliché specifies, for example, that printer drivers support only writing operations and that complex output padding is sometimes required after characters that cause large movements of the print head. Examples of low-level algorithm clichés in the device driver domain include *semaphores*, *busy-wait*, and *watermark processing*.

Examples of hardware clichés that the Apprentice will know include *serial line unit*, *printer*, and *interactive display*. A serial line unit is a

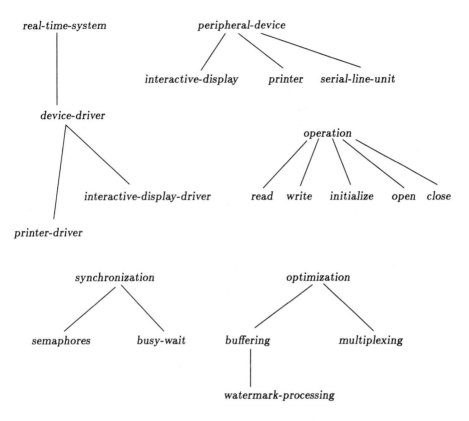

Figure 11.4 Clichés relevant to the design of device drivers.

standard bus interface used by many different kinds of hardware devices. It specifies a standard cluster of four buffer and control registers, which are used to operate the device.

Target Scenario for Design

Figures 11.5 and 11.6 show an imagined interaction between an engineer and the Apprentice in a low-level design task. This is the first part of a much longer target scenario (see [59]), in which the initial design is elaborated and changed by the engineer, with the assistance of the Apprentice. In the figures, the engineer's inputs follow the > prompts and responses from the Apprentice are in italics.

Figure 11.5 shows the initial specification provided by the engineer. This could be done interactively or prepared with a text editor and submitted all at once to the Apprentice. The specification consists of two parts. The first part describes the hardware (here an imaginary device called the K7). The second part describes a driver program for the K7.

> The "K7" is an interactive display where:
  The screen height is 4 lines.
  The screen width is 40 characters.
  The character mode is ASCII.
  Direct cursor positioning is not supported.
  The keyboard has three keys.
key		character
ACKNOWLEDGE	ACK	#O006
YES	Y	#O131
NO	N	#O116

  The bus interface is a standard SLU except that:
    Writing a 1 in Bit 1 of the XCSR initializes the device.
      Initializing the device blanks the screen and homes up the cursor.
      Initialization end is signaled the same as transmission end.
      Sending characters to the K7 and initializing the K7 cannot be
        done at the same time.

> The K7 driver is an interactive display driver where:
  Echoing is not supported
  Rubout handling is not supported.
  The basic software functions are:
    Supported: PUTC, WRITE & GETC.
    Ignored: OPEN & CLOSE.
    Not supported: READ & SEEK.
  The control codes are:
    :CLEAR - blanks the screen.
    :RESET - does a :CLEAR and flushes pending input.
    :LINE-NUMBER - returns the cursor line.
  The implementation guidelines are:
    1- Do no consing.
    2- Favor space efficiency.
    3- Defer error checking.

Figure 11.5 Target design scenario, part one, initial specification.

The specification of the K7 uses the cliché interactive display. The K7 specification contains both positive information, which describes how particular parts of this cliché are filled in (e.g., the screen height), and negative information, which states that some aspects of the cliché are not relevant (e.g., the K7 does not support direct cursor positioning).

The last five lines of the K7 specification make use of the serial line unit (SLU) cliché. The phrase "except that" indicates that the engineer is modifying the SLU cliché rather than just filling in its parts. The exception description makes use of a number of technical terms (e.g., XCSR, "initialize the device," and "blank the screen") that are defined for SLUs. This vocabulary makes it possible for the engineer to describe the exception succinctly.

The second part of the specification in Figure 11.5 concerns the driver program. As with the K7 specification, most of the specification describes how various parts of the relevant cliché are filled in (the cliché in this case is interactive display driver).

> Write code for the K7 driver.

Request for Advice: I do not know how to support :CLEAR.
Note:
  (1) :CLEAR *blanks the screen.*
  (2) The only K7 operation that blanks the screen is initialization.
Unfortunately:
  (3) Initializing the K7 homes up the cursor.
  (4) A device should not be initialized except by the INIT *function.*

> :CLEAR should home up the cursor.
> Support :CLEAR by initializing the device.

Request for Advice: I do not know how to support :LINE-NUMBER.
Note:
  (1) :LINE-NUMBER *returns the cursor line.*
  (2) No K7 operation returns the cursor line.

> Postpone.

Constraint Violation: There should be a lookahead operation.
Note: The following standard operations provide lookahead:
  (1) :ARE-CHARS-WAITING *returns* T *if there are pending input characters.*
  (2) :NUMBER-CHARS-WAITING *returns number of pending input characters.*
  (3) :PEEK *returns* NIL *if there are no pending input characters and
  returns the next character (without removing it from the input
  buffer) if a character is pending.*

> Use (2).

Figure 11.6 Target design scenario, part two, interactive dialog.

A particularly interesting part of the driver specification is the implementation guidelines section at the end. The Apprentice will use these
guidelines to decide which algorithms to pick when implementing the driver.
For example, the first two guidelines will cause the Apprentice to select algorithms that do no dynamic storage allocation and trade time for space. The
third guideline instructs the Apprentice to defer inclusion of error checking
code until after the prototype version of the driver is written and tested.
The key benefit of this postponement is not that it will save the Apprentice
coding time, but that it will save the engineer thinking time.

The interaction in Figure 11.6 illustrates that the Apprentice will be
able to detect and explain errors made by the engineer. The Apprentice will
be able to detect two kinds of errors: errors of omission (incompleteness)
and errors of commission (inconsistency). Incompleteness will be detected
using information in the cliché library. Inconsistency will be detected using
Cake's information propagation and contradiction detection facilities.

Incompleteness can be of two kinds. First, the specification may be
missing some expected information, which if provided, would allow the Apprentice to finish the implementation. In this case, the Apprentice will
request the needed information and proceed (see the interaction concerning :CLEAR in Figure 11.6). Second, the Apprentice might simply not have
enough knowledge to implement a given specification. In this case, the en-

gineer will be asked to provide specific implementation instructions (see the interaction concerning :LINE-NUMBER in Figure 11.6). Note that the engineer may postpone answering such a question. This enables the engineer to control the interaction.

Inconsistency can also be of two kinds. First, there may be inconsistency between different things the engineer says explicitly. Second, there may be inconsistency between what the engineer says and the knowledge contained in clichés (see the last interaction in Figure 11.6).

Once the problems involving :CLEAR and :LINE-NUMBER have been resolved, the engineer's input is complete enough for the Apprentice to generate executable code for the K7 driver. Exactly what this code will be like is discussed in detail in [59]. Here, suffice it to say that the central step in generating this code is choosing the right low-level clichés corresponding to the abstract clichés specified by the engineer. The Apprentice will be able to make these low-level design choices automatically based on the engineer's input and the intercliché information in the cliché library, using Cake's basic reasoning facilities.

11.3   Toward a Requirements Apprentice

The Requirements Apprentice demonstration will show how the Programmer's Apprentice can support the earliest part of the software process—requirements acquisition and analysis. This is a particularly important research area for two reasons. First, from the perspective of artificial intelligence, it is a good domain in which to pursue fundamental issues in knowledge acquisition. Second, from the perspective of software engineering, studies have indicated that errors in requirements are more costly than any other kind of error. Furthermore, requirements acquisition and analysis is not well supported by current software tools.

From Informal to Formal Descriptions

Several phases in the requirements acquisition process are worth distinguishing. The earliest phase usually takes the form of a "skull session," whose goal is to achieve consensus among a group of end-users about what they want. The requirements analyst relies on interpersonal skills in this phase. The end product of this phase is typically an *informal* description of the requirements.

Informal descriptions are characterized by, among other things, incompleteness, ambiguity, contradiction, mis-ordering of information, and the use of undefined terms. These characteristics are not (usually) due to laziness or incompetence. Informality is an essential characteristic of the human thought process. It is part of a powerful debugging strategy for dealing with complexity: Start with an almost-right description and then incrementally modify it until it is acceptable. Thus, dealing with informality in software requirements is not just a matter of being user-friendly—it is a fundamental necessity.

Most current work on software requirements tools focuses on validating *formal* descriptions (i.e., descriptions that obey a strict set of mathematical rules of form and content). The main goal of formal validation is to increase users's confidence that a given formal description actually corresponds to their desires. This can be done by applying simulation, symbolic execution, and various kinds of mathematical analysis. One thing that all of these methods have in common is that they assume the existence of a formal description to work on. None of them address the key question of how an informal description becomes a formal description in the first place.

In the area of requirements, the focus of the Apprentice will be on the transition from informal to formal descriptions. One of the goals of our research is to elaborate the initial characterization of informality given above and to develop strategies and heuristics for removing these features from informal descriptions.

Requirements Clichés

As part of our research on supporting requirements acquisition, we are codifying clichés in the area of software requirements (see Figure 11.7). Compared to implementation and design clichés, the range of clichés involved in software requirements is more open-ended. In principle, any part of the real world may be relevant to specifying a requirement. The Apprentice will be more or less useful in a given application to the extent that the relevant clichés have been codified.

The target requirements scenario concerns the requirements for a hypothetical library system (see [156] for a comparison with other approaches to the same example). Three examples of clichés in this area are *repository*, *information system*, and *tracking system*.

A repository is an entity in the physical world. The basic function of a repository is to ensure that items entering the repository will be available for later removal. There are a variety of physical constraints that apply to repositories. For example, since each item has a physical existence, it can be in only one place at a time and therefore must be either in the repository or not.

There are several kinds of repositories. Simple repositories merely take in items and then give them out. A more complex kind of repository supports the lending of items, which are expected to be returned. Another dimension of variation concerns the items themselves. The items may be unrelated or they may be grouped into classes. Example repositories include a storage warehouse (simple repository for unrelated items), a grocery store (simple repository for items grouped in classes), and a rental car agency (lending repository for items grouped in classes).

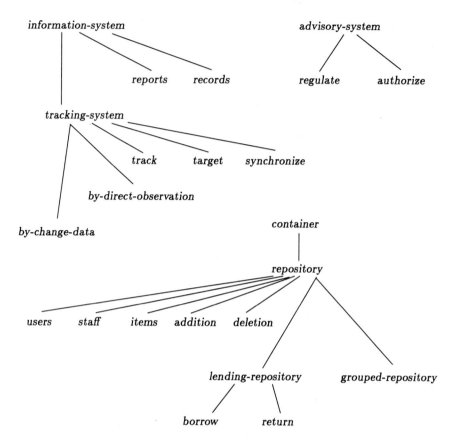

Figure 11.7 Part of a cliché library for software requirements.

In contrast to the repository cliché, the information system cliché describes a class of software systems rather than a class of physical objects. The intent of the information system cliché is to capture the commonality between, for example, personnel systems, bibliographic databases, and inventory control systems. Parts of an information system include an *information schema*, a set of *transactions* that can create/modify/delete the data, a set of *reports* that display parts of the data, *integrity constraints* on the data, a *staff* that manages the information system, and *users* that utilize the information system.

A tracking system is a specialized kind of information system that keeps track of the state of a physical object (called the *target*). The target object is assumed to have a (possibly complex) state and to be subject to various physical operations that can modify this state. The information in the tracking system describes the target object's state. The transactions modify this information to reflect changes in the target's state.

You'll get more out
of the Clydesdale Bank

Switch your Access
and Visa Cards

CB Clydesdale Bank

There are several kinds of tracking systems. A tracking system may follow several targets instead of just one. A tracking system may keep a history of the target's past states. A tracking system may operate based on direct observations of the target's state or based on observations of operations that modify the target's state. Finally, a tracking system may participate in controlling the operations on the target, rather than merely observing them. Example tracking systems include aircraft tracking systems (tracking multiple targets based on direct observations of their position) and inventory control systems (tracking a repository based on observations of operations that modify its contents).

Target Scenario for Requirements

The scenario in Figure 11.8 shows an imagined interaction between the Apprentice and a requirements analyst. This scenario is part of a larger scenario presented in [56]. In the figure, the analyst's inputs follow the > prompts, and responses from the Apprentice are in italics.

As can be seen from the form of the input, we are not trying to build a system to be used directly by the end-user. Rather, we are relying on the interpersonal skills of the analyst to facilitate the knowledge acquisition process.

The first four commands in Figure 11.8 begin the process of building a requirement by introducing the new terms *library* and *book*. Based on these four commands and the contents of the tracking system and repository clichés, the Apprentice will augment its internal model of the evolving requirement in a number of ways.

For example, since the state of a repository is the collection of items it contains (in this case, books), the Apprentice will use the constraints in the tracking system cliché to derive an information schema that provides fields for the three properties listed for books. Also based on the constraints in the tracking system cliché, an expectation will be created within the Apprentice that a set of transactions is to be defined corresponding to the typical operations on a repository.

Note that the new terms are far from fully defined at this point in the scenario. They are incomplete because many parts remain to be filled in. They are ambiguous because it is not yet clear which kind of tracking system is intended or which kind of repository a library is. Since incompleteness and ambiguity are inevitable during the early stages of constructing a requirement, the Apprentice refrains from complaining at this point. Rather, it will accept information and performs inferences on a catch-as-catch-can basis. However, if requested, the Apprentice will be able to provide a list of currently unresolved issues (see Figure 11.9) to guide the analyst in finishing the requirement.

The next four commands in Figure 11.8 begin the definition of the transactions to be supported by the database. The key terms in these commands

> Begin a requirement for a system called "LIBDB".
> LIBDB is a tracking system which tracks a "library".
> A library is a repository for "books".
> A book has the properties:
   title - a text string,
   author - a person's name,
   ISBN - a unique alphanumeric key.
> Display the transactions subsection.
> The "acquire" transaction tracks the addition of a book.
> The "checkout" transaction tracks the removal of a book.
> The "return" transaction is the inverse of checkout.

Problem: The return transaction is identical to the acquire transaction.

> Explain.

(1) The return transaction is identical to the acquire transaction.
Because:
   (2) The acquire transaction tracks the addition of a book.
   (3) The return transaction tracks the addition of a book.
   Because:
      (4) The checkout transaction tracks the removal of a book.
      (5) The return transaction is the inverse of the checkout transaction.

> Retract (4).
> The checkout transaction tracks the borrowing of a book.

Note: Assuming a library is a lending repository.

> The "retire" transaction tracks the removal of a book.
> The "purge" transaction tracks the removal of every copy of a book.

Note: The term every suggests that book is a class. If this is not the case, then the retire transaction is identical to the purge transaction.

> Redefine "book" to be a class.

Book is a class with properties:
   title - a text string,
   author - a person's name,
   ISBN - a unique alphanumeric key.

> A "copy" is an instance of a book.
> A copy has the property:
   copy number - a number unique within the class.
> Redefine transactions on a book to apply to a copy.

Redefining acquire, retire, checkout, and return.

Figure 11.8 Target requirements scenario.

are *addition* and *removal*—two of the standard operations supported by a repository.

The first command to trigger a response from the Apprentice is the analyst's attempt to define the *return* transaction. The Apprentice complains that, as currently defined, returning a book is identical to acquiring a book. (The detection of this problem will be supported by the equality reasoning facilities in Cake, in conjunction with a built-in bias that new terms should not be synonymous with old terms unless explicitly declared to be so.)

3.1.1.1 Checkout

The "checkout" transaction tracks the borrowing of a copy of a book.

INPUTS: ISBN number and copy number.

OUTPUTS: none.

PRECONDITIONS: The copy of the book uniquely identified by the
inputs must be in the roster of copies of books in the library.

EFFECT ON THE INFORMATION STORE: The input is borrowed from the
roster of copies of books in the library.

UNUSUAL EVENTS: If the input is not in the roster of copies of books
in the library, then the information system is inconsistent with the
state of the repository. A notation is made in the error log.

USAGE RESTRICTIONS: none.

Unresolved issues:
Should historical record keeping be added?
Should checking of user validity be added?
Should checking of staff member validity be added?

Figure 11.9 Requirements document fragment resulting from Figure 11.8.

Analysts will not have to deal with problems immediately—they will be
able to go on to other things leaving the problem pending. In Figure 11.8,
however, the analyst decides to deal with the problem right away. Studying the explanation generated by the Apprentice (which will be supported
using the dependency facilities of Cake), the analyst realizes that an error
was made in the definition of checkout. The analyst corrects the error by
redefining the checkout transaction in terms of borrowing.

The remaining portion of Figure 11.8 illustrates the detection of what
turns out to be a fundamental epistemological confusion on the part of the
analyst—between books as a class and books as instances. The analyst
decides that title, author, and ISBN are better thought of as properties of
a class of books, with each copy as an instance. Using the dependency
information maintained by Cake, the apprentice will be able to propagate
this conceptual reorganization throughout the requirement.

The principal result of creating a requirement using the Apprentice will
be an internal representation of the requirements as frames and plans in
Cake. This representation will eventually feed into the parts of the Apprentice concerned with design. In the meantime, however, this representation
can be used to answer queries and to generate various documents for the
requirements analyst, the end-user, and the system designer.

An example of the kind of document the Apprentice will be able to
generate is shown in Figure 11.9. As in the case of natural language input
to the Apprentice, the syntactic aspects of good English are not the key
concern here. What is important is deciding *what* to say by, for example,
choosing the appropriate level of detail.

Chapter 12

The Next Generation of CASE

The idea of computer-aided software engineering—applying the power of computers to the software process itself—has been around since the first programmers realized that programming is hard. Rapid early progress came from the introduction of assemblers and then high-level language compilers in the 1950s and early 60s. Each move to a higher level language resulted in a dramatic decrease in the program size needed for a given problem. This in turn yielded dramatic improvements in productivity by simplifying every aspect of the software process.

Stepping up again to a very high-level language has been a goal of computer science since the late 1960s. Unfortunately, there has been little success thus far in automatically compiling such languages into efficient machine code. Overall, although there have been a number of important advances in general-purpose programming languages over the past 20 years, none has had as dramatic an effect as the introduction of high-level languages.

With diminishing returns from work on general-purpose programming languages, two less general approaches to automation came to the fore in the 1970s and early 80s: domain-specific and software-task-specific support. Given a sufficiently narrow application domain, such as report generation or employee payroll, it has proven quite feasible to develop a specialized very high-level language (often called a fourth-generation language) and a program generator that compiles it into efficient machine code. It has also proven feasible to develop tools that (partially) automate specific software tasks, such as program testing or constructing a consistent version of a system.

More recently, a new movement has developed under the rubric of CASE (Computer-Aided Software Engineering). In addition to increasing

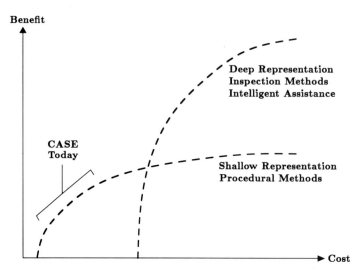

Figure 12.1 A comparison of current CASE technology (lower curve) with the technology developed for the Programmer's Apprentice (upper curve).

the power of individual software tools, CASE emphasizes the enterprise-wide integration of software support based on a central on-line repository for software objects, including requirements, designs, and source code. A general-purpose and comprehensive CASE environment supporting the integrated evolution of all software objects would be an advance as dramatic and pervasive as the move to higher level languages.

Our view of the current status of CASE is indicated by the lower curve in Figure 12.1. Rapid progress is being made. However, the day is approaching when the power of CASE tools will be limited by the technology now employed. Some tools, such as program editors, are close to these limits already. Other aspects of CASE, such as repositories, still have room for large improvement using current technology. (For a sampling of current developments in CASE, see [93, 104].)

From its start, a central goal of the Programmer's Apprentice project has been to develop technology for powerful computer support of software engineering. To date, the project has focused on how to provide intelligent assistance to an individual engineer using deeper representations and more knowledge than current CASE tools, rather than on the problems of integration and communication in a large enterprise. Although the technology we have developed has a significantly larger minimum cost (both in terms of implementing it and using it), it has the potential, as discussed below, of supporting a generation of CASE tools significantly more powerful than those that can be supported with current CASE technology (see the upper curve in Figure 12.1).

12.1   Limits of Current Technology

Essentially all current CASE tools share a common technological approach:
They use a *shallow representation* of software objects and manipulate this
representation using *procedural methods*.

Shallow Representation

For a CASE tool to operate on a given software object, it must represent
the object on line in some fashion. The choice of representation involves
a trade-off between the power of the representation and the cost of implementing it. Generally speaking, the shallower a representation, i.e., the
less information it represents explicitly, the easier it is to implement. However, the less explicitly information is represented, the harder it is for a
tool to manipulate it. For instance, it is next to impossible for a tool
that represents requirements merely as textual documents to detect logical
inconsistencies in them.

Many current CASE tools operate at the level of text, parse trees, or diagrams annotated with text. These relatively shallow representations leave
much information either implicit or totally absent. For instance, representing a program as a parse tree makes its syntactic structure explicit, but
leaves implicit the data- and control-flow structure of the underlying algorithm. As a result, the typical syntax-directed program editor provides
good support for syntactic changes. Single commands suffice to add or
delete syntactic units and the syntactic correctness of the result can be
checked. However, even a conceptually simple algorithmic change typically
requires a sequence of disconnected syntactic edits. Also, the editor has no
basis for checking the algorithmic correctness of the result.

Some CASE tools for systems analysis use a deeper level of representation. Rather than merely manipulating diagrams, they represent the
underlying information using data-dictionary and entity-relationship technology. This allows more powerful editors to be developed and a deeper
level of consistency checking.

In general, it makes sense to represent only as much information as a
given tool can take advantage of. However, current tools will eventually
reach the limits of what they can do with the representations they use.

Procedural Methods

For a CASE tool to support a given software task, it must have knowledge
about the task. In current tools, this knowledge is almost exclusively procedural. Without making use of any explicit representation of task knowledge,
the tool is simply written so that it performs the task.

Procedural methods have the advantage of enabling you to get off to a
quick start. It is typically easy to support the first round of capabilities.

However, as more and more features are added, procedural systems become progressively more difficult to modify. For example, it is relatively easy to write a program generator for a simple fourth-generation language. However, as the language is expanded, the program generator rapidly balloons into an unmaintainable monster.

12.2   Programmer's Apprentice Technology

The technology underlying the Programmer's Apprentice can be summarized in terms of three principles: *deep representation, inspection methods,* and *intelligent assistance.* Application of these principles makes it possible to overcome the limitations just discussed.

Deep Representation

The Programmers Apprentice captures algorithmic information using the Plan Calculus, described in Chapters 3–5. As compared to program text or parse trees, the Plan Calculus makes data flow, control flow, and other algorithmic features more explicit. This enables the development of a program editor (KBEmacs) in which a single command suffices to make changes that would require multiple commands in a syntax-directed editor.

To represent nonalgorithmic aspects of software, such as performance requirements, the Apprentice uses standard artificial-intelligence knowledge-representation and reasoning techniques. For example, the Requirements Apprentice, described in Section 11.3, will use frames and constraints to detect inconsistency and incompleteness in informal requirements descriptions.

An important benefit of deeper representations is that they allow a deeper level of integration between tools. A shared semantic framework enables the incremental exchange of information between tasks necessary to support a more evolutionary software process. For example the Plan Calculus is used for both analysis and synthesis tasks in the Programmer's Apprentice and enables the full exchange of information between them.

Inspection Methods

A key insight underlying the Programmer's Apprentice is that software engineers, like engineers in other disciplines, seldom reason from first principles. Rather, they rely whenever possible on their experience with standard building blocks—what we call *clichés.* Given knowledge of the clichés in a particular application area, it is possible to perform many software engineering tasks *by inspection,* as described in Chapter 2. For example, in analysis by inspection, properties of a program are deduced by recognizing occurrences of clichés and referring to their known properties.

An important advantage of inspection methods is that clichés lend themselves to declarative (nonprocedural) representation. This has two effects. First, the same library of clichés can be used in support of more than one task, e.g., implementation and recognition. Second, declarative knowledge is easier to extend. Formalizing suites of clichés and integrating them into an existing library is not trivial. However, it is much easier than modifying a collection of complex interacting procedures.

Chapters 7 and 8 show the use of low-level algorithmic clichés, such as linear search and chain enumeration, in program implementation. Chapter 10 shows the use of similar clichés in program recognition. Section 11.2 shows the use of domain-specific clichés, such as device driver and serial line unit, in program design. Section 11.3 shows the use of high-level system clichés, such as information system and tracking system, in requirements engineering.

Intelligent Assistance

Even with deep representation and inspection methods, it will not be possible (at least in the foreseeable future) to totally replace software engineers. However, the next generation of CASE can, like the Programmer's Apprentice, aim for intelligent assistance.

Rather than simply accepting and executing commands, an intelligent assistant would check the reasonableness of decisions, fill in missing details, and request advice about how to carry out complex operations. For example, in the design and requirements scenarios in Chapter 11, the Apprentice complains about problems in the engineer's input, fills in missing details using information in the cliché library, and accepts implementation advice. These abilities can contribute to both an engineer's productivity and the reliability of the final software product.

Another hallmark of an intelligent assistant is the ability to explain its actions and decisions in terms that an engineer can understand. This allows engineers to check what the tool has done. It also allows the tool to describe the problems it has encountered when it asks for advice.

Using inspection methods makes it easier for the engineer to understand what the tool is doing and for the tool to understand advice given by the engineer. The names of clichés provide the essential vocabulary for communication between the engineer and the assistant, just as they form the essential vocabulary for communication between human engineers.

12.3   Examples

In the following, we use four classes of current CASE tools to illustrate how the principles above can be applied to the next generation of CASE.

Systems Analysis

At the heart of all current systems analysis tools is some kind of diagram editor. Engineers can interactively draw boxes and arrows on the screen, with various annotations on them indicating the type of data, type of operation, etc. The editor checks that the diagrams are well formed with respect to the syntactic rules of one of the standard diagramming methodologies.

The information content of the hierarchical box-and-arrow diagrams used in systems analysis tools is typically represented at a fairly deep level. However, these tools could benefit from more emphasis on clichés and inspection methods.

The next generation of diagram editors for systems analysis could improve on current diagram editors in the same way that KBEmacs improves on current program editors. In current diagram editors, the engineer constructs a system description either from scratch or by cutting and pasting from existing diagrams, both of which can be tedious and error-prone. A library of systems analysis clichés would be more than just a collection of already constructed diagrams. Each systems analysis cliché would be a schematized diagram with associated defaults, constraints, and explanations. The library of clichés would be organized taxonomically. As in KBEmacs, the editor would keep track of how a diagram was constructed out of clichés and support later modification in the same terms.

It may also be useful to automatically recognize occurrences of clichés in existing diagrams, similar to how the Recognizer described in Chapter 10 recognizes occurrences of clichés in plans. The knowledge associated with clichés in the library may then be applied to existing diagrams.

Looking further into the future, it will be possible to deepen the representations used in systems analysis in the direction of more general logical reasoning, which could be applied, for example, to automating trade-off analysis and checking for deeper logical inconsistency and incompleteness. Intelligent assistance in some of these areas is illustrated in the Requirements Apprentice scenario in Section 11.3.

Program Construction

A variety of current CASE tools assist with program construction, including editors, cross-referencers, program generators, and component libraries. In general, these tools operate at the level of source code, sometimes augmented with parse trees, compiler symbol tables, and the like.

Moving to a representation like the Plan Calculus would increase the power of all these tools. For example, cross-referencing could be more accurate: When searching for where a variable is set, one could ignore appearances of the variable that were not in the relevant control-flow path.

Program construction tools could also benefit from the introduction of inspection methods, as illustrated by KBEmacs in Chapters 6–9. In addition, using the Plan Calculus as a representation for algorithmic clichés supports more abstract and canonical component libraries, as compared to using subroutines or program templates.

Looking further into the future, it will be possible to deepen the representations used in program construction in the direction of making design decisions explicit, as illustrated in the Design Apprentice scenario in Section 11.2.

Testing

Software testing comprises two major subtasks: defining test cases and executing them. Deeper representations (such as data and control flow) and inspection methods can help in both of these areas.

Current testing tools already make use of control-flow representations to check the *coverage* of a set of test cases, i.e., whether each path through a program is executed by some test case. Unfortunately, even when using data-flow representations, it is in general not possible to automatically construct test cases with complete coverage. Inspection methods provide a complementary approach. There are testing clichés, just as there are requirements, design, and implementation clichés. For example, it is well known that for buffered input/output routines it is a good idea to test what happens when the buffer gets full. An intelligent assistant for testing would suggest clichéd test cases based on the design of a program.

The major difficulty in executing test cases is deciding which ones to run after a design change when it is not feasible to run them all. A deeper representation would help here also: If test cases are indexed according to the design features they test, rather than just the parts of the code they exercise, it would be easier to select the most relevant tests. A modest step in this direction is demonstrated in [63].

Reengineering

The term *reengineering* has come into use recently to describe the application of CASE to existing software, i.e., software not necessarily produced using CASE tools in the first place. Approaching this problem using shallow representation and procedural methods has led to the development of a number of useful capabilities.

For example, program restructuring tools are now generally available for a number of languages. These tools, operating mostly on the level of program syntax, improve the understandability of source code by replacing go-to instructions with if-then-else, do-while, and other structured programming constructs. Other reengineering tools help a programmer understand existing software by displaying the static or dynamic structure of the code graphically and allowing the programmer to easily navigate within it.

The power of these tools to improve understandability could be increased by using an explicit representation of algorithmic structure, such as the Plan Calculus. For example, given a complete data- and control-flow analysis, it would be possible to eliminate not only dead (unexecutable) code, but also code that was executed but whose results were not used. Needless shuffling of values among intermediate variables could similarly be eliminated. It is likely that the internal operation of restructuring tools would also be simplified by using such a representation, as compared to operating directly on the source code.

A much deeper level of reengineering is to reconstruct a program's design using a library of clichés, as illustrated by the Recognizer described in Chapter 10. Once an on-line representation of its design has been obtained, an existing program can be modified at the level of design decisions, just as if it had originally been developed using a design-level CASE tool.

Totally automatic design reconstruction is not likely to be practical for programs of realistic size. Therefore, an intelligent assistance approach will be necessary. The software engineer will need to be involved in the process both to reduce the large search required and to provide specification information, such as the expected range of input values, that is missing from the source code.

Annotated Project Bibliography

The following is an annotated bibliography of the major publications produced within the Programmer's Apprentice project. For ease of reference, the publications are grouped by topic.

The Programmer's Apprentice

The following collection of references charts the general course of the Programmer's Apprentice project from its inception. The basic philosophy underlying the Apprentice was first articulated in [1, 2], which are adapted from Rich and Shrobe's 1975 master's thesis. The evolution of the philosophy since that time can be traced through a sequence of memos [3, 4, 5, 6, 7] and overview articles [8, 9, 10, 11, 12, 13]. Surveys that place the Programmer's Apprentice in the context of other research in automatic programming and intelligent software tools can be found in [14, 15, 16].

[1] C. Rich and H. E. Shrobe. Initial report on a Lisp Programmer's Apprentice. Technical Report 354, MIT Artificial Intelligence Lab., December 1976. Master's thesis.

[2] C. Rich and H. E. Shrobe. Initial report on a Lisp Programmer's Apprentice. *IEEE Trans. on Software Engineering*, 4(6):456–467, November 1978. Reprinted in D. Barstow, E. Sandewall, and H. Shrobe, editors, *Interactive Programming Environments*, pages 443–463, McGraw-Hill, New York, NY, 1984.

[3] C. Rich, H. E. Shrobe, R. C. Waters, G. J. Sussman, and C. E. Hewitt. Programming viewed as an engineering activity. Memo 459, MIT Artificial Intelligence Lab., January 1978.

[4] R. Rich, H. E. Shrobe, and R. C. Waters. Computer aided evolutionary design for software engineering. Memo 506, MIT Artificial Intelligence Lab., January 1979.

[5] H. E. Shrobe, R. C. Waters, and G. J. Sussman. A hypothetical monolog illustrating the knowledge underlying program analysis. Memo 507, MIT Artificial Intelligence Lab., January 1979.

[6] C. Rich and R. C. Waters. Abstraction, inspection and debugging in programming. Memo 634, MIT Artificial Intelligence Lab., June 1981.

[7] C. Rich and R. C. Waters. Intelligent assistance for program recognition, design, optimization, and debugging. Memo 1100, MIT Artificial Intelligence Lab., January 1989.

[8] C. Rich, H. E. Shrobe, and R. C. Waters. An overview of the Programmer's Apprentice. In *Proc. 6th Int. Joint Conf. Artificial Intelligence*, pages 827–828, Tokyo, Japan, August 1979.

[9] C. Rich and R. C. Waters. Computer aided evolutionary design for software engineering. *ACM SIGART Newsletter*, (76):14–15, April 1981. Progress report.

[10] R. C. Waters. The Programmer's Apprentice. In *Proc. CYBERSOFT-80: Int. Symp. on Cybernetics and Software*, pages 11–35, Namur, Belgium, September 1981.

[11] R. C. Waters. Programmer's Apprentice. In A. Barr and E. A. Feigenbaum, editors, *The Handbook of Artificial Intelligence*, Vol. II , pages 343–349. Morgan Kaufmann, Los Altos, CA, 1982.

[12] C. Rich. Programming apprentices. In P. H. Winston and K. Prendergast, editors, *The AI Business: The Commercial Uses of Artificial Intelligence*, pages 121–132. MIT Press, Cambridge, MA, 1984.

[13] C. Rich and R. C. Waters. The Programmer's Apprentice: A research overview. *IEEE Computer*, 21(11):10–25, November 1988.

[14] C. Rich and R. C. Waters, editors. *Readings in Artificial Intelligence and Software Engineering*. Morgan Kaufmann, Los Altos, CA, 1986.

[15] C. Rich and R. C. Waters. Artificial intelligence and software engineering. In W.E.L. Grimson and R. S. Patil, editors, *AI in the 1980's and Beyond: An MIT Survey*, pages 109–154. MIT Press, Cambridge, MA, 1987.

[16] C. Rich and R. C. Waters. Automatic programming: Myths and prospects. *IEEE Computer*, 21(8):40–51, August 1988.

KBE and KBEmacs

KBEmacs was preceded by a demonstration system called the Knowledge Based Editor (KBE). For the most part, KBE (described in [17, 18, 19]) is best viewed as a stepping stone on the way to KBEmacs. KBE supported the key capabilities of program construction using clichés and program modification in terms of its plan structure, but not much else. The only capability of KBE that was not carried through to KBEmacs was the ability to display a plan diagram for the program being edited.

KBE was extended into KBEmacs [20, 21, 22, 23] by adding support for direct editing of program text, an easy method for defining new clichés, support for constraints, support for Ada, support for the creation of comments [24], and integration with Emacs [25]. Also, the philosophy of the user interface changed significantly by our deemphasis of the Plan Calculus. *The Programmer's Apprentice* is the best single reference for KBEmacs; however, additional examples of its use are given in [21] and additional details of the underlying algorithms are given in [21, 70].

To improve the performance of KBEmacs, we have explored supporting the basic idea of constructing programs by combining clichés, without translating back and forth between program text and plans. A not very successful attempt to do this using a purely text-based editor is reported in [26]. (However, this does not mean—see [27]—that text-oriented commands should be entirely removed from program editors.) A more successful experimental program editor using parse trees is reported in [28].

The pretty printer component of KBEmacs (and KBE) is described in [29, 30, 31].

[17] R. C. Waters. The Programmer's Apprentice: Knowledge-based program editing. *IEEE Trans. on Software Engineering*, 8(1):1–12, January 1982. Reprinted in D. Barstow, E. Sandewall, and H. Shrobe, editors, *Interactive Programming Environments*, pages 464–486, McGraw-Hill, New York, NY, 1984.

[18] R. C. Waters. A knowledge-based program editor. In *Proc. 7th Int. Joint Conf. Artificial Intelligence*, pages 920–926, Vancouver, British Columbia, Canada, August 1981.

[19] R. C. Waters. The Programmer's Apprentice: Knowledge-based program editor. In *Conf. Record: IEEE Mini/Micro Northeast-84*, Session 16, pages 1–9, Boston, MA, May 1984.

[20] R. C. Waters. The Programmer's Apprentice: A session with KBEmacs. *IEEE Trans. on Software Engineering*, 11(11):1296–1320, November 1985. Reprinted in [14].

[21] R. C. Waters. KBEmacs: A step toward the Programmer's Apprentice. Technical Report 753, MIT Artificial Intelligence Lab., May 1985.

[22] R. C. Waters. KBEmacs: Where's the AI? *AI Magazine*, 7(1):47–56, Spring 1986.

[23] R. C. Waters. Reuse of clichés in the knowledge-based editor. In R. Conradi, T. M. Didrikson, and D. H. Wanvik, editors, *Advanced*

Programming Environments, Proc. Int. Workshop, pages 536–550, Springer-Verlag, New York, NY, June 1986. Lecture Notes in Computer Science Series, Vol. 244.

[24] D. S. Cyphers. Automated program description. Working Paper 237, MIT Artificial Intelligence Lab., August 1982.

[25] K. M. Pitman. Interfacing to the Programmer's Apprentice. Working Paper 244, MIT Artificial Intelligence Lab., February 1983.

[26] P.J. Sterpe. Tempest: A template editor for structured text. Technical Report 843, MIT Artificial Intelligence Lab., June 1985. Master's thesis.

[27] R. C. Waters. Program editors should not abandon text-oriented commands. *ACM SIGPLAN Notices*, 17(7):39–46, July 1982.

[28] Y. M. Tan. Ace: A cliché-based program structure editor. Working Paper 294, MIT Artificial Intelligence Lab., May 1987. Bachelor's thesis.

[29] R. C. Waters. User format control in a Lisp prettyprinter. *ACM Trans. on Programming Languages and Systems*, 5(4):513–531, October 1983.

[30] R. C. Waters. PP: A Lisp pretty printing system. Memo 816, MIT Artificial Intelligence Lab., December 1984.

[31] R.C. Waters. Pretty printing. In G.L. Steele Jr., *Common Lisp: The Language*, second edition, pages 748–769, Digital Press, Burlington MA, 1989.

Plans and Clichés

The basic ideas of plans and plan diagrams are laid out in [1], with some additional features (in particular, temporal abstraction) introduced in [46, 70]. The first comprehensive presentation of the Plan Calculus, including its semantic foundations, appeared in [32] (excerpted in [33, 34]). With regard to plan diagrams, [32] has been superseded by [35] and *The Programmer's Apprentice*. However, with regard to the formal semantics of the Plan Calculus, [32] is still the primary reference.

Like plans, the idea of software clichés originated in [1], but was greatly expanded in [32] (in particular, placing clichés in the context of inspection methods in engineering problem solving). The virtues of the Plan Calculus as a representation for software clichés are discussed in [36, 37]. For the most part, these references are superseded by *The Programmer's Apprentice*. However, [32] goes into greater detail regarding the taxonomic structure of the cliché library. Many additional examples of software clichés can be found in [21, 32, 38]. A perspective on clichés in general is given in [39].

[32] C. Rich. Inspection methods in programming. Technical Report 604, MIT Artificial Intelligence Lab., June 1981. PhD thesis.

[33] C. Rich. Multiple points of view in modeling programs. *ACM SIGPLAN Notices*, 16(1):177–179, January 1981. Proc. Workshop on Data Abstraction, Databases and Conceptual Modeling.

[34] C. Rich. A formal representation for plans in the Programmer's Apprentice. In *Proc. 7th Int. Joint Conf. Artificial Intelligence*, pages 1044–1052, Vancouver, British Columbia, Canada, August 1981. Reprinted in M. Brodie, J. Mylopoulos, and J. Schmidt, editors, *On Conceptual Modelling*, pages 239–270, Springer-Verlag, New York, NY, 1984, and in [14].

[35] C. Rich. Inspection methods in programming: Clichés and plans. Memo 1005, MIT Artificial Intelligence Lab., December 1987.

[36] C. Rich and R. C. Waters. Formalizing reusable software components. In *Proc. ITT Workshop on Reusability in Programming*, pages 152–159, Newport, RI, September 1983.

[37] C. Rich and R. C. Waters. Formalizing reusable software components in the Programmer's Apprentice. In T.J. Biggerstaff and A.J. Perlis, editors, *Software Reusability Volume II: Applications and Experience*, pages 313–343. Addison-Wesley, Reading, MA, 1989.

[38] J. Wertheimer. Derivation of a rule system pattern matcher. Technical Report 1109, MIT Artificial Intelligence Lab., June 1989. Master's thesis.

[39] D. Chapman. Cognitive clichés. Working Paper 286, MIT Artificial Intelligence Lab., April 1986.

Recognition

The best reference for the cliché recognizer described in Chapter 10 is [40], but see also [41]. The full details of the system can be found in [42]. The underlying graph parsing algorithm is described in [43]. The use of parallel processing to support graph parsing is explored in [44]. A proposal for further research on program recognition is outlined in [45].

[40] L. M. Wills. Automated program recognition: A feasibility demonstration. *Artificial Intelligence*, 1990. To be published.

[41] C. Rich and L. M. Wills. Recognizing a program's design: A graph-parsing approach. *IEEE Software*, 7(1):82–89, January 1990.

[42] L. M. Wills. Automated program recognition. Technical Report 904, MIT Artificial Intelligence Lab., February 1987. Master's thesis.

[43] D.C. Brotsky. An algorithm for parsing flow graphs. Technical Report 704, MIT Artificial Intelligence Lab., March 1984. Master's thesis.

[44] P. M. Ritto. Parallel flow graph matching for automated program
     recognition. Working Paper 310, MIT Artificial Intelligence Lab.,
     July 1988.

[45] L. M. Wills. Determining the limits of automated program
     recognition. Working Paper 321, MIT Artificial Intelligence Lab.,
     June 1989. PhD proposal.

Automated Reasoning

One of the initial motivations behind the design of the Plan Calculus was
to facilitate automated reasoning about programs (see [1, 37]). Automated
reasoning using plans was the primary focus of Shrobe's work [46], with
particular attention to reasoning about side effects [47].

Recently, we have focused on implementing the Cake hybrid knowledge-
representation and reasoning system described in Section 11.1. Since Cake
is still under development, there is not yet a comprehensive reference describing it. However, the basic concepts behind the system are laid out
in [48, 49, 50]. In addition, there are a number of papers that describe
various specific aspects of the system [51, 52, 53, 54]. (FRAPPE is the name
given to the bottom three layers of Cake—see Figure 11.2, page 193.)

[46] H. E. Shrobe. Dependency directed reasoning for complex program
     understanding. Technical Report 503, MIT Artificial Intelligence
     Lab., April 1979. PhD thesis.

[47] H. E. Shrobe. Dependency directed reasoning in the analysis of
     programs which modify data structures. In *Proc. 6th Int. Joint Conf.
     Artificial Intelligence*, pages 829–835, Tokyo, Japan, August 1979.

[48] C. Rich. Knowledge representation languages and predicate calculus:
     How to have your cake and eat it too. In *Proc. 2nd National Conf. on
     Artificial Intelligence*, pages 193–196, Pittsburgh, PA, August 1982.

[49] C. Rich. The layered architecture of a system for reasoning about
     programs. In *Proc. 9th Int. Joint Conf. Artificial Intelligence*, pages
     540–546, Los Angeles, CA, 1985.

[50] D. Brotsky and C. Rich. Issues in the design of hybrid knowledge
     representation and reasoning systems. In *Proc. Workshop on
     Theoretical Issues in Natural Language Understanding*, pages 32–38,
     Halifax, Canada, May 1985.

[51] Y. A. Feldman and C. Rich. Reasoning with simplifying assumptions:
     A methodology and example. In *Proc. 5th National Conf. on
     Artificial Intelligence*, pages 2–7, Philadelphia, PA, August 1986.

[52] Y. A. Feldman and C. Rich. Bread, Frappe, and Cake: The
     gourmet's guide to automated deduction. In *Proc. 5th Israeli Symp.
     on Artificial Intelligence*, Tel Aviv, Israel, December 1988.

[53] Y. A. Feldman and C. Rich. Principles of knowledge representation and reasoning in the FRAPPE system. In *Proc. 6th Israeli Symp. on Artificial Intelligence*, Tel Aviv, Israel, December 1989.

[54] Y. A. Feldman and C. Rich. Pattern-directed invocation with changing equalities. *Journal of Automated Reasoning*, to appear.

Requirements

The principles and goals of the Requirements Apprentice (see Section 11.3) are best described in the original memo [55] (excerpted in [56]). Work on the Requirements Apprentice demonstration has been going on for about two years and, as described in [57], is now approximately two-thirds complete.

[55] C. Rich and R. C. Waters. Toward a Requirements Apprentice: On the boundary between informal and formal specifications. Memo 907, MIT Artificial Intelligence Lab., July 1986.

[56] C. Rich, R. C. Waters, and H. B. Reubenstein. Toward a Requirements Apprentice. In *Proc. 4th Int. Workshop on Software Specification and Design*, pages 79–86, Monterey, CA, April 1987.

[57] H. B. Reubenstein and R. C. Waters. The Requirements Apprentice: An initial scenario. In *Proc. 5th Int. Workshop on Software Specification and Design*, Pittsburgh, PA, May 1989.

Design

Work on the Design Apprentice (see Section 11.2) is just beginning [58]. The complete target scenario for the Design Apprentice can be found in [59]. In-depth discussion of one particular aspect of design—the use of simplifying assumptions—can be found in [60].

Designing programs using clichés has many advantages with respect to productivity and reliability; however, it can lead to a loss of efficiency. An approach to improving the efficiency of programs and designs by rearranging the computation of intermediate results is proposed in [61].

[58] Y. M. Tan. A program design assistant. Working Paper 327, MIT Artificial Intelligence Lab., June 1989. Master's proposal.

[59] C. Rich and R. C. Waters. The Programmer's Apprentice: A program design scenario. Memo 933A, MIT Artificial Intelligence Lab., November 1987.

[60] C. Rich and R. C. Waters. The disciplined use of simplifying assumptions. *ACM SIGSOFT Software Engineering Notes*, 7(5):150–154, December 1982. Proc. ACM SIGSOFT Second Software Engineering Symp.: Workshop on Rapid Prototyping.

[61] R. J. Hall. Program improvement by automatic redistribution of intermediate results. Working Paper 305, MIT Artificial Intelligence Lab., May 1988. PhD proposal.

Debugging

Under the umbrella of the Programmer's Apprentice, four different approaches to assisting with program debugging have been investigated. The Sniffer system [62] identifies bugs in a program using a library of bug clichés. The Testing Assistant [63] keeps track of test cases applied to a program during its construction and can automatically retry the relevant test cases after modifications to the program. The Debussi system [64] assists in localizing bugs, using a general dependency-based approach and the Plan Calculus. The work described in [65] investigates various ways of categorizing software errors.

[62] D.G. Shapiro. Sniffer: A system that understands bugs. Memo 638, MIT Artificial Intelligence Lab., June 1981. Master's thesis.

[63] D. Chapman. A program testing assistant. *Comm. of the ACM*, 25(9):625–634, September 1982.

[64] R. I. Kuper. Dependency-directed localization of software bugs. Technical Report 1053, MIT Artificial Intelligence Lab., May 1989. Master's thesis.

[65] S. M. Levitin. Toward a richer language for describing software errors. Working Paper 270, MIT Artificial Intelligence Lab., May 1985. Bachelor's thesis.

Program Translation

As discussed in [66], the Plan Calculus and cliché recognition provide significant leverage on the task of high-quality program translation. A prototype system for translating between Cobol and Hibol (a very high-level business data processing language) is described in [67]. The use of a global translation approach to support compilation into extremely efficient object code is discussed in [68]. A system that applies source-to-source transformations (a kind of simple cliché recognition) as a means of improving the quality of translation is described in [69].

[66] R. C. Waters. Program translation via abstraction and reimplementation. *IEEE Trans. on Software Engineering*, 14(8):1207–1228, August 1988.

[67] G. Faust. Semiautomatic translation of Cobol into Hibol. Technical Report 256, MIT Lab. of Computer Science, March 1981. Master's thesis.

[68] R.D. Duffey II. Formalizing the expertise of the assembler language programmer. Working Paper 203, MIT Artificial Intelligence Lab., September 1980. Master's proposal.

[69] T. R. Kennedy III. Using program transformations to improve program translation. Memo 962, MIT Artificial Intelligence Lab., May 1987. Master's thesis.

Temporal Abstraction and Iteration

The concept of temporal abstraction was first presented in [70] (excerpted in [71, 72]) and elaborated in [32, 46]. Because temporal abstraction allows iterative programs to be composed of iterative clichés in the same simple manner that numerical expressions are composed of numerical functions, it is an important source of the power of KBEmacs. A series of macro packages [73, 74, 75, 76, 77, 78] have been implemented that separate the concept of temporal abstraction from the rest of KBEmacs and make it directly available in Lisp. The latest of these macro packages [79, 80, 81] is available as a portable Common Lisp macro package.

[70] R. C. Waters. Automatic analysis of the logical structure of programs. Technical Report 492, MIT Artificial Intelligence Lab., December 1978. PhD thesis.

[71] R. C. Waters. A method for analyzing loop programs. *IEEE Trans. on Software Engineering*, 5(3):237–247, May 1979.

[72] R. C. Waters. A method for automatically analyzing programs. In *Proc. 6th Int. Joint Conf. Artificial Intelligence*, pages 935–941, Tokyo, Japan, August 1979.

[73] R. C. Waters. LetS: An expressional loop notation. Memo 680a, MIT Artificial Intelligence Lab., February 1983.

[74] R. C. Waters. Expressional loops. In *11th Annual ACM Symp. on Principles of Programming Languages*, pages 1–10, Salt Lake City, UT, January 1984.

[75] R. C. Waters. Efficient interpretation of synchronizable series expressions. *ACM SIGPLAN Notices*, 22(7):74–85, July 1987. *Proc. ACM SIGPLAN '87 Symp. on Interpreters and Interpretative Techniques*.

[76] R. C. Waters. Obviously synchronizable series expressions: Part I: A user's manual for the OSS macro package. Memo 958a, MIT Artificial Intelligence Lab., March 1988.

[77] R. C. Waters. Obviously synchronizable series expressions: Part II: Overview of the theory and implementation. Memo 959a, MIT Artificial Intelligence Lab., March 1988.

[78] R. C. Waters. Using obviously synchronizable series expressions instead of loops. In *Proc. 1988 IEEE Int. Conf. on Computer Languages*, pages 338–346, Miami, FL, October 1988.

[79] R.C. Waters. Optimization of series expressions: Part I: User's manual for the series macro package. Memo 1082, MIT Artificial Intelligence Lab., December 1989.

[80] R.C. Waters. Optimization of series expressions: Part II: Overview of the theory and implementation. Memo 1083, MIT Artificial Intelligence Lab., December 1989.

[81] R.C. Waters. Series. In G.L. Steele Jr., *Common Lisp: The Language*, second edition, pages 923–955, Digital Press, Burlington MA, 1989.

Bibliography

[82] H. Abelson and G. J. Sussman. *Structure and Interpretation of Computer Programs.* McGraw-Hill, New York, NY, 1985.

[83] A. V. Aho, J. D. Ullman, and J. E. Hopcroft. *The Design and Analysis of Computer Algorithms.* Addison-Wesley, Reading, MA, 1974.

[84] G. Arango and P. Freeman. Modeling knowledge for software development. In *Proc. 3rd Int. Workshop on Software Specifications and Design*, pages 63–66, London, England, 1985.

[85] F. T. Baker. Chief programmer team management of production programming. *IBM Systems Journal*, 11(1), 1972.

[86] R. M. Balzer. A 15 year perspective on automatic programming. *IEEE Trans. on Software Engineering*, 11(11):1257–1267, November 1985.

[87] D. R. Barstow. An experiment in knowledge-based automatic programming. *Artificial Intelligence*, 12(1 and 2):73–119, 1979. Reprinted in [14].

[88] D. R. Barstow. A perspective on automatic programming. *AI Magazine*, 5(1):5–27, Spring 1984. Reprinted in [14].

[89] D. R. Barstow. Domain-specific automatic programming. *IEEE Trans. on Software Engineering*, 11(11):1321–1336, November 1985.

[90] S. K. Basu and J. Misra. Some classes of naturally provable programs. In *2nd Int. Conf. on Software Engineering*, San Francisco, CA, 1976.

[91] R. M. Burstall and J. L. Darlington. A transformation system for developing recursive programs. *Journal of the ACM*, 24(1), January 1977.

[92] T. E. Cheatham. Reusability through program transformation. *IEEE Trans. on Software Engineering*, 10(5):589–594, September 1984. Reprinted in [14].

[93] E. J. Chikofsky. *Computer-Aided Software Engineering (CASE)*. IEEE Computer Society Press, Los Alamitos, CA, 1989.

[94] O. J. Dahl, E. Dijkstra, and C. A. R. Hoare. *Structured Programming*. Academic Press, Boston, MA, 1972.

[95] J. B. Dennis. First version of a data flow procedure language. In *Proc. Symp. on Programming*, pages 241–271, Univ. of Paris, Paris, France, April 1974.

[96] J. Domingue. Itsy: An automated programming advisor. Technical Report 22, The Open Univ., Human Cognitive Research Lab., Milton Keynes, England, June 1987. PhD thesis.

[97] V. Donzeau-George. A structure-oriented program editor: A first step towards computer assisted programming. In *Proc. Int. Computing Symp.*, Antibes, France, 1975.

[98] J. Doyle. A truth maintenance system. *Artificial Intelligence*, 12:231–272, 1979.

[99] J. Earley. An efficient context-free parsing algorithm. Carnegie-Mellon Univ., Computer Science Dept., 1968. PhD thesis.

[100] H. Ehrig, M. Nagl, G. Rozenberg, and A. Rosenfeld, editors. *Graph-Grammars and Their Application to Computer Science*. Springer-Verlag, New York, December 1986. Lecture Notes In Computer Science Series, Vol. 291.

[101] S. F. Fickas and R. Brooks. Recognition in a program understanding system. In *Proc. 6th Int. Joint Conf. Artificial Intelligence*, pages 266–268, Tokyo, Japan, August 1979.

[102] R. E. Fikes and N. J. Nilsson. STRIPS: A new approach to the application of theorem proving to problem solving. *Artificial Intelligence*, 2:189–208, 1971.

[103] R. W. Floyd. Assigning meaning to programs. In J. T. Schwartz, editor, *Mathematical Aspects of Computer Science*, pages 19–32. American Math. Society, Providence, RI, 1967. Vol. 19.

[104] C. Gane. *Computer-Aided Software Engineering: The Methodologies, the Products, and the Future*. Prentice Hall, Englewood Cliffs, NJ, 1990.

[105] S. L. Gerhart. Knowledge about programs: A model and case study. In *Proc. Int. Conf. on Reliable Software*, pages 88–95, June 1975. Published as ACM SIGPLAN Notices, 10(6).

[106] J. A. Goguen, J. W. Thatcher, and E. G. Wagner. An initial algebra approach to the specification, correctness, and implementation of abstract data types. In R. Yeh, editor, *Current Trends in Programming Methodology, Vol. IV*. Prentice Hall, Englewood Cliffs, NJ, 1978.

[107] I. P. Goldstein. Summary of MYCROFT: A system for understanding simple picture programs. *Artificial Intelligence*, 6(3), 1975.

[108] C. Green and D. R. Barstow. On program synthesis knowledge. *Artificial Intelligence*, 10(3):241–279, 1978. Reprinted in [14].

[109] C. Green, D. Luckam, R. Balzer, T. Cheatham, and C. Rich. Report on a knowledge-based software assistant. Technical Report 195, Rome Air Development Center, Griffiss AFB, NY, 1983. Reprinted in [14].

[110] J. V. Guttag. Abstract data types and the development of data structures. *Comm. of the ACM*, 20(6):396–404, June 1977.

[111] M. T. Harandi and F. H. Young. Template based specification and design. In *Proc. 3rd Int. Workshop on Software Specifications and Design*, pages 94–97, London, England, 1985.

[112] D. Harel. Statecharts: A visual formalism for complex systems. *Science of Computer Programming*, 8, 1987.

[113] C.A.R. Hoare. An axiomatic basis for computer programming. *Comm. of the ACM*, 12(10):576–583, October 1969.

[114] K. E. Huff and V. R. Lesser. A plan-based intelligent assistant that supports the process of programming. *ACM SIGSOFT Software Engineering Notes*, 13(5):97–106, November 1988. Proc. ACM SIGSOFT/SIGPLAN Software Engineering Symp. on Practical Software Development Environment, Boston, MA. Also published as ACM SIGPLAN Notices, 24(2).

[115] Y. I. Ianov. The logical schemes of algorithms. In *Problems of Cybernetics*, pages 82–140. Pergamon Press, 1960. Vol. 1, English translation.

[116] W. L. Johnson and E. Soloway. PROUST: Knowledge-based program understanding. *IEEE Trans. on Software Engineering*, 11(3):267–275, March 1985. Reprinted in [14].

[117] V. Jonckers. Exploring algorithms through mutations. In *7th European Conf. on Artificial Intelligence*, pages 556–568, Brighton Centre, England, July 1986. Vol. 1.

[118] E. Kant. Understanding and automating algorithm design. *IEEE Trans. on Software Engineering*, 11(11):1361–1374, November 1985.

[119] E. Kant. Interactive problem solving using task configuration and control. *IEEE Expert*, pages 36–49, Winter 1988.

[120] D. E. Knuth. *The Art of Computer Programming*, Volumes 1, 2, and 3. Addison-Wesley, Reading, MA, 1968, 1969, 1973.

[121] J. Laubsch and M. Eisenstadt. Domain specific debugging aids for novice programmers. In *Proc. 7th Int. Joint Conf. Artificial Intelligence*, pages 964–969, Vancouver, British Columbia, Canada, August 1981.

[122] J. Z. Lavi. Improving the embedded computer systems software process using a generic model. In *Proc. 3rd Int. Workshop on Software Specifications and Design*, pages 127–129, London, England, 1985.

[123] B. H. Liskov and J. Guttag. *Abstraction and Specification in Program Development*. McGraw-Hill, New York, NY, 1986.

[124] B. H. Liskov and S. N. Zilles. Specification techniques for data abstractions. *IEEE Trans. on Software Engineering*, 1(1):7–19, March 1975.

[125] M. Lowry. Algorithm synthesis through problem reformulation. In *Proc. 6th National Conf. on Artificial Intelligence*, pages 432–436, Seattle, WN, July 1987.

[126] F. J. Lukey. Understanding and debugging programs. *Int. Journal of Man-Machine Studies*, 12:189–202, 1980.

[127] R. Lutz. Program debugging by near-miss recognition and symbolic evaluation. Technical Report CSRP.044, Univ. of Sussex, England, 1984.

[128] R. Lutz. Diagram parsing — A new technique for artificial intelligence. Technical Report CSRP.054, Univ. of Sussex, England, 1986.

[129] Z. Manna. *Mathematic Theory of Computation*. McGraw-Hill, New York, NY, 1974.

[130] Z. Manna and R. Waldinger. A deductive approach to program synthesis. *ACM Trans. on Programming Languages and Systems*, 2(1):90–121, January 1980. Reprinted in [14].

[131] B. P. McCune and J. S. Dean. Advanced tools for software maintenance. Technical Report 313, Rome Air Development Center, Griffiss AFB, NY, December 1982.

[132] R. Medinia-Mora and P. H. Feiler. An incremental programming environment. *IEEE Trans. on Software Engineering*, 7(5), September 1981.

[133] M. L. Miller and I. Goldstein. Problem solving grammars as formal tools for intelligent CAI. In *Proc. Assoc. for Computing Machinery*, 1977.

[134] H. Mills. Chief programmer teams, principles, and procedures. Report FSC 71-5108, IBM Federal Systems Division, 1971.

[135] M. L. Minsky. *Society of Mind*. Simon and Schuster, New York, NY, January 1987.

[136] M. L. Minsky. A framework for representing knowledge. In P. H. Winston, editor, *The Psychology of Computer Vision*. McGraw-Hill, New York, NY, 1975.

[137] J. Misra. A technique of algorithm construction on sequences. *IEEE Trans. on Software Engineering*, 4(1):65–69, January 1978.

[138] M. S. Moriconi. A designer/verifier's assistant. *IEEE Trans. on Software Engineering*, 5(4):387–401, July 1979. Reprinted in [14].

[139] W. R. Murray. Heuristic and formal methods in automatic program debugging. In *Proc. 9th Int. Joint Conf. Artificial Intelligence*, Los Angeles, CA, August 1985.

[140] J. M. Neighbors. The Draco approach to constructing software from reusable components. *IEEE Trans. on Software Engineering*, 10(5):564–574, September 1984. Reprinted in [14].

[141] H. Partsch and R. Steinbruggen. Program transformation systems. *ACM Computing Surveys*, 15(3):199–236, 1983.

[142] G. R. Ruth. Intelligent program analysis. *Artificial Intelligence*, 7:65–85, 1976. Reprinted in [14].

[143] E. D. Sacerdoti. Planning in a hierarchy of abstraction spaces. *Artificial Intelligence*, 5(2):115–135, 1974.

[144] E. D. Sacerdoti. The nonlinear nature of plans. In *Proc. 4th Int. Joint Conf. Artificial Intelligence*, pages 206–214, Tblisi, Georgia, USSR, September 1975.

[145] R. C. Schank and R. P. Abelson. *Scripts, Plans, Goals, and Understanding*. Lawrence Erlbaum, Hillsdale, NJ, 1977.

[146] D. R. Smith. KIDS — A knowledge-based software development system. Technical Report KES.U.88.7, Kestrel Institute, Palo Alto, CA, October 1988.

[147] D. R. Smith, G. B. Kotik, and S. J. Westfold. Research on knowledge-based software engineering environments at Kestrel Institute. *IEEE Trans. on Software Engineering*, 11(11):1278–1295, November 1985.

[148] E. Soloway and K. Ehrlich. Empirical studies of programming knowledge. *IEEE Trans. on Software Engineering*, 10(5):595–609, September 1984. Reprinted in [14].

[149] E. Soloway et al. MENO-II: An intelligent programming tutor. *Journal of Computer-Based Instruction*, 10(1 and 2), Summer 1983.

[150] R. M. Stallman. EMACS: The extensible, customizable self-documenting display editor. In *Proc. ACM SIGPLAN/SIGOA Symp. on Text Manipulation*, Portland, OR, June 1981.

[151] G. L. Steele Jr. *Common Lisp: The Language*. Digital Press, Burlington, MA, 1984.

[152] G. J. Sussman. Slices at the boundary between analysis and synthesis. In J. C. Latombe, editor, *Artificial Intelligence and Pattern Recognition in Computer-Aided Design*. North-Holland, Amsterdam, March 1978. Proc. IFIP Working Conf., Grenoble, France.

[153] Symbolics, Inc., *Lisp Machine Documentation (Release 4)*, Cambridge, MA, 1984.

[154] T. Teitelbaum and T. Reps. The Cornell Program Synthesizer: A syntax-directed programming environment. *Comm. of the ACM*, 24(9):563–573, September 1981.

[155] U.S. Department of Defense, U.S. Govt. Printing Office. *Military Standard Ada Programming Language*, February 1983. ANSI/MIL-STD-1815A-1983.

[156] J. M. Wing. A study of 12 specifications of the library problem. *IEEE Software*, pages 66–76, July 1988.

[157] N. Wirth. *Systematic Programming, An Introduction*. Prentice Hall, Englewood Cliffs, NJ, 1973.

[158] W. A. Wulf, R. L. London, and M. Shaw. An introduction to the construction and verification of Alphard programs. *IEEE Trans. on Software Engineering*, 2(4):253–265, December 1976.

List of Clichés

Systems

information-system, 202
tracking-system, 202
  by-change-data, 202
  by-direct-observation, 202
advisory-system, 202
real-time-system, 197

Iteration

linear-search, 14, 25
  exhaustive-linear-search, 18
generation, 71
  counting-down, 72
  cdr-generation, 72
filtering, 72
accumulation, 73
  sum, 73, 105
  product, 73
  count, 106
  max-accumulation, 186
  min-accumulation, 186
termination, 74
enumeration, 18, 28
  cdr-enumeration, 14, 89
    trailing-cdr-enumeration, 16
  file-enumeration, 118
  chain-enumeration, 122

Sets

set-add, 39
find-if-present, 18
set-retrieve, 40, 181
    hash-table-retrieve, 178, 181

Sequences

select-term, 182
new-term, 52
alter-term, 55
accumulate, 76
    max-accumulate, 186
    min-accumulate, 186
generate, 76
filter, 76
truncate, 76
earliest, 182

Numerical

difference, 42
times, 48
increment, 52
decrement, 60
negate, 64
negative, 64
equal-one, 60

Index